PRAISE FOR *LEND ME A TENOR*

"One of the two great farces by a living writer."

The New York Times

"*Lend Me A Tenor* is a remarkable piece of theatre . . . a masterpiece!"

The London Times

"Fills the theatre with the sound of laughter."

(London) Sunday Express

PRAISE FOR *MOON OVER BUFFALO*

"*Moon Over Buffalo* packs more comic genius onto the stage than anything in recent memory!"

USA Today

"Comedy Triumphant. A completely side-splitting joy. Just go by 45th Street around 8 o'clock and you'll hear the theatre rollicking."

WCBS-TV

"The funniest show in New York . . . The comedy has audiences rolling in the aisles. The second act has a show-within-a-show spoof of 'Private Lives' with everybody in the wrong costumes reading the wrong lines. This has to be one of the most hysterical things ever put onstage. I have seen *Moon Over Buffalo* three times! I expect you to see it once."

Liz Smith, *New York Post*

LEND ME A TENOR
AND OTHER PLAYS

BY
KEN LUDWIG

ALSO BY KEN LUDWIG

PLAYS

Divine Fire

Postmortem

Sullivan & Gilbert

Be My Baby

Twentieth Century
(from the play by Hecht and MacArthur)

Treasure Island
(from the novel by Robert Louis Stevenson)

The Three Musketeers
(from the novel by Alexander Dumas)

The Fox on the Fairway

The Game's Afoot

MUSICALS

Crazy For You
(with the music and lyrics of George and Ira Gershwin)

The Adventures of Tom Sawyer
(with the music and lyrics of Don Schlitz)

An American in Paris
(with the music and lyrics of George and Ira Gershwin)

LEND ME A TENOR
AND OTHER PLAYS

BY

KEN LUDWIG

CONTEMPORARY PLAYWRIGHTS
SERIES

A Smith and Kraus Book
Hanover, New Hampshire

A Smith and Kraus Book
Published by Smith and Kraus, Inc.
177 Lyme Road, Hanover, New Hampshire, 03755
www.smithandkraus.com / (888) 282-2881

Leading Ladies © 2006 by Ken Ludwig
Lend Me A Tenor © 1984 under the title *Opera Buffa* by Kenneth Ludwig; © 1986, 1989
    by Ken Ludwig
Moon Over Buffalo © 1996 by Ken Ludwig
Shakespeare in Hollywood © 2005 by Ken Ludwig

First Edition: November 2010
10 9 8 7 6 5 4 3 2 1
Manufactured in the United States of America
Design and production by Julia Hill Gignoux, Freedom Hill Design
Cover image: Designed by Dewynters, London Ltd., permission given for
reproducing by Dewynters, London Ltd., copyright Dewynters, London Ltd.

Library of Congress Control Number: 2010938329

FOR MY CHILDREN, OLIVIA AND JACK,
WITHOUT WHOM I WOULD HAVE WRITTEN
AT LEAST FIVE MORE PLAYS

AND FOR MY BROTHER, GENE,
WITHOUT WHOM THERE WOULD BE
NO PLAYS AT ALL

CONTENTS

ACKNOWLEDGMENTS

My thanks to my wife, Adrienne, who is not only the beloved mother of our children but also editor, proofreader extraordinaire, and muse. My thanks also to my children, Olivia and Jack, who are the light of my life; to the rest of my family: Gene, Carol, Abigail, Elizabeth, and David Ludwig; to my dear friends and unflagging supporters Jim and Mary Davidson, Peter Herzberg, Simon Reade, Marty and Lenore Schneiderman, Rita Braver, Bob Barnett, Richard Clifford, Derek Jacobi, Harry and Kathie Teter, Tappan and Robin Wilder, Janet and Christopher Griffin, Ira Dosovitz, Buddy Karelis, Lynn Redgrave, Gail Paster, Sandy McClatchy, Eric Schaeffer, John Rando, Gregg Henry, Kenny Stilwell, Charles Williams, J. W. Morrissette, and Barbara Mowatt; to my remarkable manager Rosey Strub; to my excellent publishers at Samuel French, including Abbie Van Nostrand and Ken Dingledine; to Jonathan Lomma, Peter Franklin, Gilbert Parker, and Patricia Macnaughton, fine advisors all; to Billie Sandler, who was my wonderful assistant for many years; and to her successors Kristin Sandoval and Rebecca Borden.

Comedy is not just a happy as opposed to an unhappy ending, but a way of surveying life so that happy endings must prevail.

LOUIS KRONENBERGER

INTRODUCTION

The joy I have taken in writing plays over the years is incalculable. When I get an idea for a new play, I am never happier. "This time," I say to myself, "it's *Twelfth Night* or bust. How can I miss with this Italian tenor blowing in from the train station? Or this pair of intrepid English actors who mix up their *Hamlet* with their *Henry the Fifth*? Or this over-the-hill Cyrano who becomes crazed with ambition when he hears about the visiting movie producer?" When such notions swim past my mind's eye, and I think about how they can make us laugh and sit on the edge of our seats and yet somehow be turned inside out so that they might tell us something about ourselves, my heart does a sort of somersault, and I start sharpening my pencil with a glee that I did not possess the day before.

The urge to write begins with the desire to imitate, and I have dreamt for many years of living in the Illyria of *Twelfth Night* and the "old-fashioned house" of *She Stoops to Conquer;* in the Litchfield inn of *The Beaux' Stratagem* and the Yonkers feed store of *The Matchmaker.* These are lands of pure comedy that make us glad to be alive and happy to be participating in this elusive element of our humanity that we call "art."

I came across a speech not long ago by a man named Karl Paulnack. Paulnack is the director of the music division of the Boston Conservatory, and he addressed the following remarks to the parents of an incoming class of students in an effort to convince them that their children — all of whom could have gone instead to law school or medical school — had not erred in choosing art as a way of life:

"The first people to understand how music really works were the ancient Greeks. And this is going to fascinate you: the Greeks said that music and astronomy were two sides of the same coin. Astronomy was seen as the study of relationships between observable, permanent, external objects, and music was seen as the study of relationships between invisible, internal, hidden objects. Music has a way of finding the big, invisible moving pieces inside our hearts and souls and helping us figure out the position of things inside us."

I believe that the same can be said about all the arts, from drama and poetry to painting and sculpture. Indeed, I have staked my life on this simple but earth-shattering proposition: that art can reorder our hearts.

Like the Rev. Canon Chasuble in *The Importance of Being Earnest*, I will speak metaphorically: I believe that inside our hearts are building blocks that can, over time, become chipped and disordered and lose all sense of harmony and beauty. I believe that we begin in beauty when we are children and become disordered over time. If we look at the ruins of ancient Rome we can see the beauty of what was; and this kind of beauty can be reordered with a hammer and chisel. The blocks in our souls need drama and music, painting and sculpture to repair them.

Drama, it seems to me, is the least obvious of the arts, perhaps because it has so much of the practical about it. There is something rough and ready about drama — a playwright, after all, is a wright, a maker of things in a practical sense. When I write a new play, I have the feeling that I am rolling up my sleeves and getting down to work — and I like that about the process. First, I need to dream as deeply and as profoundly as I can; and then it is time to sharpen my pencil and scratch it all out on a lined piece of yellow paper. Similarly, actors need very practical skills. They must learn their lines, put on costumes and makeup, and make their exits and their entrances. It is not surprising that we do not blink an eye when we see the Mechanicals in *A Midsummer Night's Dream* rehearsing a play. Quince is a carpenter and Snug a joiner. Their hands are rough. And yet it is entirely natural that they should be putting on a play, because plays are sturdy things, the way the houses that they build are sturdy.

The metaphor of houses (here comes Chasuble again) is a good one, I believe, because one of the most satisfying things about plays, especially comedies, is their architecture. *What* the playwright has chosen to describe is generally of paramount importance to our night in the theater. But *how* he tells his tale is frequently so wrapped up in the tale itself that the two are inseparable.

In this age of television, there is a tendency to equate the notion of dramatic comedy with jokes and joking, and nothing could be further from the truth. Without good proportions and a kind of spatial balance, no play will ever succeed. If a play is to have any real claim on our attention, it must have a solid structure, even — or perhaps especially — if that structure is virtually invisible. Think of *A Midsummer Night's Dream*. It is astonishing for its poetry, it is remarkable for its story, and it is dazzling in its wealth of characters: but it is also utterly astounding for its architecture, which enhances everything else inside it. Five acts and four separate plots; the outer two acts set in Athens with

Theseus and Hippolyta, the inner three in the Wood with the fairies; four couples, two sets of lovers with dizzying permutations, and a local weaver and his friends who are rehearsing yet another play — and every moment is crystal clear. Structurally, the play is a kind of miracle. And, like a great house, you do not think about the architecture, you just admire the building. The beauty of great stage comedy is bound up with the skill of plotting and the artistry of storytelling.

I was teaching a class on theater recently when one of the students asked me what my plays are "about." I do not usually think of my plays that way, but on reflection, I suppose there are several answers.

Lend Me A Tenor, I think, is about parents versus children: the tearing down by youth of the barriers set up by the older generation who seek to foil the natural urges of their children. Youth comes out on top, of course, as it has in comedy since the age of Plautus. At the same time, *Lend Me A Tenor* is about the encouragement of youth by their natural heroes, who are usually, ironically, of their parents' generation. I think the play is also about finding yourself within yourself and not letting yourself get stopped when you know for certain what resides in your heart. Therefore, I suppose, it is about myself at the time I wrote it. I was a young playwright, trying to survive, who believed he had something inside himself worth saying. Was I any different in this way from the rest of the world at my age? I think not.

I have always thought of *Moon Over Buffalo* as being quite similar to *Lend Me A Tenor*, but the similarities are in tone and not in theme. *Moon Over Buffalo*, ultimately, is about second chances and about the courage that is needed to take a second chance. There is something finally valiant about George and Charlotte. They do not give up, even in the face of almost certain defeat. The play is also about the recovery of romance, another kind of second chance.

Leading Ladies continues the theme of second chances, although Leo and Jack are probably on their tenth or eleventh chance, and the adversity in Leo's case is almost paralyzing. To overcome his desperation, Leo needs to dream and then to act on his dreams. Meg is equally desperate, but in a quieter way. Her whole life hangs in the balance, and she faces the terrible issue of compromise. The play is also, I think, about social barriers. Meg ultimately does something that is remarkably courageous that tears her previous beliefs in half.

Shakespeare in Hollywood has a whole different set of concerns. It is about falling in love and dreaming. It is about myths and magic. It is also about a time in our history when censorship took on frightening proportions both in the world of film and the world at large. Also, it became increasingly clear to me as I wrote *Shakespeare in Hollywood* that the world of the Hollywood studio system of the 1930s had a number of similarities to the world of *A Midsummer Night's Dream*. Is Hermia so very different from a glamorous movie star who attracts every hot-blooded male she bumps into? Does Helena not remind us of the typical Girl Friday who blossoms from a thorn to a rose? Is Bottom not a sort of good-natured cowboy's sidekick who is overeager to be helpful? And could Oberon and Titania's stormy marriage not be ripped from yesterday's Hollywood tabloid? The Wood Near Athens, it turns out, is a very theatrical place. And making *A Midsummer Night's Dream* — indeed the whole world of Shakespeare — accessible to a new audience through a familiar metaphor was certainly one of the results I was after.

To the extent that there are themes common to all of the plays in this volume, and perhaps to my work as a whole, I believe that they are bound up with the nature of good fellowship and humanity — where we can find it, how we can sustain it, how we can lose it, and what it is worth. The plays in this volume do their best to move the ball closer to the kind of world where we would all like to live, a world of sensible optimism and an honest heart. And if that heart has been reordered by miracles like drama and music, then all the better.

Ken Ludwig
2010

LEND ME A TENOR

Pictured (L–R): J-Smith Cameron (Maggie), Jeff Brooks (Bellhop),
Philip Bosco (Saunders), Jane Connell (Julia), Caroline Lagerfelt (Diana),
Victor Garber (Max), Tovah Feldshuh (Maria), Ron Holgate (Tito Merelli)

ORIGINAL PRODUCTION

The play was first presented on August 1, 1985, at the American Stage Festival in Milford, New Hampshire. The set designer was John Falabella, the costume designer was David Murin, the lighting designer was John Gisondi, and the music coordinator was John Clifton. It was directed by Larry Carpenter with the following cast:

MAX	Walter Bobbie
MAGGIE	Christine Rose
SAUNDERS	George Ede
TITO	Ronald Holgate
MARIA	Judith Roberts
BELLHOP	Joe Palmieri
DIANA	Linda Lee Johnson
JULIA	Bella Jarrett

ORIGINAL LONDON PRODUCTION

The play was subsequently presented on March 6, 1986, by Andrew Lloyd Webber for The Really Useful Theatre Company at the Globe Theatre, London. The set and costume designer was Terry Parsons and the lighting designer was Michael Northen. It was directed by David Gilmore with the following cast:

MAX	Denis Lawson
MAGGIE	Jan Francis
SAUNDERS	John Barron
TITO	Ronald Holgate
MARIA	Anna Nicholas
BELLHOP	Edward Hibbert
DIANA	Gwendolyn Humble
JULIA	Josephine Baker

ORIGINAL BROADWAY PRODUCTION

The play was first presented in New York City on March 2, 1989, at the Royale Theater by Martin Starger and The Really Useful Theatre Company. The set designer was Tony Walton, the costume designer was William Ivey Long, the lighting designer was Paul Gallo, the production stage manager was Steven Beckler, the stage manager was Clifford Schwartz, the assistant to the director was Lori Steinberg, the sound was by Aural fixation, the general manager was Robert Kamlot, the music coordinator was Edward Strauss, and hair was by Angela Gari. It was directed by Jerry Zaks with the following cast:

MAX	Victor Garber
MAGGIE	J. Smith-Cameron
SAUNDERS	Philip Bosco
TITO	Ronald Holgate
MARIA	Tovah Feldshuh
BELLHOP	Jeff Brooks
DIANA	Caroline Lagerfelt
JULIA	Jane Connell

BROADWAY REVIVAL

The Broadway revival of *Lend Me A Tenor* was presented on April 4, 2010, by The Araca Group, Stuart Thompson, Carl Moellenberg, Rodney Rigby, Olympus Theatricals, Broadway Across America, and The Shubert Organization at the Music Box Theatre, New York. The set designer was John Lee Beatty, the costme designer was Martin Pakledinaz, the lighting designer was Kenneth Posner, the sound designer was Peter Hylenski, and the stage manager was David O'Brien. It was directed by Stanley Tucci with the following cast:

MAX	Justin Bartha
MAGGIE	Mary Catherine Garrison
SAUNDERS	Tony Shalhoub
TITO	Anthony La Paglia
MARIA	Jan Maxwell
BELLHOP	Jay Klaitz
DIANA	Jennifer Laura Thompson
JULIA	Brooke Adams

AUTHOR'S PREFACE

The first production of *Lend Me A Tenor* took place at the American Stage Festival in Milford, New Hampshire, and starred the great actor-director Walter Bobbie as Max. Soon after this production, I met an English director named David Gilmore who was visiting the United States to cast a West End revival of *Annie Get Your Gun*. David had happened to see a production of my play *Sullivan & Gilbert* that was being produced at the time by the Kennedy Center, and as we discussed it, he asked me casually what else I had written lately. I told him about *Lend Me A Tenor*, and he took a copy home to England with him.

A few days later, David called me from his home in Wimbledon and said that he had enjoyed the play. He said that he would like to direct it and, moreover, would like to show it to a "producer friend" of his. I remember thinking at the time, "If I just hand this play over to David, he's going to think I don't have any real connections of my own and that I don't know how to deal in big-time theater circles." With this imbecilic notion in my head, as though my brain had been invaded by some alien species with the ability to make humans stupid at a moment's notice, I said "Well, David, I don't know . . . I don't want the play to look shopped around. I do have interest from some big-time producers. Who's your friend?" To which he answered, "Andrew Lloyd Webber."

Fortunately, the aliens from the Planet Idiot left my brain as quickly as they had entered, and I said calmly, "Well that's nice. Why don't we show it to him."

Two days later, the telephone rang, and an English voice came over the line and said, "How do you do? This is Andrew Lloyd Webber. You don't know me." I said that I had, in fact, heard of him and was delighted to be speaking with him. He then said that he thought that *Lend Me A Tenor* was the funniest play he had ever read and asked me if I had licensed the performance rights to anyone else yet. I said no. He asked if he could acquire them. I said yes. And that was that.

Two weeks later, I found myself on a plane to London. Within an hour of landing, I joined Andrew and his friend Richard Stilgoe (the librettist of *Starlight Express* and colibrettist of *The Phantom of the Opera*) at the American Bar at the Savoy Hotel. As always (I came to learn) Andrew was brimming with energy and ideas, and he could not have been kinder or more supportive. He has always reminded me of Charles Dickens — bursting with new projects and filled with the seemingly endless energy to accomplish them. The first words out of Andrew's mouth were not "Nice to meet you," or "Welcome to

London." They were, without preamble: "Listen, Ken, I have a *great* idea for the poster! Covent Garden is about to produce *Otello* with Placido Domingo, and I think I can arrange a deal where we both use similar posters and help each other with publicity!" I have never had a better producer.

True to his word, Andrew had *Lend Me A Tenor*, directed by David Gilmore, open in the West End at the Globe Theatre (now called The Gielgud) within six months of that first call to Washington. The production starred Denis Lawson and Jan Francis and enjoyed a long, healthy run.

On opening night in London, Andrew threw a generously lavish party at the Piccadilly Hotel in central London. I remember that in the weeks preceding the party, the guest list had gotten longer and longer; and when my wife, Adrienne, and I entered the ballroom on the arms of Andrew and his wife, Sarah Brightman, there were hundreds of guests in a scene out of *War and Peace*, including stars, politicians, and personalities of the highest order.

My most vivid recollection is the moment after we walked in the door, when Andrew turned to me and said, "Ken, I would like you to meet a friend of mine. This is Sir Edward Heath." At which point Andrew walked away, taking Adrienne and Sarah with him, leaving me alone with the former prime minister of Great Britain.

I did not know quite what to say to this *eminence gris*, and in typical English fashion, he said nothing as well. So we stood there silently for at least two full minutes. Finally, finding the silence unbearable, I ventured a tentative, nervous question: "How did you like the play, sir?"

He coughed. Sniffed. Took his time. Finally, in a rumbly, phlegmy voice, he said slowly, ". . . The first act was too long." That was it. That was all he said. Not another word. And then we stood there for another two minutes of embarrassed silence with neither of us speaking.

At last, a trifle defensively, I ventured, "Well, the truth is, sir, it's pretty hard to write a play." To which he promptly replied, "It's even harder to run the British government" and walked away.

Lend Me A Tenor was produced on Broadway by Andrew and the American film producer Martin Starger. This time out, the director of the play was Jerry Zaks and the play starred Victor Garber, Phil Bosco, Tovah Feldshuh, and Ron Holgate, each one of whom was greater than the other. Ron, one of the glorious wonders of American musical comedy (he won a Tony Award for playing Richard Henry Lee in *1776*) was with *Lend Me A Tenor* from the very beginning at the American Stage Festival and continued with the play in London and New York.

In London, the play was nominated for a number of awards, including the Olivier Award for Best New Comedy, and in New York, we garnered seven Tony nominations and won two of them. The 2010 Broadway revival received three Tony nominations including Best Revival. The play has been translated into at least twenty languages and is performed somewhere in the world every night of the year. —*KL*

CHARACTERS

MAX, assistant to Saunders

MAGGIE, Max's girlfriend

SAUNDERS, Maggie's father, manager of the Cleveland Grand Opera
Company

TITO MERELLI, a world-famous tenor, known also to his fans as
Il Stupendo

MARIA, his wife

BELLHOP, a bellhop

DIANA, a soprano

JULIA, chairman of the Opera Guild

PLACE AND TIME

The action takes place in a hotel suite in Cleveland, Ohio, in 1934.

ACT I
Scene One: Early afternoon on a Saturday in September
Scene Two: Four hours later

ACT II
Scene One: That night, about eleven o'clock
Scene Two: Fifteen minutes later

LEND ME A TENOR

ACT I

SCENE ONE

*An elegant suite in a first-rate hotel in Cleveland, Ohio. Early afternoon on
a Saturday in September, 1934.*

*Two rooms: a sitting room stage right and a bedroom stage left with a
connecting door that swings open into the bedroom. Up center in each room
is a door to the corridor. In the sitting room, a large window (facing a street,
several stories below) and a door to the kitchenette. In the bedroom, two more
doors, both along the outside wall, one (upstage) to the closet, the other (downstage) to the bathroom. Six doors in all.*

*The furniture consists, at a minimum, of a sofa, pouf, radio, and coffee
table in the sitting room; and a bed and bureau in the bedroom.*

*As the house lights go down, we hear music: a recording of "La donna è
mobile" from Verdi's* Rigoletto, *sung thrillingly by a world-class tenor.*

*When the lights come up, Maggie, late twenties, pretty and quirky, is
alone onstage, sitting on the pouf in the sitting room. She listens rapturously
to the music, which by now is coming from the radio (and now sounds scratchy
as an old recording). She is entirely caught up in the sensual sound of the tenor's
voice. She sways to the music and mouths the words.*

*After several seconds, Max, midthirties and rumpled, enters the sitting
room from the corridor. He wears glasses. He also wears a scarf, indicating
that he's just been outdoors. He enters hurriedly, with urgency.*

He looks around the room, confirming in an instant that Tito isn't there.

MAX: *(Over the music.)* Maggie — !

MAGGIE: Shhh!

MAX: Did he call?!

MAGGIE: No. Now will you wait!

*(Max sighs. He looks at his watch. Then he notices Maggie's reaction to the
music; she's swaying in rapture. The aria ends, and Maggie falls backward.)*

RADIO ANNOUNCER: The magnificent voice of Tito Merelli, brought to you in
honor of his live appearance this evening with the Cleveland Grand Opera
Company —

(Max turns off the radio.)

MAX: He wasn't on the train.

MAGGIE: Oh my God. He is so wonderful. When he does that last note, I almost can't breathe.

MAX: Maggie, he wasn't there! *(The phone rings. Max grabs it.)* Hello?! . . . No, sir, I couldn't find him.

SAUNDERS: *(Through the phone.) Goddammit! Where the hell is he?!*

MAX: *(To Maggie.)* It's your father. *(Into the phone.)* I don't know! I looked everywhere. I asked the conductor. I had him paged. I-I-I'm sorry, I just —

(The sound of Saunders hanging up.)

MAX: Sir? . . . Sir? *(Max hangs up.)* He's gonna kill me.

MAGGIE: He will not. He'd have nobody to yell at. At least nobody who takes it the way you do.

MAX: Maggie, the man is two hours late! The rehearsal starts in *ten minutes*!

MAGGIE: He'll be here, Max. This is Tito Merelli. He's a genius. They just don't think like other people.

MAX: So what are you saying? He's a grown man and he can't tell time?

MAGGIE: I'm just not worried, okay? *(Pause.)* Oh, Max, just think of it. Tonight. The curtain rises and he walks onstage. And suddenly there's nothing else in the world but that . . . that *voice*.

(Pause.)

MAX: I can sing too, you know.

MAGGIE: Oh, Max — *(She laughs out loud.)*

MAX: I can! What are you — "Oh, Max."

MAGGIE: You don't sing like Tito Merelli.

MAX: Not yet. Okay?

MAGGIE: You don't.

MAX: In your opinion. It's a matter of taste.

MAGGIE: It is not! I wish you wouldn't fool yourself. He's a star, Max. He sings all over the world. He's in *Life* magazine!

MAX: So is Mussolini.

MAGGIE: And he's very sensitive.

MAX: How do you know that?

(Beat. She realizes she's caught.)

MAGGIE: *(Casually.)* Because I met him. Last year.

MAX: You did? You never told me that.

MAGGIE: It was no big thing. When I was in Italy with Daddy, we went to La

Scala and he was in *Aida.* Then afterwards we went backstage and . . . well, there he was, all by himself, behind the curtain. He was wearing a sort of . . . loincloth and his whole body was pouring with sweat. Anyway, he looked up and saw us and do you know what he did, Max. He kissed my palms.

MAX: Yeah. So what?

MAGGIE: It was romantic.

MAX: He's Italian! They kiss everything!

MAGGIE: Fine, forget it.

MAX: Meatballs. Cheese. Cold cuts.

MAGGIE: Max —

MAX: If it *moves*, they kiss it.

MAGGIE: *Max!*

MAX: So what else happened?

MAGGIE: Nothing. *(Pause.)* Of any importance.

MAX: Something else happened?

MAGGIE: Not really.

MAX: Something sort of happened.

MAGGIE: It wasn't important.

MAX: What happened!

MAGGIE: It was nothing! Oh — ! *(Reluctantly, embarrassed.)* I fainted.

MAX: You fainted?

MAGGIE: It must have been the heat and all the excitement. I remember thinking suddenly, my God, it's like an oven back here. And we were talking and he sort of . . . stared right at me, and then I . . . blacked out.

MAX: Oh great. I mean this is terrific. My fiancée meets this — this sweaty Italian guy and she keels over.

MAGGIE: From the heat! And I'm not your fiancée, Max.

MAX: Wait a minute. Did I ask you to marry me or not? Huh? Remember that? What did you-you black out during the proposal?

MAGGIE: I heard it, Max, and I said no.

MAX: You said you'd think about it.

MAGGIE: *(Taking his hand.)* Max. I'm just not ready yet. I want something special first. Something wonderful and romantic.

MAX: I'm not romantic? I don't believe this. What do you call a rowboat at three A.M., huh? Moonlight shimmering on the water. Nobody for miles.

MAGGIE: You lost the oars.

MAX: But it was fun! It turned out fun!

MAGGIE: We spent thirty hours in a rowboat, Max.

MAX: That's not the point!

MAGGIE: I haven't had any flings, Max.

MAX: Flings?

MAGGIE: Flings.

MAX: I've been asking you to fling with me for three years! I begged you!

MAGGIE: I don't mean that! I just feel that I need some . . . wider experience.

MAX: Oh. Sure. I get it. You mean like Diana.

MAGGIE: Diana?

MAX: Desdemona. Soprano.

MAGGIE: Oh, her.

MAX: She's flinging her way through the whole cast. All the men are getting flung out. You should see the guy who plays Iago. He's supposed to be evil. He can hardly walk.

MAGGIE: Max —

MAX: He's limping now —

MAGGIE: Max, listen. Let's be honest. When you kiss me, do you hear anything? Special?

MAX: Like what?

MAGGIE: Like . . . bells.

MAX: You wanna hear bells?

MAGGIE: I guess it sounds stupid, doesn't it?

MAX: Yeah. It does.

MAGGIE: Just forget it.

(A knock at the door.)

SAUNDERS: *(Offstage.)* Max!

MAX: *(Torn.)* Maggie —

MAGGIE: I said forget it!

(More knocking.)

SAUNDERS: *(Offstage.)* Max!

MAX: Coming!

(Max opens the door, and Saunders rushes in. Midfifties, authoritarian, and very upset.)

SAUNDERS: Well? Any word?!

MAX: Not yet.

SAUNDERS: Goddammit!!

MAX: I-I-I'm sorry.

MAGGIE: Max!

SAUNDERS: *(To Maggie.)* What the hell are you doing here?

MAGGIE: I'm sure I can be here if I want to.

SAUNDERS: Wrong.

MAGGIE: Daddy — !

SAUNDERS: Do you know what time it is?

MAX: It's almost one.

SAUNDERS: Do you know what that means?

MAX: He's late.

SAUNDERS: It means he's late!!!

(Saunders takes a grape from the fruit bowl.)

MAX: I-I wouldn't worry, sir. I mean, I'm sure he'll get here.

SAUNDERS: Do I seem worried, Max?

MAX: No! No.

MAGGIE: Max!

MAX: I mean . . . well . . . yeah. You do.

SAUNDERS: I do? How interesting. In that case, perhaps you can tell us what extrasensory Maxian perception has led you to form this startling and erroneous conclusion.

(He pops the grape in his mouth.)

MAX: That . . . that's wax fruit.

(Saunders blows the grape across the room [into the audience].)

SAUNDERS: Goddammit!!

MAGGIE: Daddy!

MAX: I'm sorry!

SAUNDERS: Call the station!

MAX: I was just there —

SAUNDERS: CALL THE STATION!

MAX: Yes, sir.

(He goes to the phone, finds the phone book, and looks for the number.)

MAGGIE: Daddy, have you taken your pills?

SAUNDERS: Yes, yes.

MAGGIE: You're lying, Daddy.

(She rummages through her handbag and comes up with a bottle of pills.)

SAUNDERS: I am perfectly capable of controlling my own nervous system. Where would Lauritz Melchior be today if he'd taken phenobarbital?

MAGGIE: Open wide.

SAUNDERS: Margaret . . .

MAGGIE: Mouth!

(He sticks out his tongue, she puts the pill on it, and he swallows it. The phone rings. They all freeze. Then Max reaches for it.)

SAUNDERS: No! He's been in an accident. I can feel it. *(It rings again.)* He's lying in the gutter, stinking drunk on cheap Chianti.

(It rings again.)

MAGGIE: Max.

SAUNDERS: All right! Pick it up!

(Max picks it up.)

MAX: *(Into the phone.):* Hello? . . . Yes it is . . . Oh no. That's terrible.

SAUNDERS: He's dead. Selfish bastard.

MAX: *(To Saunders.)* It's Mrs. Leverett. The rehearsal's starting.

SAUNDERS: Give me that! *(He grabs the phone. Suddenly charming.)* Madam Chairman, how very kind of you to c — No. No, he hasn't quite arrived yet . . . Julia . . . Jul- . . . Juli- . . . Julia! Will you calm down! . . . What? . . . *(He sighs.)* . . . I see . . . Well, if I may, I will leave that decision in your capable hands. Right. Good-bye. *(He hangs up.)* It appears that the Opera Guild Collation Committee has decided to serve shrimp mayonnaise at the intermission, the refrigerator has broken down and the temperature backstage is a hundred degrees.

MAX: So what do we do?

SAUNDERS: We play it by ear. If the shrimp stays pink, the audience gets it. If it turns green, we feed it to the stagehands.

MAX: Shall I call the station?

SAUNDERS: No. I've changed my mind. I want the line open. *(To Maggie.)* And I want you out of here.

MAGGIE: Why?

SAUNDERS: Because I said so.

MAGGIE: Daddy!

SAUNDERS: Max and I have some business to discuss.

MAGGIE: I won't say a word.

SAUNDERS: Out.

MAGGIE: I'll wait in the bedroom.

SAUNDERS: Wrong.

MAGGIE: But I want to see him! You said I could. You promised!

SAUNDERS: Well I lied, you nitwit! Now get out!

MAGGIE: Max thinks I should stay. Don't you, Max?

(Pause.)

MAX: I-I think he's right.

MAGGIE: I see.

SAUNDERS: Good-bye, my dear.

MAX: *(To Maggie.)* I'm — I'm sorry.

>*(Maggie spots the key to the room on the table next to her. Without them seeing it, she picks up the key and takes it with her, with her handbag.)*

MAGGIE: *(At the door, ignoring Max.)* See you later . . . Daddy.

>*(She exits to the corridor, closing the door behind her. Max feels like a crumb.)*

SAUNDERS: I've got a thousand of Cleveland's so-called cognoscenti arriving at the theater in six hours in black tie, a thirty-piece orchestra, twenty-four chorus, fifteen stagehands, and eight principals. Backstage, I have approximately fifty pounds of rotting shrimp mayonnaise, which, if consumed, could turn the Gala Be-a-Sponsor Buffet into a mass murder. All I don't have is a tenor. Time.

MAX: One-fifteen. *(Pause.)* I'm-I'm really sorry, sir. I wish there was something I could do to help.

SAUNDERS: It's not your fault, Max. I wish it was. The question now is what to do if that irresponsible Italian jackass doesn't arrive.

MAX: I-I have an idea about that, actually.

SAUNDERS: You do?

MAX: Yeah. I mean, sort of.

SAUNDERS: Well, spit it out, Max.

MAX: The thing is — I mean, I was just-just thinking that — well — I mean — I could do it.

SAUNDERS: Do what?

MAX: Sing it. Otello. Sort of — step in. You see, I-I've been to all the rehearsals and I know the part and I-I mean, I could do it. I know I could.

SAUNDERS: Otello? Big black fellow.

MAX: Yes, sir.

SAUNDERS: Otello, Max. He's huge. He's larger than life. He loves with a passion that rocks the heavens. His jealousy is so terrible that we tremble with irrational fear for our very lives. His tragedy is the fate of tortured greatness, facing the black and gaping abyss of insensible nothingness. It isn't you, Max.

MAX: It-it could be. I mean, if I had the chance.

SAUNDERS: *(Turning directly front, addressing the audience.)* "Ladies and gentlemen. May I have your attention, please. I regret to inform you that Mr. Tito Merelli, the greatest tenor of our generation, scheduled to make his American debut with the Cleveland Grand Opera Company in honor of our tenth anniversary season, is regrettably indisposed this evening, but . . . BUT! . . . I have the privilege to announce that the role of Otello will be sung tonight by a somewhat gifted amateur making his very first appearance on this, or indeed any other stage, our company's very own factotum, gopher, and all-purpose dogsbody . . . Max!" Do you see the problem?

MAX: I guess so.

SAUNDERS: Old women would be trampled to death in the stampede up the aisles.

MAX: I see what you mean.

SAUNDERS: Time.

MAX: One-twenty. *(A depressed silence. Saunders picks up a grape and starts chewing. Then he realizes and spits it out and starts stamping on it in his fury. Meanwhile, the phone rings. Max picks it up.)* Hello? What? Could you speak more slowly, please.

SAUNDERS: If it's Julia, tell her she can take the shrimp and stuff it up her —

MAX: *(To Saunders.)* Sir! It's him! He's in the lobby!

(Saunders runs to the phone and grabs it.)

SAUNDERS: *(Into the phone, all charm.)* Signor Merelli! Benvenuto a Cleveland! I will be down *immediamente. Presto. (He hangs up.)* All right, Max. This is it. You have your instructions. Key word, Max.

MAX: Glue.

SAUNDERS: Glue. You will stick to him like

MAX: glue

SAUNDERS: and you will not let him out of your

MAX: sight.

SAUNDERS: You will drive him to the rehearsal and then drive him back. You will give him whatever he wants except

MAX: liquor and women.

SAUNDERS: At the performance, you will lead a spontaneous

MAX: standing ovation

SAUNDERS: then return him to the reception, keeping him

MAX: sober

SAUNDERS: with his hands

MAX: to himself

SAUNDERS: at which point he can

MAX: drop dead

SAUNDERS: for all we care. Good.

MAX: Good.

(Break. Saunders crosses to the corridor door, pauses.)

SAUNDERS: Max!

MAX: Sir?

SAUNDERS: Get rid of that fruit bowl.

(Saunders exits, pulling the door closed behind him. Simultaneously, Maggie enters quickly through the bedroom/corridor door and closes it quietly. Then she darts to the bathroom and enters it, slamming the door behind her in her haste. As Max is entering the kitchenette with the fruit, he hears the door slam and stops, puzzled. Still holding the fruit, he walks into the bedroom and looks around. He opens the closet door. No one there. He goes to the bathroom door, opens it, and Maggie, who was holding the doorknob inside, is yanked into the room.)

MAX: *(Horrified.)* Maggie!

MAGGIE: Is he here?

MAX: No! But he's coming up!

MAGGIE: *(Excited.)* Oh, Max!

MAX: Maggie, do you realize what this looks like? I mean, waiting for him in the bathroom! *(A knock at the sitting room/corridor door.)* He's here!

MAGGIE: *(In raptures.)* Oh, Max!

MAX: With your father!

MAGGIE: Bye, Max.

(She steps back into the bathroom and closes the door.)

MAX: Maggie!

SAUNDERS: *(Offstage.)* Ma-ax. The door is *locked*, Max.

MAX: Coming! *(He heads for the sitting room. Stops.)* Fruit! *(Which he is still holding. Back to the bathroom.)* Maggie! Door!

(Maggie comes out, annoyed.)

MAGGIE: Max!

MAX: Fruit! *(He hands it to her.)*

MAGGIE: *(Touched, accepting it.)* Thank you, Max.

(She steps back in and Max slams the door.)

SAUNDERS: *(Offstage.)* Ma-ax! Open the door, please!

MAX: Coming!

(He rushes into the sitting room, closing the connecting door. At the corridor door, he stops abruptly. Adjusts himself. Opens the door. Saunders enters.)

SAUNDERS: *(Offstage — then on.)* MAX!!

MAX: Hi.

SAUNDERS: *(Glaring murderously, then smiling broadly.)* Thank you.

> *(He steps aside, permitting Maria and Tito Merelli to enter the sitting room. Maria is a Sophia Loren type: busty, proud, and excitable. Tito is imposing. Both of them speak, not surprisingly, with Italian accents.)*

SAUNDERS: My friends, your suite.

MARIA: So are you, I'm a-sure.

> *(She flings her fur stole at Max.)*

SAUNDERS: Thank you. I'll make the introductions, shall I? Signora Merelli, whom we did not expect, but could not possibly be more pleased to have with us. And Signor Tito Merelli, who needs no introduction. My assistant, Max.

MARIA: *Ciao.*

TITO: *(Handing his hat and coat to Max.)* How do you do. John.

MAX: Uh, Max.

SAUNDERS: *(Enunciating.)* Max.

TITO: John!

MAX: *(Shrugging.)* He can call me John, if he wants —

MARIA: My husband would like a-the john. He throws up.

> *(Maggie sticks her head out of the bathroom. During the following, she tiptoes across the bedroom to listen.)*

SAUNDERS: Oh, the *john.* Yes, of course. Right this way.

TITO: *Grazie.*

> *(Tito and Saunders head for the john.)*

MAX: *(To Maria.)* The john. We-we misunderstood, you see, we usually say the STOP!!! *(Maggie freezes. Saunders and Tito stop. They haven't entered the bedroom yet, but Tito has opened the connecting door partway.)* There-there-there's one in the lobby. It's much-much nicer. Cleaner.

SAUNDERS: Are you all right, Max?

MAX: Me? Fine. I just — they've got this terrific bathroom in the lobby. It's in-incredible.

SAUNDERS: I'm sure that this one is peachy, Max.

MAX: No. No it isn't. Trust me.

TITO: John!

SAUNDERS: This way. I'm awfully sorry.

> *(Saunders leads Tito into the bedroom by which time Maggie has caught on and disappears into the closet, closing the door behind her.)*

TITO: *Grazie.*

MARIA: *(To Max.)* Forgive a-my husband, eh? *(She shouts.)* He's a-stupid!

TITO: SHUT UP!

MARIA: SHUT UP A-YOUSELF!

(Tito enters the bathroom and slams the door. During the following, Saunders listens at the bathroom door, concerned.)

MARIA: *(To Max.)* He eats a-like a fat a-pig. We have a-food on the train. He eats a-too much. Then we arrive, he wants a-lunch. "Don't eat," I tell 'im. "You get a-sick. You wone be happy." He eats a-like a pig. Two plates. Why, eh? Why?! Because he likes a-bosoms.

MAX: Bosoms?

MARIA: He wants a-bosoms. Is that normal? You tell me. Eh?

MAX: Well, it's-it's-it's I'd say it's unusual.

SAUNDERS: *(Returning to the sitting room, jovial.)* What is so unusual, Max?

MAX: Mr. Merelli, apparently, he-he'd like to have bosoms.

SAUNDERS: Well . . . that's wonderful.

MARIA: The waitress — eh? — she leans a-way over. "You wanna seconds?" He likes a-bosoms, he says a-sure. He's not hungry! He wants a-more bosoms.

MAX: Oh.

SAUNDERS: I see. *(A knock at the corridor door.)* Excuse me.

(Saunders opens the door to find the Bellhop, who enters carrying two suitcases and a vanity case. Immediately, he bursts into the famous aria from The Barber of Seville.*)*

BELLHOP: *(Singing.)* Largo al factotum
della citta, largo!
La ran la, la ran la,
la ran la, la!

SAUNDERS: Shut up!

BELLHOP: Where is he?!

MAX: Bathroom.

SAUNDERS: Max!

MAX: Sorry.

SAUNDERS: Luggage in the bedroom, thank you.

BELLHOP: Yes, *sir*!

(Max leads him to the bedroom.)

SAUNDERS: *(To Maria.)* I'm awfully sorry about that. You'd think that people would have better manners.

MARIA: Hey, it's okay. No big deal, eh? It happens a-ten times a day. Phone rings, I pick it up, I get *Pagliacci*. I go to the butcher, he skins a-the chicken, he sings a-me *Carmen*.

(The phone rings.)

SAUNDERS: *(To Maria.)* Excuse me.

BELLHOP: *(Singing at bathroom door, through the keyhole.)* Presto a Bottega, che l'alba e gia, presto —

MAX: Hey!!

SAUNDERS: *(Into the phone.)* Yes? Hello, Julia . . . Yes, he is!

(Saunders turns his back and during the following, carries on a silent conversation with Julia.

As Max lays the fur stole and Tito's hat and coat on the bed, the Bellhop opens the closet door, revealing Maggie standing in the doorway. However, he doesn't see her, having turned away to get the suitcases. Max, however, sees her and reacts. Beat. Max slams the door.

The Bellhop looks up, sees that Max has slammed the door and sighs at Max with annoyance. He returns to the closet door and opens it again — again turning away without seeing Maggie. As he picks up the two suitcases, Maggie runs out of the closet and hides behind the closet door.

As the Bellhop enters the closet with the suitcases, Max opens the bedroom/corridor door and motions to Maggie to leave. She sticks her head out from behind the closet door and shakes it no. As the Bellhop reenters from the closet, she disappears again.

The Bellhop goes to the bed and gathers up the stole, coat, and hat — at which point, Maggie runs around the closet door and back in the closet, slamming the door behind her. This is followed immediately by Max slamming the corridor door. The Bellhop looks at one door, then the other, then at Max, who feigns innocence, as though nothing has happened.

The Bellhop shrugs and walks to the closet with the wraps. He opens the door and Maggie is standing there. He stares at her for a moment, then wordlessly, he hands her the hat, coat, and fur. She nods as if to say "thank you" and smiles wanly. The Bellhop closes the door on Maggie. He turns front, dazed — then shrugs and heads for the sitting room. Before leaving the bedroom, however, he stops and gives Max the thumbs-up and hits him on the arm as if to say "way to go." Then he goes into the sitting room, followed by Max, who closes the connecting door behind him.)

SAUNDERS: *(Into the phone.)* Julia, as soon as possible! . . . No he's fine . . . Julia, he is perfectly all right! . . . Yes!

(As he talks to Julia, the Bellhop comes over with his hand out. Saunders hands him a coin.)

BELLHOP: *(Looking at the tip.)* He's got to be kidding.

SAUNDERS: Out! Now!

BELLHOP: That's pathetic.

SAUNDERS: *(Into the phone.)* I'm sorry, Julia. We have a bellhop on our hands who is not only rude, but apparently brainless.

BELLHOP: Nice guy.

SAUNDERS: *(He hangs up.)* I believe you owe this lady an apology.

BELLHOP: I do?

SAUNDERS: I would say so, yes.

BELLHOP: Fine. *(To Maria.) Mia signora, mi dispiace. Non volevo disturbarla. Se l'ho offesa, chiedo scusa, chiedo scusa.* [My dear lady, I'm sorry. I did not intend to bother you. If I have offended you, I certainly beg your forgiveness.]

MARIA: *Non e niente, l'assicuro.* [I assure you, it's of no importance.]

BELLHOP: *Grazie, la saluto.*

MARIA: *Ciao.*

(The Bellhop gives Saunders a look, then exits to the corridor, closing the door behind him.)

MAX: I hope Mr. Merelli is all right.

MARIA: Phh!

(At this point, Tito emerges from the bathroom, holding the fruit bowl, puzzled by it. He looks sick. He puts it on the bureau, then sits on the bed.)

SAUNDERS: I don't suppose this sort of thing affects his singing. I mean, he will go on?

MARIA: You got a-women in the opera?

SAUNDERS: Women? Well yes, of course. Fourteen.

MARIA: He wouldn't miss it, believe me. You know why? Eh? Because he's got a . . . *(She gropes.)* . . . a . . . What's a-the word. Starts a-with *p.*

SAUNDERS: P?

MAX: Pride?

SAUNDERS: Personality?

MARIA: All men, they got this thing. It starts a-small, it gets a-big, and it makes a-trouble.

SAUNDERS: P?

MAX: Privates?

MARIA: Passion! He's got a big a-passion!

MAX: Oh.

SAUNDERS: I see.

(*Tito enters the sitting room.*)

MAX: Mr. Merelli!

SAUNDERS: Are you all right?

TITO: Me? I'm a-fine. *Perfetto.*

MARIA: *(Derisively.)* Hoo!

TITO: I'm a-okey-dokey. I feel like ten bucks.

MARIA: Look at 'im, eh? He looks a-like a sick dog.

TITO: I'm tip a-top.

MARIA: Liar!

TITO: Shut up!

MARIA: Phh!

TITO: A little stomach. It's nothing. I'm a-fine. A few more minutes, I'm gonna be even better.

SAUNDERS: Better?

MARIA: That's what I thought. I'll get a-you pills.

(*She gets up.*)

TITO: *(A familiar argument.)* I done take pills.

MARIA: You need a-pills!

TITO: No! I'm a-Merelli! Merelli says a-no!

MARIA: What's a-matter? You got a girl in there?

TITO: Yeah. Sure. I got a girl. In fact, I got two girls. Both a-naked. Go ahead! Look!

MARIA: Some day, you gonna wake up in a-you bed, you gonna be a soprano!

TITO: *(To Max.)* Jealousy, eh? Jealousy! It's a-terrible.

MARIA: *(Overlapping, to Saunders.)* In my heart, he makes a-me sick.

TITO: *(Overlapping.)* She's a crazy woman.

MARIA: *(Overlapping.)* Because he's a-stupid. He's got a-no brains.

TITO: *(Overlapping.)* All the time it's a-jealousy, jealousy, jealousy —

MARIA: SHUT UP!

TITO: SHUT UP A-YOUSELF!

(*Maria slams into the bedroom. Huffing in unison, Tito and Maria both sit, he on the sofa, she on the bed. During the following, Maria calms herself, then lies on the bed and flips through a copy of* Vogue.)

SAUNDERS: So . . . I uh, I don't mean to be pushy, but I really do think we ought to be going.

TITO: Sure. Okay. Thanks a-for everything. See you tonight.

SAUNDERS: No. Sorry. I meant all of us. To the rehearsal.

TITO: ME?

SAUNDERS: Right.

(Tito considers it.)

TITO: No. No, I done think so. You want the truth, I'm not so good.

SAUNDERS: You're not?

TITO: No.

SAUNDERS: What's the matter?

TITO: I'm a-sick. I eat too much. I'm a-stupid.

SAUNDERS: Signor Merelli. I don't think you understand. You see, I have a hundred people at the theater. *Cento persona.* They're waiting for you.

TITO: Hey. You done get it. I'm gonna sing right now, I'm gonna throw up on the soprano.

SAUNDERS: I don't believe this.

TITO: Hey! Done worry, okay? Tonight I'm gonna be there. I'm a-Merelli. I done miss performance.

SAUNDERS: But you don't know the stage directions! The-the tempos!

TITO: I sing Otello fifty times. Is no big deal.

SAUNDERS: And what about the costume fitting?

TITO: I bring a-my own. It's in the suitcase. You wanna see? In fact, I bring a-two costumes. Just in case.

SAUNDERS: You can't do this.

TITO: I wear my own costume at Vienna Staatsoper, Covent Garden. You think in Cleveland I'm gonna suffer?

(The phone rings. Saunders grabs it.)

SAUNDERS: *(Into the phone.)* Yes? . . . OH MY GOD!!! . . . I'll be right there. Just keep looking! . . . Jul- . . . Juli- . . . JULIA, DON'T PANIC!

(He hangs up.)

MAX: Trouble?

SAUNDERS: They lost the music. All of it.

TITO: That's not good.

SAUNDERS: All right, now listen. I want an answer and I want it now. Are you coming or not?

TITO: Not.

SAUNDERS: Right. That's settled. Max!

MAX: Sir?

SAUNDERS: If there's a problem of any kind, I want you to call me. Immediately.

MAX: Yes, sir.

SAUNDERS: I'll be at the theater.

MAX: Right.

(Tito groans.)

SAUNDERS: Max!

(He motions for Max to join him at the door.)

MAX: Sir?

SAUNDERS: He needs some sleep. Do whatever you have to.

MAX: Yes, sir.

(Saunders exits. Tito leans back on the sofa. He doesn't notice at first that Max is still there. Then he does.)

TITO: You stay here?

MAX: Yes. I-I-I mean if you don't mind.

TITO: Sure. Help a-youself. *(He belches, pats his stomach.) Scusi.*

MAX: You really are sick, aren't you?

TITO: It's okay. I'm gonna live. In my village, they got a saying — "Nobody ever dies from a-gas." And believe me, they know.

MAX: Yeah, but-but maybe you should take those pills. I mean, they might help.

TITO: Thanks, a-no. I need sleep, not a-pills. I gotta relax. Take a deep breath. It's not so easy, eh?

MAX: Why not?

TITO: Why not. Today it's a-Cleveland, Monday New York. Rushing every place. I live in hotels. I'm gonna have children, they gonna look like bellhops.

MAX: I see.

TITO: I get tense, I feel a-sick — then I can't sing nothing.

MAX: Nothing?

TITO: Singing. It's like a-life, eh? You gotta relax, take it easy. You get a-tense, you finished.

MAX: I know what you mean. I-I sing myself, a little.

TITO: You?

MAX: Yeah. I-I-I mean, not like you. I wish I could.

TITO: Hey. Done knock yourself down. It's no good. To sing, you need a-confidence. You gotta say, "I'm a-the best. I'm a-Max. I sing good."

MAX: I know. I-I-I mean that's the problem. Whenever I sing in front of people, I-I get tense. I tighten up. I can't help it.

TITO: That's it, eh? That's a-me, now. My doctor, he says take a-pills. Phenobarbital. It makes-a you sleep. But I'm a Merelli. I done take pills.

MAX: *(To himself.)* Phenobarbital.

(During the following, Max picks up Saunders' bottle of phenobarbital from the table, where Maggie left it.)

TITO: Hey! I got it. We have a drink. A little wine, eh?

MAX: Hm? No! No, I-I-I don't think that's such a — *(He looks at the bottle of pills.)* Well. All right.

TITO: You got a-glasses? I got a good Chianti.

MAX: I-I don't know.

TITO: You gonna join me.

(He heads for the bedroom.)

MAX: Right. Okay. One glass!

(Max disappears into the kitchenette as Tito enters the bedroom. Maria is lying on the bed, on her stomach, still reading Vogue.*)*

TITO: *Ciao.*

MARIA: *Ciao.*

(She ignores him. Tito looks at her.)

TITO: Eh. *Bellezza.* I'm a-sorry. Okay?

MARIA: Phh.

TITO: I get a-tense. It's too much. It's a-my fault.

MARIA: Yeah.

TITO: Hey. Listen. We take a vacation. Soon. *(He sits on the bed.)* Greece, eh? We get a boat. We sail a-the islands. Sleep all day. On the sand. *(He's rubbing her backside.)* Just a-two, eh. Like a-the old days. Clams. Big lobster. Suck a-the claws.

MARIA: *(Warming considerably.)* Tito . . .

TITO: *Bellezza.*

(They get intimate. She's kissing his neck.)

MARIA: Close a-door.

TITO: Huh?

MARIA: Close a-door.

TITO: Now?

MARIA: Close.

TITO: Maria. I got a stomach. No joke.

MARIA: I make a-you better. Fix you up.

TITO: No. Hey. Not now, okay? I-I can't do it!

(She stops, angry.)

MARIA: Pig!

TITO: Maria!

MARIA: You got a girl.

TITO: I got nobody.

MARIA: You got a girl! So done lie!

TITO: Maria —

MARIA: Three weeks — nothing! Not once, eh?

TITO: I'm sorry. I get a-tense. I-I got a stomach!

MARIA: I wanna be a nun, I'll join a-the church! At least sometimes I have a-some fun. I sing a-hymns. Pluck a-chickens!

TITO: She's crazy. My wife, she's a-crazy.

MARIA: Oh sure, I'm a-crazy. I hate a-trains, I'm a-crazy. I hate hotels. I'm a-crazy. I got a-empty bed, and I'm a-crazy!

TITO: Maria, I'm a sick a-man!

MARIA: SO TAKE A-YOU PILLS!

TITO: *(Angry.)* Fine. Okay. I take a-pills! *(He goes to the vanity case and takes out his bottle of pills.)* You wanna pills, I take a-pills. Look! Hey! Two pills. No. *Four* pills!

MARIA: Two!

TITO: Four!!

MARIA: Oh!

TITO: Okay? Happy?
(He puts the bottle on the bedside table.)

MARIA: Phh!

TITO: I take a-pills, I got a happy wife. Happy marriage!
(He pulls a bottle of Chianti from the vanity case.)

MARIA: Now you gonna be sick.

TITO: So what? My girl in the closet, she's not gonna care.

MARIA: Pig!

TITO: SHUT UP!

MARIA: SHUT UP A-YOUSELF!
(Maria slams into the bathroom. Tito slams into the sitting room.)

TITO: Max!
(He paces, upset. Max enters from the kitchenette with two glasses.)

MAX: Are you all right?

TITO: I'm a-peachy. Just a-fine. I done relax, I'm gonna blow up! Open!
(He hands Max the bottle.)

MAX: *(Taking it.)* Uh, s-sorry. Corkscrew?

TITO: Eh? Oh yeah. Corkascrew. Sure. I'm a-stupid!
(Tito enters the bedroom, grabs the vanity case, and sits on the bed. As he looks for the corkscrew, Max unscrews the top from the bottle of phenobarbital and

pours several pills into one of the glasses. He thinks for a moment, then pours more pills. Beat. Then adds a few more for good measure. By this time, Tito has found the corkscrew. He slams back into the sitting room as Max pockets the bottle of pills. Tito grabs the Chianti and starts opening it.)

TITO: Jealousy, eh? That's all I get is a-jealousy. Back a-stage. Girls, they come a-see me. Nice girls. They wanna my autograph. That's it. They say, "Hello, Tito. We love a-you, Tito." Maria, she goes a-nuts.

MAX: I'll pour.

(Max takes the bottle, fills Tito's glass, and hands it to him. Then he puts his finger into Tito's glass and stirs. Tito watches, startled, then bemused. He looks at Max. Max removes his finger and acts as if nothing's wrong. Beat.)

TITO: Hey. Join me.

MAX: Gee, I-I-I don't really —

TITO: Drink!

MAX: Right. *(He pours some wine into his own glass and raises it.)* Well. Down the hatch.

(Tito pauses. Then ceremoniously, proud to know the local ritual, he puts his finger into Max's glass and stirs. Max looks sick.)

TITO: *Salut.*

(Tito drains his glass as Max watches. For a moment, Tito senses something strange; then he sighs with pleasure at the effect of the wine. Max is clearly relieved.)

MAX: I think you're going to feel a lot better now.

TITO: I hope so, eh? 'Cause worse would be impossible.

(Tito sits down heavily.)

MAX: You-you might even take a nap. Who knows.

TITO: Sure. Who knows. *(He picks up the bottle and starts pouring himself more wine.)* Miracles happen, eh?

MAX: *(Trying to stop him.)* Mr. Merelli, I-I-I —

TITO: Tito! You call me Tito. 'Cause I like you.

MAX: Uh . . . right. Tito. *(It's too late. The wine is poured.* Max *takes the bottle.)* Good year. *(He puts the bottle down as far from Tito as possible.)*

TITO: *Salut.*

(As Tito drinks, the bathroom door swings open, and Maria stalks into the bedroom.)

MARIA: *(To herself.)* No more! That's it! I'm a-finished with that man!

(During the following, she finds a pen and a piece of paper in her vanity case, then sits on the bed and starts to write her farewell note to Tito.)

TITO: *(Relaxing.)* Hey. Max. Sing a-me something.

MAX: Huh?

TITO: You sing, I listen. Maybe I help, eh? Make a-pointer.

MAX: Gee, that's awfully — Now?

TITO: Sure. Why not? Free lesson.

MAX: Well, I-I-I suppose . . .

TITO: Come on. Let's hear. Stand up!

MAX: *(Standing.)* Right. Is there, uh, anything special?

TITO: Pick a-you favorite. Go.

MAX: Right. *(He is nervous and embarrassed. He clears his throat, then gropes for the right pitch.)* Ahem . . . Okay . . . *(Without much confidence, he starts to sing. He's chosen the tenor line of the duet "Dio, che nell'alma infondere" from Act II, Scene One of Verdi's* Don Carlo. *He sings without accompaniment and not very well.)*
> *Dio, che nell'alma infondere*
> *Amor volesti e speme —*

TITO: Stop! *(Max stops.)* Okay. You're a-tight, eh? Tense. Is no good. You gotta relax. Be you.

MAX: I-I-I'm trying. I —

TITO: Okay, now shake a-youself.

MAX: Huh?

TITO: Shake! Like this. *(Standing by now, he shakes his body, arms flailing in a singer's exercise.)* Come on! *(Tentatively,* Max *imitates him.)* Move! *(Max lets loose. They both move around the room, arms flailing.)* Good. Okay. Now the throat. It's a-tight. It's gotta be loose. Like this. *(He rolls his head in a circle, around his shoulders, simultaneously singing a note.)* Ahhh . . .

MAX: *(Joining.)* Ahhh . . .
> *(They continue for a few seconds, then stop. Max holds his forehead to stop the dizziness.)*

TITO: Now . . . together.
> *(They sing "ah," roll their heads and move around the room, arms flailing. After a few seconds, Tito stops and watches Max, who eventually notices that he's doing it alone. He straightens up.)*

TITO: Now a trick, eh? You gotta hear the music. Before you sing. You gotta hear everything. The orchestra, the chorus —

MAX: *(Enthusiastic.)* I-I know what you mean!

TITO: Everything! It's in a-you heart!

MAX: Right!

TITO: Okay. Shh! Listen!

> *(Silence. Then four notes, pizzicato, from the orchestra — which is now in their heads. A fifth note swells and they begin the duet.)*

MAX/TITO: *(Singing, with full orchestra.)*

> *Dio, che nell'alma infondere*
> *amor volesti e speme,*
> *desio nel cor accendere*
> *tu sei di liberta;*
> *desio accendere, accender nel cor*
> *tu sei di liberta.*
> *Giuriamo insiem di vivere*
> *e di morire insieme.*
> *In terra, in ciel*
> *congiungere ci puo,*
> *ci puo la tua bonta.*
> *Ah! Dio che nell'alma, [etc.]*

> *(Their duet gets progressively more confident and dramatic. Meanwhile, Maria stands, having finished her note. She scans it with tears in her eyes, folds it in half, and props it on the bed, on top of the pillow. Note: The paper should be distinctive and easy to recognize — lavender, perhaps. She picks up her vanity case, heads for the door to the corridor, and opens it. She stops. She forgot something — her fur stole. She goes to the closet, opens it, and Maggie falls out, having fallen asleep inside, against the door. The following is heard over the singing, as it occurs during the quiet second verse.)*

MAGGIE: How do you do. I realize this may look a little strange, but I can explain it — *(Maria stifles a growl of anger, then reaches into the closet, takes the stole, and turns away.)* You see, I thought, well, why not hide in the closet. *(Stole in one hand, vanity case in the other, Maria stalks out.)* Wait! You don't understand! I don't even know him!

> *(Maggie runs out after Maria, closing the door behind her. Meanwhile, Tito and Max finish their duet.*)*

---

*Note: It is important to deliver the full duet as edited by the author of the play: i.e., including the last seven lines of Act I, Scene Two of the opera — the big ending of the scene that finishes the duet with a bang. In the Broadway revival of 2010, these last seven lines were inadvertently omitted, which may have been confusing for those who saw the play. To hear the complete music required, including the proper internal cut in the Verdi opera, producers of the play should refer to the Samuel French recording.

TITO/MAX: *(Singing.)*

> *Vivremo insiem e morremo insiem!*
> *Sarà l'estremo anelito,*
> *sarà, sarà un grido, un grido:*
> *Libertà!*
> *Vivremo insiem, morremo insiem!*
> *grido estremo sarà:*
> *Libertà!*

TITO: Haha!

MAX: Haha!

TITO: That's a-wonderful! That's a-beautiful! You sing a-beautiful!

MAX: *(Overlapping.)* I-I-I see what you mean! I felt so good! I mean, I-I felt relaxed!

TITO: Ohh! That was work, eh? Hoo!

MAX: It was great!

> *(They calm down.)*

TITO: Hey. Guess what. I think I'm a-tired.

MAX: Oh. I-I'm sorry. I —

TITO: No! That's a-good. I'm gonna sleep.

MAX: Oh. Oh good! That-that's great.

TITO: *(Yawning.)* Yahh! Hoo. *(He stands up unsteadily.)* Max. You wake a-me, eh? Six-thirty.

MAX: Right. Sure. I promise. *(Tito heads for the bedroom.)* Uh . . . Tito, thanks, for the lesson.

TITO: Hey. You sing good. No joke. You got real promise.

MAX: Thanks.

TITO: We talk a-more, later. Okay?

MAX: Sure. And if you need anything, just holler.

> *(Tito goes into the bedroom and closes the door. Max, who feels wonderful, sits and daydreams. He sips his Chianti. Tito is exhausted now — drugged, in fact. He realizes that Maria isn't there. He looks around. He calls toward the bathroom.)*

TITO: Maria! Hey. I'm gonna sleep. Okay? *(No answer.)* Maria. I'm gonna sleep . . . *(He knocks.)* Okay? *(No answer. He shrugs, and with a groan, stretches out on the bed until he comes nose to nose with Maria's note. He picks it up and reads it. Pause. A scream.)* NOOOO!!! *(Max bounds out of his chair and runs to the bedroom.)* No! No! No! *(He drops the note on the bedside table.)*

MAX: *(Flying into the bedroom.)* What happened?!

TITO: Impossible!

MAX: What?!

TITO: No!!

MAX: WHAT HAPPENED?!!

TITO: She's a-gone! Maria!

MAX: Gone where?

TITO: *(Shaking Max.)* Gone! Gone! She's a-gone!

MAX: Tito!!!

TITO: *(Releasing him.)* She's a-left me! For good!

MAX: Are you sure?

TITO: SHE'S A-GONE!

MAX: Now-now-now wait a second. Maybe she went downstairs. For-for a magazine.

TITO: Look! Look!! No case! *(He flings open the closet door.)* No fur!

MAX: I guess she's gone.

TITO: MARIA!! NO! NO! NO!

MAX: Tito! CALM DOWN!

TITO: *(Sitting.)* Max . . . Max . . .

MAX: Now listen! We-we-we can look for her. We'll look in the lobby —

TITO: It's a-my fault. I give her trouble. She's not a-happy. *(Crying.)* Me! I make her unhappy!

MAX: Tito . . .

TITO: She hates a-me. I wanna kill myself.

MAX: She'll come back. You'll see.

TITO: I'm gonna kill myself!

    (He jumps up and runs into the sitting room.)

MAX: Stop!

    (Max runs after him. Tito looks wildly around the room for his instrument of destruction. He picks up the Chianti bottle and tries to stab himself with it. No good. He tosses it away and Max catches it, still chasing him.)

TITO: I'm gonna kill myself! I live a-no more!!

MAX: Calm down!

TITO: No more!

MAX: Hey, please!

TITO: She hates a-me! I hate a-myself!

    (Tito rushes into the kitchenette.)

MAX: No, Tito!

(Max follows him. Noise of a struggle.)

MAX: *(Offstage.)* Tito, stop it!

TITO: *(Offstage.)* Get away!

MAX: *(Offstage.)* Don't! Hey!

(A crash — a drawer of cutlery hitting the floor. A second later, Tito rushes out, followed by Max. Tito is holding a fork.)

MAX: Tito!

TITO: I'm gonna kill myself!!!

MAX: *Put down that fork!!!*

TITO: She hates a-me! It's all over!

MAX: Tito! This is not an opera! Please! Put it down!

(Tito drops the fork and collapses onto the sofa, exhausted.)

TITO: Oh, Max! *Max!*

MAX: It's all right. You'll be fine.

TITO: She's a-gone.

MAX: It's not your fault.

TITO: Oh, Maria. Maria . . .

MAX: She'll come back. You'll see. *(Tito picks up the Chianti bottle and starts to drink.)* Hey! Hey, no! Stop! *(He takes the bottle.)* Come on. Get up. Let's get you to bed.

TITO: I can't.

MAX: LET'S GO!

(Max pulls Tito to his feet and, holding him up, leads him to the bedroom.)

TITO: Max, she hates a-me.

MAX: Nooo. She loves you. She'll come back.

TITO: I wanna kill myself.

MAX: Into bed. Come on.

(He lays Tito down on the bed. Throughout the following, Tito becomes increasingly limp and dizzy. His speech slurs with exhaustion.)

TITO: Bed . . .

MAX: You'll get a good sleep. You'll feel a lot better. I promise.

TITO: Sleep . . .

MAX: We'll take off your shoes.

(He pulls Tito's shoes off. It's a struggle.)

TITO: Shoes . . .

MAX: Uuuh! There. I'll bet that feels good. Huh? Now close your eyes . . . I'll be right inside . . .

TITO: Max!

MAX: Huh?

TITO: Max. Done leave me! Stay! Please!

MAX: Okay. Right. I'm here.

TITO: *(Faintly.)* Stay . . .

MAX: I-I-I'm right here. Here I am. See? Okay?

TITO: *(Fainter.)* Sleep . . .

MAX: Shhh. That's right. A good sleep . . . Off you go . . .

    (Pause. All is quiet. Max sits on the edge of the bed.)

TITO: Max!

MAX: *(Falling off the bed.)* I'm right here!

TITO: Max . . . sing . . .

MAX: *(Getting back on the bed.)* Huh?

TITO: Maria. She sings a-me. I sleep . . .

MAX: Oh. I see.

TITO: *(Faint.)* Sing . . .

MAX: Right. *(He clears his throat.)* Is there, uh . . . anything special?

TITO: Sing!

MAX: Sing.

    (Max tries feebly to get the pitch, as before. Then he remembers the lessons and
    shuts his eyes to conjure up the orchestra. A French horn sounds the pitch in
    Max's head. He looks up and smiles. Then softly he begins to sing the tenor
    line from the Don Carlo *duet.)*

MAX: *(Singing.) Dio, che nell'alma infondere*
    amor volesti e speme,
    desio nel cor accendere [etc.]
    (As Tito falls asleep, he reaches for Max's hand and holds it. Max pats Tito's
    hand and continues singing. The lights fade as the sound of the orchestra takes
    over the musical theme.)

SCENE TWO

    Four hours later. About 6:30 P.M. Max and Tito are asleep. Max is in the sit-
    ting room on the sofa. Tito is stretched out on the bed, under the covers. As the
    music fades, the telephone starts ringing. Max wakes up, disoriented. He an-
    swers the phone.

MAX: Hello?

BELLHOP: *(Singing through the phone.)*
   Largo al factotum
   della citta, largo!
   La ran la, la ran la,
   la ran la, la!

MAX: Thank you —

BELLHOP: *(Through the phone.)* It's six-thirty! This is your wake-up call!

MAX: *(Into the phone.)* Thanks . . . Hm? . . . No. He's sleeping . . . No, you can't meet him . . . Not now! N — *(Max sighs.)* Look. All right. If you bring up some coffee, you can meet him for a second . . . I promise!

BELLHOP: *(Through the phone.)* Yahoooo!

   (There's a knock at the sitting room/corridor door.)

MAX: *(Hanging up the phone.)* Coming! *(Max goes to the door and opens it. It's Diana. She's in her midthirties. Beautiful and very sexy.)* Diana.

DIANA: Hi, Max. *(She strolls in, looks around.)* Nice place.

MAX: Yeah. Well, you know. Tito Merelli.

DIANA: Of course.

   (She wanders into the room, in no hurry.)

MAX: How was rehearsal?

DIANA: Not too bad. Considering I had to sing the duets by myself.

MAX: Yeah, I'm-I'm sorry about that. He'll be there tonight, though. No problem.

DIANA: It might work better that way.

   (Max looks at his watch.)

MAX: Diana . . . is there, uh, anything I can do for you?

DIANA: I just thought I'd stop by and say hello. I thought it might be preferable to meeting him onstage.

MAX: Gee, that's-that's nice of you, but the thing is, he's uh, he's sleeping right now. He's taking a nap.

DIANA: *(Sitting.)* I can wait. There's no hurry.

MAX: Yeah, well — actually, I-I thought it might be better if I got him to the theater first and then he could meet everybody at the same time. I mean, I've got to wake him, and he has to get ready and-and he might want some time alone. If you see what I mean.

DIANA: Do you know what he could do for me, Max? One call from Tito Merelli, and I'd be at the Met in two days.

MAX: Yeah —

DIANA: So you see, Max, it's very important to me that I get to know him. Spend a little time with him. Do you understand?

MAX: Yeah, I do. I really do. Except right now, the thing is just to get him there and-and then later, you'll have plenty of time. I mean he'll-he'll be here tomorrow. Right? Okay.

(Pause.)

DIANA: You're very cute, Max. Has anyone ever told you that before?

MAX: Sure. My-my mother. My aunt Harriet.

DIANA: Anyone single?

MAX: My uncle Bud.

DIANA: You aren't going to let me see him, are you, Max?

MAX: Later. I promise. I'll-I'll arrange it so you have lots of time with him. Alone. Okay? I promise.

DIANA: Will you give him a message for me?

MAX: Sure. Anything.

DIANA: Tell him this.

(She puts her hand behind Max's neck and kisses him on the lips. It's a very long kiss. He doesn't know what to do with his arms. She breaks it off.)

MAX: YAHH!! I'll tell him. Of course he might misunderstand.

DIANA: See you later, Max.

(She picks up her purse and exits, closing the door. Max sighs with relief.)

MAX: *(He looks at his watch.)* Oh jeez. *(He hurries to the connecting door and knocks.)* Tito. It's time to get up. *(He opens the door and switches on the bedroom light.)* Sorry. *(Max leaves the door open and turns back into the sitting room. During the following, he picks up the Chianti bottle and glasses and heads for the kitchenette. Tito continues sleeping.)* I ordered some coffee, but if you want anything else, I can call downstairs. *(Max goes into the kitchenette, then comes out again a moment later, having disposed of the bottle and glasses.)* Are you hungry? Tito? *(No answer. Max goes to the connecting door, looks in the bedroom, and sees that Tito is still asleep.)* Tito. It's time to get up. You'll be late. *(Max enters the bedroom and walks to the bed. He shakes Tito.)* Hey, come on. I hate to wake you, but it's quarter to seven. *(No response.)* Tito . . . Let's go! *(He pulls Tito up by the arms and releases him. Tito flops back on the bed.)* What's the matter? Tito, wake up! *(He shakes him harder.)* Tito! *(No response. Max straightens up and stares at Tito, suddenly afraid. Something is definitely wrong. He then notices a folded note on the bedside table — Maria's note, which happens to be next to Tito's bottle of pills. He hesitates, then picks up the note and reads it. Reading.)* "By the time you get this, I'll be gone forever." *(Max stiffens, looks at Tito, then back at the note.)* "After what has happened, it's just not worth to me the pain and unhappiness of staying around anymore. The fun is gone and now, so am I. *Ciao.*" *(He stares at the note, horrified. He then sees the bottle of pills and picks it up. It's empty.)* Tito! Wake up! *(He shakes him violently.)* Tito, for God's sake! *(A knock at the sitting room/corridor door. Max doesn't hear it and continues shaking Tito.)* Tito, can you hear me? Tito! Please! Tito!

SAUNDERS: *(Offstage.)* Max?

MAX: *(Shaking him again.)* Tito, wake up! Please wake up! *Come on! (Suddenly, Max stops shaking him. He realizes that it's no use. Tito is gone. Max is white as a sheet.)* Oh my God.

SAUNDERS: *(Offstage, knocking.)* Open the door, Max!

MAX: *(Calling.)* C-coming! One second! *(Max looks at Tito sadly. He's lost a friend.)* Tito. I'm so sorry.

SAUNDERS: *(Offstage, still knocking.)* Max! Open the door!

(Max turns away and walks into the sitting room, closing the connecting door behind him. He's in a daze, but makes it to the corridor door and opens it. Saunders enters, in white tie for the evening's festivities.)

SAUNDERS: Well thank you, Max. I hope that wasn't too much trouble. *(No response.)* And how is Il Stupendo? Has he recovered yet?

MAX: Recovered?

SAUNDERS: You said on the telephone he was upset. His wife . . . ?

MAX: Oh. Right.

SAUNDERS: Which frankly didn't surprise me at all the way they carried on. I was fully expecting one of them to pull a knife. *(No response.)* Is he feeling better? . . . Max?

MAX: Hm?

SAUNDERS: Is he feeling better?

MAX: Sir . . . he's dead.

(Pause.)

SAUNDERS: Well I'm not surprised. It must really take it out of you having your wife just walk out the door.

MAX: Sir —

SAUNDERS: Of course it doesn't have to be the best performance he ever gave. Just get him onstage at this point —

MAX: *Sir.*

SAUNDERS: Max?

MAX: He's dead. I mean he . . . he's dead. He killed himself.

(Long pause.)

SAUNDERS: Who?

MAX: Tito.

(Pause.)

SAUNDERS: Merelli?

MAX: *(Nodding, he's choked up.)* He's in the bedroom.

(Saunders eyes Max. Then walks to the connecting door.)

SAUNDERS: Is this a joke?

MAX: *(A sob.)* No.

(Saunders opens the door and steps inside. Max follows him to the door. Saunders looks at Tito. He walks to the bed and pauses. He shakes Tito's shoulder. No response. Gingerly, he opens one of Tito's eyelids. Nothing. Pause.)

SAUNDERS: Jesus Christ.

MAX: I know.

SAUNDERS: What happened?!

MAX: He-he got upset. About his wife. He took the whole bottle.

SAUNDERS: Jesus Christ!

MAX: He left a note —

(Saunders snatches the note from Max. He pores over it, as Max continues.)

MAX: I-I-I knew he was upset — he got so excited. I-I mean he grabbed a fork and said he'd kill himself, but then he-he calmed down and he just-just wanted to rest.

SAUNDERS: *(Squinting at the note.)* "The *fur* is gone?"

MAX: *(Looking.)* "Fun." "The fun is gone and now, so am I."

SAUNDERS: Oh my God.

MAX: I-I thought he was exaggerating.

SAUNDERS: They'll crucify me.

MAX: It's not your fault.

SAUNDERS: They'll want their money back! *(Pause.)* Italian bastard. I knew he'd get me. *(To Tito.)* Are you satisfied?! HUH?!

MAX: Sir —

SAUNDERS: *(Climbing onto the bed and shaking Tito violently in a rage.)* ARE YOU PROUD OF YOURSELF??!! FEEL BETTER NOW??!! *AHHH-HHHH!!!*

MAX: *(Trying to pull Saunders off.)* SIR, CALM DOWN!!

(Finally, after several more seconds, Saunders stops.)

SAUNDERS: Why me? He could have waited until tomorrow. He could have jumped out of the window after breakfast.

MAX: We sang a duet together. I mean I-I really liked him.

(Saunders climbs off the bed.)

SAUNDERS: *(Bitter.)* Well, I guess that wraps it up. End of the road. *Arriverderci.* *(Suddenly he attacks the body again.)* AHHHH!!!

MAX: SIR!!

(Saunders stops. Stands up. Then kicks the bed. Max covers Tito, head and all, with the blanket. Saunders walks into the sitting room, and Max follows him.)

SAUNDERS: I'll have to make an announcement, of course. A few brief words, nothing elaborate. Ladies and gentlemen — Mr. Tito Merelli killed himself this afternoon, thereby depriving many of us . . . of a great pleasure. It was universally acknowledged that he sang like an angel, but apparently he wanted to prove it. In short, our star for the evening has departed this world in a final gesture of selfishness and deceit unrivalled in the history of comic opera!

MAX: I think maybe I should make the announcement.

(Saunders runs for the connecting door to get at Tito again, but Max grabs him.)

SAUNDERS: Ahhhhhhhhhh!

MAX: We-we could still do the performance. I think we should.

SAUNDERS: Oh oh oh absolutely. We can prop him up and play a record. Add a few lines about how he was wounded in the Battle of Cyprus, then carry him around the stage on a stretcher!

MAX: I-I-I mean the understudy.

SAUNDERS: The understudy. Of course! My God, you've solved the whole problem! Skip the announcement, stick a note in the program, "The role of Otello will be sung by Albert Rupp." And then if there is anyone still in the audience when he takes his bow, they can stone him to death! The ultimate operatic experience! One thundering orgasm of insane violence! Make *Salomé* look like *The Merry Widow!*

MAX: Sir, I think you ought to calm down.

SAUNDERS: Right! Good point! We don't want two dead bodies around here. Just think of the smell. Put everybody at the Gala Buffet right off their shrimp!

MAX: Sir! Let's just-just sit down for a minute. Okay? Sir? *(Saunders is dazed.*

Numb. Slowly he sits. Max sits next to him. Pause.) These things happen, sir.

SAUNDERS: *(A last lunge, Max grabs him.)* AHH!

MAX: It's not your fault. It was just — unlucky, that's all. I mean everybody'll understand.

SAUNDERS: Yes. Of course they will. And then they'll fire me. Ungrateful cruds. *(Pause. The rage is over. Black despair. After several seconds, however, Saunders smiles. Then he chuckles. More chuckles. Then he breaks into laughter; genuine, if slightly hysterical.)*

MAX: What's so funny? . . . Sir? . . .

SAUNDERS: Ohhh! . . . I was just thinking. They probably wouldn't know the difference. Albert Rupp. Black his face. Huge wig, lots of padding. If we didn't tell the audience, they'd think he was Tito Merelli.

MAX: Think so? *(He thinks about it. Then chuckles.)* I think you're right. *(He starts to laugh, in spite of himself — which sets off Saunders again.)* They probably wouldn't know —

SAUNDERS: They'd give him a standing ovation!

MAX: Bring down the house! *(They both laugh uproariously, out of control. They can't stop. Finally.)* Ohhh . . .

SAUNDERS: Ohhh . . .

MAX: It wouldn't work.

SAUNDERS: I know.

MAX: I mean the company would know it was him —

SAUNDERS: Of course.

MAX: And the story would leak out —

SAUNDERS: And then the audience would hang me. Yes, I realize that.

MAX: If he wasn't in the company, I bet it would work.

SAUNDERS: But he is.

MAX: Yeah. Too bad.

(Long pause. Slowly, a light dawns in Saunders' brain. He rolls it over in his mind, then turns his head and looks at Max. Max sees him and smiles amiably. He doesn't realize what Saunders is thinking. Then he sees the stony, maniacal look in Saunders' eyes and suddenly Max looks nervous.)

SAUNDERS: *(Quietly.)* Max.

MAX: Forget it. It wouldn't work. They'd spot me in ten seconds.

SAUNDERS: No they wouldn't.

MAX: Hey, stop it. The answer's no.

SAUNDERS: Max . . .

MAX: You're out of your mind. I don't even look like him.

SAUNDERS: Black face. Lots of hair . . .

MAX: Hey. We were joking. This is life. It's called reality. Remember that?

SAUNDERS: You could do it, Max. I know you could.

MAX: *(Starting to panic.)* Hey. Look. Just-just one second, okay? I don't speak Italian. I-I-I-I-I hardly speak English.

SAUNDERS: You wouldn't have to speak Italian. Just sing it.

MAX: Look-look-just-just okay? They'd know. They would know. It's me. Max.

SAUNDERS: No they wouldn't! That's the point! They've never seen him before. They're expecting *him,* not *you.*

MAX: Yeah, but-but-but-but . . .

SAUNDERS: They want to see him, Max. They want to say they've seen him.

MAX: But it's an opera! Four acts!

SAUNDERS: You know the part. You admitted it.

MAX: I can hum it! In the bathtub!

   (The phone rings.)

SAUNDERS: You know every single note, I know you do —

MAX: Wrong! There's a few at the end, I-I get mixed up —

SAUNDERS: Aha! *(Into the phone.)* Yes?

MAX: *(Pacing.)* You're out of your mind!

SAUNDERS: *(Into the phone.)* Yes, Julia.

MAX: I mean, you're crazy! Okay? You're nuts!

SAUNDERS: *(Into the phone, he can't hear.)* What? *(To* Max.) Be quiet.

MAX: They could arrest me! It's called impersonation. Big crime —

SAUNDERS: *(Into the phone.)* No, Tito is much better. He's fine…

MAX: No, he isn't. He's dead. He's not fine. Fine is living!

SAUNDERS: *(Into the phone.)* No! Now, Julia, just listen. Don't come up . . . No. Just stay *downstairs.* Well, frankly, he's still a bit upset about his wife, and I think it's better if we meet you backstage.

MAX: That's better. That is better. Because he's dead!

SAUNDERS: *(Into the phone.)* Yes, just Max . . . Right. Fine. See you there. *(He hangs up.)*

MAX: That was a mistake.

SAUNDERS: Max . . .

MAX: No.

SAUNDERS: I'm begging you, Max. I'm on my knees. *(He is.)*

MAX: No!

SAUNDERS: Look at me! Max. You can do it, believe me!

MAX: I can't!

SAUNDERS: A thousand people! They're getting dressed now. They've got tickets at fifty dollars each, Max. That's fifty thousand dollars!

MAX: Sir —

SAUNDERS: My whole career! My life, Max. My children. It's all in your hands. *(Saunders grabs Max around the knees and sobs. He looks up. No reaction. He sobs harder, sinking to Max's ankles.)*

MAX: Ohhhh, *crap!*

SAUNDERS: I'll never forget this, Max.

MAX: I bet.

(Saunders jumps to his feet and races into the bedroom. Max, now speechless with fear, follows him. During the following, Saunders takes one of the suitcases from the closet and puts it on the bed next to Tito.)

SAUNDERS: I have it all figured out. It's simple. You change here, makeup, the works. Then we drive to the theater just in time and suddenly, bang, you're onstage.

MAX: Oh God.

SAUNDERS: Between the acts, you'll stay in your dressing room. Locked up. Then, after it's over, it's straight to the car, drive back and we're finished.

MAX: What about, uh . . . *(He nods at Tito.)*

SAUNDERS: No problem. Tomorrow morning, we break the news. He took the pills *after* the performance and passed away quietly during the night. This is it. *(The costume. Saunders rummages through the suitcase.)* Costume . . . makeup . . . wig . . . *(A knock at the sitting room/corridor door. They both freeze.)* Who's that?

MAX: How should I know?!

SAUNDERS: I'll take care of it. You just change, and make it quick.

(He hands Max the suitcase and heads for the sitting room.)

MAX: Sir?

SAUNDERS: *(Stopping.)* Yes, Max?

MAX: Wish me luck.

SAUNDERS: We don't need luck, Max.

MAX: Thanks.

(Max enters the bathroom. Saunders leaves the bedroom and closes the door.)

SAUNDERS: We need a miracle. *(He walks to the sitting room/corridor door.)* Who is it?

JULIA: *(Offstage.)* It's me, Henry. Open the door.

SAUNDERS: Julia! I told you not to come up!

JULIA: *(Offstage.)* Open the door, Henry! *(Saunders opens the door. Julia enters. She's about sixty and wears a silver dress covered in sequins. She strikes a pose.)* How do I look? The truth.

SAUNDERS: Like the Chrysler Building.

JULIA: I knew you'd like it. *(She sweeps in and twirls around.)* It's straight from Paris. Haute couture. I feel like one of those fancy French tarts.

SAUNDERS: Julia, for God's sake —

JULIA: Now, don't be cross, Henry. I couldn't bear waiting backstage anymore. Not with those shrimp. I could hardly breathe. Besides, I thought I might cheer him up. The woman's touch. Suddenly before he knows it he'll feel vital again. Totally alive.

SAUNDERS: No, I don't think so.

JULIA: You know what this reminds me of? That opera, the one with the snow falling, and the violins and everybody's hungry all the time.

SAUNDERS: Julia, please! Just *listen*!

JULIA: I'm listening, Henry.

SAUNDERS: I want you to go to the theater. Now. All right? As a favor to me.

JULIA: Oh, Henry. You know how I feel about you.

SAUNDERS: *(Moving toward the door.)* Good. Off you go —

JULIA: But it's just so silly. I'm here already.

SAUNDERS: But you won't be soon. You'll be at the theater.

JULIA: *(Logically.)* Not if I'm here. I can't be in two places.

SAUNDERS: You won't be in two places. You won't be here.

JULIA: Why not?

SAUNDERS: Because you'll be there.

JULIA: But why bother? I'm already here —

SAUNDERS: Julia, please — ! *(A knock at the door.)* Now what?!

JULIA: *(Sitting.)* I think it's the door.

(Saunders stops halfway to the door, returns to stand just behind Julia, and raises his arm as though he's going to slug her over the head, backhanded. He controls himself and returns to the door.)

SAUNDERS: *(At the door.)* Who is it?!

BELLHOP: *(Offstage.)* Room service. Coffee for two.

SAUNDERS: We didn't order any coffee.

BELLHOP: *(Offstage.)* You did so! Ask Max!

SAUNDERS: Well, it's cancelled!

JULIA: *(Going to the door.)* Oh stop it, Henry. You can't just let him stand there.

SAUNDERS: Don't — !

(She opens the door. The Bellhop enters, holding a tray with a coffee service on it. He also has a camera hanging around his neck. He leaves the door open.)

BELLHOP: Thank you, madam.

JULIA: On the table, please.

SAUNDERS: And then get out.

JULIA: He's only doing his job, Henry.

SAUNDERS: Well, he can do it somewhere else.

BELLHOP: Shall I pour, madam?

JULIA: Thank you, that would be very nice.

SAUNDERS: Julia, I want you out of here!

BELLHOP: He's not very friendly, is he?

SAUNDERS: Julia, please! You promised!

JULIA: I wonder what's keeping Mr. Merelli?

BELLHOP: Is he getting dressed?

JULIA: Apparently.

BELLHOP: *(Going to the connecting door.)* Perhaps he needs some help with his buttons. You know these opera stars, they're helpless —

SAUNDERS: STOP! *(The Bellhop stops, his hand on the doorknob.)* Take one step into that room and I will *kill* you.

BELLHOP: Fair enough. I'll wait out here.

SAUNDERS: You're not waiting anyplace, you're getting out!

BELLHOP: Fine . . . As soon as I meet him. *(He sits.)*

SAUNDERS: You're not meeting him.

BELLHOP: Max promised. That's why I brought the coffee. I'm a bellhop, not a waiter.

SAUNDERS: Listen, you — !!

(In a burst of anger, Saunders grabs the Bellhop by his shirtfront and hoists him to his feet. Simultaneously Maggie appears at the sitting room/corridor door dressed for the evening. She carries a single red rose.)

JULIA: Henry!

BELLHOP: Help!

MAGGIE: *(Rushing in.)* Daddy!

BELLHOP: Help!

MAGGIE: What are you doing?

SAUNDERS: *(To the Bellhop.)* Are you getting out?

BELLHOP: I'm getting wrinkled.

MAGGIE: Daddy, stop it! What's the matter?

(Saunders drops the Bellhop.)

BELLHOP: *(Smoothing himself out.)* We had a slight misunderstanding. Then he went insane.

SAUNDERS: *(To Maggie.)* What the hell are you doing here?

MAGGIE: I came to see Mr. Merelli. To-to wish him luck.

SAUNDERS: Well, you're not going to, so get out!

MAGGIE: Daddy, what's the matter with you? Has something happened?

SAUNDERS: *(After a slight pause.)* No.

JULIA: He's been under a lot of strain lately. Haven't you, Henry?

SAUNDERS: No!

BELLHOP: Yes, you have, Henry. I can tell.

SAUNDERS: Get him out of here. I'm warning you.

MAGGIE: *(To the Bellhop.)* This isn't like him at all.

BELLHOP: Oh yes it is.

SAUNDERS: Get out!! Now!!

BELLHOP: All right!! *(With dignity.)* I will be happy to leave —

JULIA: *(To Saunders.)* There.

BELLHOP: As soon as I get one picture.

SAUNDERS: Give me the camera.

BELLHOP: No.

SAUNDERS: *(Advancing.)* Hand it over, you little twit!

BELLHOP: *(Retreating.)* Stay away from me!

MAGGIE: Daddy!

JULIA: Henry!

(Saunders chases the Bellhop around the sofa, with Maggie and Julia chasing Saunders.)

BELLHOP: *Hold it!*

(The Bellhop snaps a picture of the other three, who pose momentarily without realizing it. Then immediately the chase resumes.)

SAUNDERS: I want the camera!

(As the chase continues in the sitting room, the bathroom door opens and Max emerges, dressed head to foot as Otello in colorful doublet, hose, boots, and cape. His face and neck are blackened with makeup, and he wears black gloves and a large black wig. He also wears his glasses. He staggers into the bedroom, visibly quaking. He makes it to the connecting door and puts his ear against it. The action in the sitting room has continued without a break.)

JULIA:: Henry!

BELLHOP: Help!

SAUNDERS: *(To Maggie.)* Get the camera! Maggie!

JULIA: Henry, let him take the picture.

BELLHOP: Henry!

SAUNDERS: Gotcha! *(He grabs him.)*

BELLHOP: All right! Okay! I give up!

SAUNDERS: Little creep!

> *(Max raps sharply on the connecting door. The others freeze and turn to the noise.)*

JULIA: It's him!

MAGGIE: He must be ready.

JULIA: *(Calling.)* Mr. Merelli? Is that you?

MAX: *(From the bedroom, after a slight pause.)* Ciao.

SAUNDERS: Jesus Christ.

JULIA: *(Calling.)* We're all waiting for you.

MAX: *(Heavy accent.)* Please. Send a-me in a-da room, a-Meester Sounders.

JULIA: What a beautiful accent.

MAGGIE: *(Nudging him.)* Daddy . . .

SAUNDERS: I heard him, thank you.

JULIA: *(Calling.)* He'll be right in!

SAUNDERS: Julia. Maggie. I'm asking you for one last time to leave the room.

MAGGIE: But I've got to talk to him!

SAUNDERS: Margaret —

MAGGIE: It's important!

JULIA: Oh, Henry, don't be such a pill. He has to meet us sometime.

MAGGIE: Please?

JULIA: *(To Maggie.)* Now don't you worry. You're staying right here. And so am I.

MAX: *(From the bedroom.)* 'Allo?

JULIA: Henry. Go inside!

SAUNDERS: You're going to regret this, Julia.

JULIA: You always say that and I never do.

MAX: 'Allo?!

SAUNDERS: I'm coming!! *(He goes to the connecting door and turns the knob.)* It's me.

> *(Max hides behind the door as Saunders backs into the bedroom, shielding it from the others. He closes the door — then sees Max and jumps backward.)*

SAUNDERS: Good God!

> *(Julia, Maggie, and the Bellhop are by this time listening at the door, straining to hear what's happening.)*

MAX: *(Loud.)* I can't do it!!

SAUNDERS: *(Hissing.)* Keep it down!

MAX: *(Whispering.)* I can't do it!

SAUNDERS: Max. You look terrific!

MAX: You're crazy!

SAUNDERS: You'll be wonderful!

MAX: No I won't. Believe me.

MAGGIE: *(In the sitting room, to Julia.)* What are they saying?

JULIA: I can't hear a thing.

(The Bellhop, Maggie, and Julia disperse from the door.)

SAUNDERS: You'll get a curtain call just for the costume.

MAX: Fine. Then you wear it!

SAUNDERS: Max, we have a bargain. You promised.

MAX: I know. I'm sorry. I'll-I'll-I'll make it up to you. I'll pay you money. Big money —

SAUNDERS: Now just relax! Sit down! You're wound up over nothing.

MAX: *(Sitting, hysterical.)* Nothing . . .

SAUNDERS: Think of it, Max. Your voice, alone, fills the theater to the second balcony. No one breathes . . .

MAX: *(Removing his glasses.)* Including me. That's the trouble.

SAUNDERS: You can do it, Max.

MAX: I can't.

SAUNDERS: It's your big break. Everything you've ever dreamed about —

MAX: I can't even walk! *(Increasingly panicked.)* I-I-I'm shaking all over! I'm losing weight!

SAUNDERS: Max —

MAX: Please!! I'll do anything else! I promise!

SAUNDERS: Max, get a hold of yourself!

MAX: *(Near tears.)* You don't understand! *I can't do it!!* I'm sorry.

(Pause. Saunders realizes that it's no use. He sighs heavily. He's done all he can.)

SAUNDERS: All right, Max. Go change. I'll make an announcement. I suppose it wouldn't have worked anyway.

(Saunders steels himself, grimly, and leaves the bedroom, closing the door behind him. Max remains where he is and doesn't move.)

JULIA: Well?!

MAGGIE: Where is he?!

BELLHOP: What happened?!

SAUNDERS: Please. I have a short announcement to make. Mr. Merelli has been under a great deal of strain lately. Indeed, as some of you know, today was not one of his better days.

JULIA: Henry!

MAGGIE: What's the matter?!

JULIA: Is he sick?!

SAUNDERS: Mr. Merelli . . . has unexpectedly taken ill.

(Stunned silence.)

MAGGIE: Oh no.

SAUNDERS: He will not be singing in this evening's performance.

JULIA: Henry, you must be joking!

SAUNDERS: I'm afraid not.

JULIA: *(Horrified.)* Oh my God! *(She sits.)* Henry, do something!

SAUNDERS: There's nothing I can do.

JULIA: Oh my God!

MAGGIE: It's my fault. It's all my fault.

SAUNDERS: Maggie —

MAGGIE: It is!

JULIA: Henry, talk to him! Tell him it's too late to get sick! Say something!

SAUNDERS: I tried, believe me.

(Without warning, Maggie bolts toward the bedroom.)

MAGGIE: Mr. Merelli!

SAUNDERS: Maggie!

(Too late. She swings the door open. Max sees Maggie and bounds to the door. To prevent her from seeing Tito's body, he advances into the sitting room, closing the connecting door behind him.)

MAGGIE: Please! I've got to talk to you! *(Max is speechless. So are the others.)* Mr. Merelli, I-I know you've had a bad day, and-and you aren't feeling well. And I'm sure you don't feel like singing tonight, after what happened. But the thing is, everybody's counting on you. I mean, they've all been waiting, for months, and . . . and looking forward to it. And it really won't matter if it isn't your very best, I mean just so it's *you*. And . . . and I know it's asking a lot, but . . . if you could do it — even the first act — we'd all be so grateful. So . . . Could you? Please?

(Max is stunned. He looks at Maggie. Then at Saunders. Then back at Maggie. Pause.)

MAX: *(Shrugging, speaking with an accent.)* Sure, why not, eh?

(All hell breaks loose. Maggie, Julia, and the Bellhop surround him, all talking at once. The following three speeches are simultaneous.)

MAGGIE: Oh thank you! Thank you so much! You have no idea how much this means to me. I mean, I know it'll be a strain for you, after what happened —

JULIA: Oh, Mr. Merelli! I cannot tell you what a relief this is to me. And on behalf of the Opera Guild, I want to thank you, from the bottom of my heart, for your courage and-and sacrifice in the face of adversity —

BELLHOP: What a guy. *(Pumping his hand.)* Mr. Merelli, my name's Frank, and I've always wanted to meet you since I was this high. And I've got to tell you that everything I've read about you is true. I mean I'm really impressed —

SAUNDERS: HOLD IT!! *(They fall silent.)* If we don't leave immediately, he'll miss the curtain.

BELLHOP: Oh my God. I've got to change! I'll see you there! *(He exits, running.)*

SAUNDERS: Julia. Shall we go?

JULIA: Yes of course. I fly on wings of song. *(She exits.)*

SAUNDERS: Maggie?

MAGGIE: I'm coming. *(Saunders exits. Max turns away, but Maggie hasn't left yet.)* Oh, Mr. Merelli, I've got to talk to you!

MAX: Huh? Hey. We talk later, eh? I, uh, got to prepare myself —

MAGGIE: It's about your wife. I did something terrible!

MAX: Moggie. Pleese. *(Pause.)* There are some few moments when we done look back and done look ahead. And for that a-one moment, we have a-music, we have a-happiness, we have a-hope. Eh? That's all.

MAGGIE: *(Handing him the rose she brought with her.)* This is for you.

MAX: *(Accepting it.)* Grazie.

(She extends her hand, and they shake. But Max doesn't let go. He turns her hand over and gives her a lingering kiss on the palm. She stares at him, speechless, looks at her hand, then reels out of the room, light-headed. Max watches her exit. He's stunned. Long pause. Then he falls to his knees, sobbing with fear. In the process, he drops the rose. After a moment, he hears [and we hear] two voices — his own and Tito's — singing the final moments of the Don Carlo duet that they sang in Scene One. The music grows louder and swells in beauty. Max listens to it, then sees the rose and picks it up and smells it. His courage grows. He gets to his feet and stands up straight and tall. As the music

continues, Max turns majestically and walks to the corridor door, arms out, cape billowing behind him. At the threshold, he pauses and turns back. He comes to the footlights, acknowledges the thundering applause in his head, throws a kiss to the audience, and then turns again and hurries out of the door to his debut.

At this moment — in the bedroom — the covers on the bed move, and Tito sits up with an effort, pulling the covers from his face. Groggy and heavily drugged, he looks around, as . . .)
(The curtain falls.)

END OF ACT I

ACT II

SCENE ONE

Later that night, about eleven P.M. There is one striking difference from the last time we saw the suite: the bed is empty and Tito is gone. In addition, the bathroom and connecting doors are both ajar, and the sitting room/corridor door is in the closed position, but not pulled shut. In the darkness, we hear the final, serene moment of the Otello-Desdemona duet, "Gia nella notte densa." As the duet ends, the lights come up, and we hear someone knocking at the sitting room/corridor door.

MAGGIE: *(Offstage.)* It's open.

JULIA: *(Offstage.)* That's odd. *(Julia and Maggie enter, cautiously at first. Both are dressed as in the previous scene.)* Tito . . . ?

MAGGIE: *(Calling.)* Mr. Merelli . . . ?

JULIA: *(Into the bedroom.)* Tito . . . ?

MAGGIE: I guess he's not back yet.

JULIA: *(Puzzled.)* Apparently not.

(She pulls the connecting door closed.)

MAGGIE: *(Relaxing now, collapsing onto the sofa.)* Oh my God. Wasn't he wonderful?

JULIA: Wonderful isn't the word, my dear. He was box office all the way. *(The telephone rings.)* I wonder who that could be.

MAGGIE: Maybe it's him.

JULIA: *(Into the phone.)* Hello? . . . No he isn't back yet, I'm afraid. Who is this, please? *(Startled.)* Oh my goodness. Is anything . . . Julia Leverett. Chairman of the Opera Guild.

MAGGIE: Who is it?

JULIA: *(To Maggie.)* The police.

MAGGIE: Police?!

JULIA: *(Into the phone.)* Oh dear. I see . . . Well that's good . . . Oh dear! . . . Oh good . . . Oh dear . . . I certainly will. Thank you very much. Good-bye.

MAGGIE: Well?

JULIA: It's very sad actually. Apparently some lunatic dressed as Otello tried to get into the theater tonight. He said he was Tito Merelli.

MAGGIE: Oh no.

JULIA: When they wouldn't let him in, he started screaming in Italian, so the stage manager called the police.

MAGGIE: Did they get him?

JULIA: Well, they arrested him and dragged him off, but he got away down an alley. Apparently the man's demented. When they grabbed him, he actually hit a policeman.

MAGGIE: Oh my God.

JULIA: They're sending two of their men over to keep an eye out.

MAGGIE: I hope nothing happens.

JULIA: That's all we need at the reception is some lunatic on the rampage. We'll have enough of those already when the board starts drinking. *(She heads for the door.)* I suppose we'd better go. They'll start arriving any minute now.

MAGGIE: Maybe I should wait here. I-I could tell him that you're looking for him. I mean, I just want to be helpful.

JULIA: Of course you do. And I won't tell Max if you don't.

MAGGIE: Max? It's none of his business.

JULIA: Isn't it?

MAGGIE: He didn't even show up tonight.

JULIA: *(Teasing.)* If I see him downstairs, shall I tell him you're looking for him?

MAGGIE: No, thank you.

JULIA: How about Tito?

MAGGIE: Aunt Julia —

JULIA: See you later, my dear.

(Julia exits, closing the door behind her. Maggie pauses for a moment, then goes to the telephone and clicks for the operator.)

MAGGIE: *(Into the phone.)* Stage door of the Opera House please . . . Hello, Harry? It's Maggie Saunders . . . Just fine. How are you? . . . Yes it was. It was fabulous. I was just wondering, is . . . is Max around backstage by any chance? . . . *(Disappointed.)* Oh . . . Not at all? . . . No, that's all right. It's nothing special. *(The sound of the sitting room/corridor door being unlocked. Maggie looks up, says quietly.)* Thanks, Harry. Bye.

(She hangs up. The door opens and Max enters. He's still in full costume and makeup. He doesn't see her.)

MAGGIE: Hi.

MAX: *(Startled.)* Ciao.

(Max strolls into the room, full of confidence and swagger. Maggie is suddenly

nervous, being alone with "Tito." She tries to make conversation, but Max isn't helping.)

MAGGIE: I-I hope you don't mind me being here. The door was open — I mean, we knocked first, but you weren't here. Which I guess you know, since you were somewhere else. So then I waited, because I have a message from Aunt Julia. Mrs. Leverett. She's not really my aunt, actually. She's an old friend, but I call her Aunt Julia in case you're wondering. Anyway, she asked me to-to wait here and remind you that she hopes you'll make a speech at the reception. Just a few words, and I'm sure they'd really appreciate it, if you feel like it, which you probably don't, which is understandable, and that's the message.

(Pause.)

MAX: Thanks. That's a-very nice of you, eh? To give a-me the massage.

(He realizes his mistake with the word and turns away, rolling his eyes.)

MAGGIE: It was nothing really.

MAX: It's a-very sweet.

(Pause. She continues to stare at him.)

MAGGIE: So. I-I guess I ought to be going.

MAX: Yeah? That's a-too bad.

MAGGIE: It is?

MAX: Yeah. For me, eh?

MAGGIE: *(Very pleased.)* Oh. Well. I don't *have* to go. If you don't think so. I mean it's your bedroom. Suite. Rooms. Of course, I'm sure you'd like to just relax a little now and take off my clothes. Your clothes! Off. Change your clothes, into something more comfortable. So I probably shouldn't be here for that. If you don't think so.

MAX: Hey. I'm gonna tell you something, it's gonna shock a-you, eh?

MAGGIE: I doubt that.

MAX: It's gonna be a big a-surprise. Okay?

MAGGIE: Okay.

MAX: Tonight, when I'm a-singing my love song to Desdemona . . . I'm a-thinking of you.

MAGGIE: Me?

MAX: *Gia nella notte densa s'estingue ogni clamor. Tuoni la guerra e s'inabissi il mondo se dopo l'ira immense vien quest'immenso amor.* Now, in the dark a-night, all big sounds, they die away. The guns can a-roar, the whole world can collapse, if, after this immense destruction, there comes this immense a-love.

MAGGIE: Me? *(He kisses her on the lips. She responds. Bells start to ring — all kinds of bells in a long peal of ecstasy. Maggie breaks away and looks up, acknowledging them, then grabs Max in a kiss of passion. They both feel breathless and hot.)* I want to bear your children!

MAX: Me too!

(They start kissing again, but Maggie breaks it.)

MAGGIE: But what about your wife?

MAX: My wife? Oh my *wife.* That wife.

MAGGIE: Maria.

MAX: Maria. She . . . she's uh . . . Heh. This is gonna surprise you, eh? *(Grave.)* She's not a-my wife.

MAGGIE: She's not?

MAX: No. She pretends she's a-my wife. She likes to think so, eh? It's a-very sad.

MAGGIE: Oh, Tito! *(They go at it again, with even more enthusiasm, both of them getting hotter by the second. Without warning, there's a knock at the door.)* Oh hell!

(Maggie faces front, and we see now that her face is smudged all over with Max's black makeup.)

MAX: Yeah?!

SAUNDERS: *(Offstage.)* Open up.

MAGGIE: Oh my God! It's my father!

(She runs to the mirror to compose herself — and sees her face and screams. Then she pulls a hankie from her purse and tries to get the makeup off.)

MAX: *(Buying time.)* Who's the-ere?

SAUNDERS: *(Offstage.)* It's me.

MAX: Who is "me," please?

SAUNDERS: *(Offstage.)* Who do you think it is, you jackass! Now open the door!

(Maggie has finished now as best she can. Max looks at her and she nods okay.)

MAX: *(Opening the door.)* Ciao.

(Saunders enters carrying white tie and tails for Max on a hanger.)

SAUNDERS: Where have you been?! I've been looking all over — Maggie!

MAGGIE: *(Shielding her face.)* Hi, Daddy.

SAUNDERS: What are you doing here?

MAGGIE: I-I just came up to deliver a message to Mr. Merelli.

SAUNDERS: Oh. Oh I see. To Mr. Merelli.

MAGGIE: Aunt Julia wants him to speak at the reception.

SAUNDERS: Well, we'll have to see about that now, won't we? I'm sure that Mr. Merelli is awfully tired. Aren't you?

MAX: Hm? Yeah. Sure. *(He yawns.)*

MAGGIE: Well . . . I guess I ought to be going then.

SAUNDERS: What a good idea.

MAGGIE: It was nice meeting you, Mr. Merelli. I hope to see you again sometime.

MAX: Me too, eh?

MAGGIE: *Soon.*

MAX: Soon?

MAGGIE: *(Nodding hard at the door.)* You certainly *unlocked* the *door* to our hearts this evening.

MAX: Thanks.

MAGGIE: And will again, I'm sure.

MAX: *(Not getting it.)* I hope a-so, eh?

MAGGIE: So I won't even say good-bye. Just *au revoir.*

MAX: *Ciao. (Maggie exits. Max closes the door; in his own voice.)* Well?

SAUNDERS: Max, Max, Max. We did it, you crazy bastard!

MAX: We?

SAUNDERS: *(Exploding.)* A complete triumph! They floated, they suffered, they cried their eyes out.

MAX: I guess I was okay then.

SAUNDERS: Max. Let me put it this way. I owe you one.

MAX: No you don't. You owe me several.

SAUNDERS: You're right. I do. And if there's any little favor you can think of, Max, any trifling thing —

MAX: Next season.

SAUNDERS: Hm?

MAX: I thought I'd start out next season with Don José in *Carmen.*

SAUNDERS: Oh.

MAX: Then Rodolfo in *La Boheme,* then finish off with something lighter, like *Die Fledermaus.*

SAUNDERS: Max —

MAX: Sir?

SAUNDERS: It just so happens, I have another idea. An inspiration. A flash of genius. You're going to love it.

MAX: Yeah?

SAUNDERS: *(Smiling cunningly.)* Verdi's *Requiem.*

MAX: I don't get it.

SAUNDERS: Requiem! Mass for the dead. Who is dead, Max?

MAX: Tito! I almost forgot.

SAUNDERS: Well I didn't, and I have it all figured out. Tomorrow morning we arrive together. We knock at the door, no answer, so we get the manager. He lets us in and "Oh-my-God, the man is dead! Tito! Tito! What have you done?" Too late. He's gone. Within the hour, it hits the wire service, and by Monday we've got every newspaper and magazine in the country here. So —I call a press conference. I make a short and touching statement: "We, of the Cleveland Grand Opera Company, we who were graced by the final warblings of that immortal voice, which is no more, we will honor the memory of Il Stupendo a week from today at eight o'clock with a single performance of Mr. Merelli's favorite and sadly appropriate work of music — Verdi's *Requiem.*"

MAX: Was that his favorite?

SAUNDERS: How the hell should I know?!

MAX: Sorry.

SAUNDERS: The point is, you idiot, it'll put us on the map! The publicity will be incredible. I couldn't have planned the whole thing better if I'd strangled him myself. Now guess, Max, guess who will sing the tenor solos in the *Requiem.* Hm?

MAX: Me?

SAUNDERS: You.

MAX: Thanks.

SAUNDERS: Now look, I've got to get downstairs to that stupid reception, so here's the drill. Put this on, *(Handing him the white tie and tails.)* turn back into Max. Then wait in here, with the door locked, and do not, under any circumstances, let anyone in. I'll make Tito's excuses downstairs, and then, when the reception's over, I'll come back up and we'll both leave. All right? Good. Now go change.

(He heads for the door.)

MAX: Uh . . . Sir?

SAUNDERS: Max?!

MAX: I, uh . . . I just want to say that I-I really liked him, and I don't think you ever quite realized what a . . . a really nice man he was. I mean, before he died.

SAUNDERS: Max. Believe me —I loved him like a brother. But there's nothing we can do for him now. It's just too late.

MAX: I guess so.

SAUNDERS: If it's any comfort to you, Max, just remember — from here on out, it's clear sailing. Absolutely nothing can go wrong.

(Saunders exits, closing the door behind him. Simultaneously, the bedroom/corridor door bursts open and Tito enters. He, too, is dressed as Otello, in exactly the same costume and makeup that Max is wearing. Tito is in a state of panic. Exhausted and bedraggled, he pants heavily from running. His eyes dart madly in every direction as he leans against the door, gasping for air.

Also simultaneously, a siren wails from the street below as though a police car is pulling up at the hotel. Max walks to the window and looks down. Tito hears the siren and dives into the closet, closing the door behind him. Max shrugs and heads for the bedroom. As he reaches the connecting door, he hesitates and braces himself.)

MAX: Poor Tito. *(He sighs, covers his eyes and enters the room, heading for the bathroom. Max doesn't want to see Tito's body. He couldn't bear it. And yet, he can't help himself. He separates his fingers and glances at the bed, then covers his eyes again and turns away. Poor Tito! He continues into the bathroom and closes the door. Offstage.)* Oh my God! *(Max runs out of the bathroom without the white tie and tails and, closing the door behind him, stares at the bed, dumbfounded. He tears away the covers, looks under the bed and around the room. No Tito!)* Oh my God!! *(He hesitates for a split second, then runs out of the bedroom into the corridor, closing the door behind him.)* MISTER *Saunders*!!

(Pause. Slowly the closet door opens and Tito emerges. He looks around and listens. Not a sound. He sighs heavily, then totters cautiously through the bedroom and into the sitting room. He looks around the room. He feels certain now that he's safe at last and sinks onto the sofa and closes his eyes. At which point, Julia enters through the sitting room/corridor door and sees Tito from the back, sitting quietly on the sofa. She smiles, then walks silently into the room and covers his eyes with her hands.)

JULIA: Guess who?

TITO: YIY!!

(He bounds to his feet and stares at her.)

JULIA: Now, aren't you ashamed of yourself. Sitting here quietly enjoying yourself, while everyone downstairs is simply dying to meet you.

TITO: Excuse me please, but who are you?

JULIA: You're angry with me, aren't you?

TITO: Angry?

JULIA: Here I am, haranguing you about the reception when I haven't even told you how magnificent you were tonight. Tito. My dear man. *(Sitting and leaning back seductively, lowering her voice to the bass range.)* How can I ever thank you?

TITO: For what?

JULIA: For what? For what you did this evening!

TITO: I didn't do nothing! It wasn't me!

JULIA: No it wasn't you. You're right. It was Otello. There, onstage, in flesh and blood. It was beauty and it was life. It was love and it was pain. And as I sat there in the theater, watching you tonight, hanging on your every note, I thought to myself: Now, at this moment, I am hearing the greatest performance of any opera star that has ever lived!

TITO: I was good, eh?

JULIA: Words cannot express it.

TITO: I think I'm a-gonna siddown, okay? *(He does.)*

JULIA: You poor thing. You've had a bad day, haven't you?

TITO: Yeah.

JULIA: Of course you have, and you've been very brave. But, Tito, dear Tito. You will come down to the reception, won't you? For just a few minutes?

TITO: No. I done think so.

JULIA: But, Tito, you promised me!

TITO: I did?

JULIA: Tito Merelli. I'm surprised at you. How could you possibly disappoint me like this? Me. Julia.

TITO: I'm sorry, eh?

JULIA: And I'm sorry, too. For I simply will not take no for an answer. Do you understand? I will not budge from this spot until you agree. Not one inch. *(She folds her arms and stands firm.)* There are times, I'm afraid, when one simply has to apply the iron glove in the velvet hand. Especially if one hopes to get the bird.

TITO: *(Thinking.)* Okay. I give up.

JULIA: You do?

TITO: Yeah.

JULIA: Oh, Tito, you're wonderful! I knew you wouldn't let us down. Let's go!

TITO: No. Hey. *(He turns on the charm and takes her hand.)* Julia. I'm a-tired, eh? I need a few minutes to, uh, get off a-my feet, wash a-my face. Okay, Julia?

JULIA: *(Aroused.)* Oh my dearest, dearest Tito. You've made me so very happy. I only wish there was something I could do for you. *(Lowering her voice and trying again.)* Can you think of anything?

TITO: Yeah. Go.

JULIA: I understand. Poor baby. You need some time alone. *(He ushers her to the door.)* Every minute shall seem an hour, and every hour a second. And so I fly.

(She exits, closing the door.)

TITO: Jesus Christ! *(He thinks for a moment about what to do — then springs into action. He rushes into the bedroom, grabs his suitcase and puts it on the bed to pack. Then a thought strikes him.)* Train station. *(He hurries into the sitting room toward the phone book. He finds it and rifles through it searching for "train station.")* Train, train, train. *(At this moment, the sitting room/corridor door opens, and Diana enters, wearing the slinkiest, most inviting dress imaginable. She closes the door quietly. By this time, Tito has found the appropriate page and heads back toward the bedroom, scanning the column.)* Tractor. Trailers. Trophies.

DIANA: Hi there. *(Tito stops dead. He looks at Diana — and drops the phone book to the floor.)* Surprised to see me? *(He nods his head yes and wheezes.)* I told you I might drop in. Didn't you believe me? *(He shakes his head no and wheezes.)* Are you all right?

TITO: Dry . . . dry throat.

DIANA: Then perhaps I should order some champagne. What do you think?

TITO: Sure. Great.

DIANA: May I use the phone? *(Diana walks to the telephone. Tito watches her, fascinated. She picks up the phone and clicks for the operator. Into the phone.)* Room service, please. *(As she waits, she smiles at Tito. He smiles back. Into the phone.)* Yes, I'd like to order a bottle of champagne. *(To Tito.)* Is Mumm all right?

TITO: She's fine, thank you.

DIANA: *(Into the phone.)* Yes. That'll be fine. *(She hangs up.)* Well. You certainly are a fast operator, I must say. I barely know you, and here we are, alone in your hotel room with a bottle of champagne on the way up.

TITO: I'm just a tricky guy, eh?

DIANA: Come here.

TITO: Huh?

DIANA: Come here. *(She sits on the sofa and motions him to sit beside her. He does, cautiously. She faces him directly.)* Tito. Can I ask you a question?

TITO: Sure. Hey.

DIANA: I want you to be totally honest with me. All right? Do you promise?

TITO: Cross a-my heart.

DIANA: Brutal, if necessary.

TITO: Nooo . . .

DIANA: Yes. Please.

TITO: Okay.

(Pause.)

DIANA: Was I good tonight?

TITO: Good?

DIANA: I'm sure it's difficult to make any lasting judgments, after having done it with me only once. But would you say I was . . . exciting tonight?

TITO: *(Trying to work it out.)* We spent a-some time together, eh?

DIANA: We certainly did.

TITO: Yeah . . .

DIANA: Now I want the truth. Just take the big moment at the end. Would you say it was something special? *(No answer.)* I can take it, believe me, Tito. I'm a professional.

TITO: A pro-? Oh my God. A *professional*!

DIANA: *(Hurt.)* You don't think so?

TITO: No I do! I promise!

DIANA: Well then? How was I? *(Pause.)* Tito?

TITO: I'm trying to remember!

DIANA: *(Bitterly.)* I suppose you're telling me I was no good.

TITO: No! Hey! You-you were great! You were fantastic!

DIANA: You're only saying that —

TITO: No I swear! You-you were unbelievable! It went a-by so fast, I can hardly remember.

DIANA: Oh, Tito. Do you mean it?

TITO: Yeah. Sure.

DIANA: Thank God. I'm so relieved.

TITO: Heh. This, uh, profession. You take it a-pretty serious, eh?

DIANA: It's all I've ever wanted to be since I was a little girl. Isn't that awful?

TITO: It's terrible.

DIANA: Of course my mother was in the business.

TITO: Ah.

DIANA: And my father was too.

TITO: You father?

DIANA: I guess you could say it's in my blood.

TITO: You got something in your blood?!

DIANA: Does it show?

TITO: No! No! You look-a fine.

DIANA: And you thought I was good tonight. I mean really, really good?

TITO: Oh yeah. Great.

DIANA: You have no idea what this means to me, Tito. Coming from you.

TITO: Heh, thanks.

DIANA: I was so afraid you were disappointed. I mean, it's just so hard to tell with all those people there.

TITO: *(After a slight pause.)* People?

DIANA: You really are incredible, aren't you. You've had so much experience, you don't even notice them. I think that's wonderful.

TITO: People?!

DIANA: Tito.

TITO: Eh?

DIANA: Now, Tito, just supposing that I really am as good as you think. And supposing that I have the confidence and the stamina to make it in the big time, in New York . . .

TITO: Yeah?

DIANA: I was wondering if, perhaps, you'd like to introduce me to some of your friends. Is that possible, Tito?

TITO: Hey. I'm not so sure, eh?

DIANA: Producers. Directors. The ones that matter. What about your agent?

TITO: My agent, she's a woman.

DIANA: So? That's all right with me.

TITO: It is?

DIANA: Of course! I wouldn't care if she was a kangaroo! The important thing is whether she's good or not. Right?!

TITO: I guess.

DIANA: All I'd need with her is five minutes. And if she doesn't think I'm special, at least I tried. I had a chance! Tito?

TITO: Hey. I do my best, okay?

DIANA: You will?

TITO: If that's a-what you want.

DIANA: Tito. How can I ever thank you?

TITO: My pleasure, eh?

DIANA: It will be. I promise. *(She kisses him, passionately. Almost at once we hear a knock at the sitting room/corridor door.)* Oh see who it is!

(Tito gets up, reluctantly, and goes to the door.)

TITO: Who is, please?

MAGGIE: *(Offstage.)* It's me. Maggie.

TITO: *(To Diana, whispering.)* Who's Moggie?

DIANA: She's Henry's daughter. I suppose she wants your autograph or something.

MAGGIE: *(Offstage.)* Open up!

TITO: *Minuto!*

DIANA: *(Taking her purse.)* Go ahead, but just get rid of her as soon as you can. I'll slip into something more comfortable. How does that sound?

TITO: I like it.

DIANA: Keep warm.

(She throws him a kiss and exits into the bathroom, closing the door. Tito watches her go, then closes the connecting door.)

MAGGIE: *(Offstage.)* Tito! *(Tito opens the door to the corridor. Maggie hurries in and quickly closes the door. Breathless.)* I slipped out during one of the speeches, so I don't think anybody noticed. Of course I might have been going to the ladies' room or out for a walk, I mean there's nothing wrong with that, except I think I looked suspicious.

TITO: How do you do.

MAGGIE: A lot better, now that I'm here. Are you all right?

TITO: I'm a-fine, thank you.

MAGGIE: Good.

(She advances into the room and takes a breath.)

TITO: So.

MAGGIE: So.

TITO: I think I know why you come, eh?

MAGGIE: I guess you do.

TITO: You want a-my autograph.

MAGGIE: Is that what you call it in Italian?

TITO: In Italian is *autografo.*

(Maggie turns her back on Tito, afraid to look at him. During the following, she doesn't see what Tito's doing — which is looking around on the table for a pen and a piece of paper.)

MAGGIE: And what's the word for "love" in Italian? *Amore?*

TITO: *(Searching.)* Hey, that's good. You speak a-the language, eh?

MAGGIE: I never would have believed that anything like this could have ever happened,

TITO: Life is funny, eh?

MAGGIE: It certainly is.

> *(By now, Tito has found the pen and paper and sits on the sofa, facing away from Maggie, to use the coffee table to write on.)*

TITO: So, what would you like me to say, eh? *(Writing.)* "Moggie . . . "

MAGGIE: Tito . . .

TITO: I get to that.

MAGGIE: *(Still facing away from him.)* Tito . . . Before we go any further, I want you to know that I've never done anything like this before.

TITO: No?

MAGGIE: No. Which doesn't mean that I regret it. Not for a second.

TITO: Hey. I done mind. Honest.

MAGGIE: *(Pale.)* You "don't mind"?

> *(They face each other.)*

TITO: Is no big deal, eh? I do it all the time.

MAGGIE: Well. Then maybe we should just forget all about it.

TITO: No! Hey. For me is a pleasure. A privilege. It makes me feel proud, eh?

MAGGIE: Do you mean that?

> *(They turn away from each other again.)*

TITO: Sure. And I'm gonna make it a-very special. Just a-for you. *(He reads.)* "Moggie."

MAGGIE: I *want* it to be special, Tito! I want it to be everything I've ever dreamed of!

TITO: Hey. I do my best, okay? *(Maggie unzips her dress and pulls it down around her. Reading.)* "Moggie." *(Writing.)* "A very special a-person . . ." *(Maggie's dress drops to the floor, and she steps out of it. Writing.)* "And beautiful to look at."

MAGGIE: Thank you.

TITO: *(Signing with a flourish.)* "Merelli." So. Now you gonna have a-my name forever.

MAGGIE: *(Hushed, thrilled.)* Your name? Forever?

TITO: *(Feeling the paper.)* Should last pretty good.

> *(Maggie turns and looks at him. It's a dream come true.)*

MAGGIE: Oh, Tito!

> *(He turns in surprise at the tone of her voice and sees her in her underwear.)*

TITO: YIY! *(He drops the pen and paper.)*

MAGGIE: I'm yours. All yours.

(She goes straight for him and pushes him backward onto the sofa, kissing his face and neck.)

TITO: Moggie!

MAGGIE: Tito! *(If he could have stopped her, it's too late now. She's all over him. He's struggling for air — when without warning, there's a knock at the door. Very insistent. They both freeze.)* Holy cow! Are you expecting anybody?

TITO: No.

SAUNDERS: *(Offstage.)* Max?!

TITO: Max?

MAGGIE: *(Horrified.)* Oh my God! It's Daddy!

TITO: Daddy?

MAGGIE: *(Jumping up.)* If he finds me here like this, he'll kill you!

TITO: Keel?

MAGGIE: He'll go crazy! I've got to hide!

SAUNDERS: *(Offstage, knocking.)* Max?!

(Maggie heads toward the bedroom.)

TITO: No!

(Too late. Maggie opens the door and enters the bedroom. Tito runs in after her.)

MAGGIE: Closet or bathroom?

TITO: Closet!

MAGGIE: You're right! *(She runs to the closet and opens the door.)* Just tell him you haven't seen me!

TITO: I haven't seen you.

(She kisses him quickly, then disappears into the closet, closing the door. At which point, the bathroom door opens, and Diana enters. She wears a towel.)

DIANA: Is she gone yet?

TITO: Not yet.

DIANA: Well, get rid of her!

TITO: I do my best.

DIANA: Perhaps I'll take a bubble bath. Then you can join me.

TITO: Bubble? I wone be long.

(She exits back into the bathroom, closing the door. Tito sighs, then runs into the sitting room, closing the connecting door as he goes, then runs to the corridor door and opens it.)

SAUNDERS: *(Offstage.)* Max!

TITO: *Ciao.*

(*Saunders glares at him and enters.*)

SAUNDERS: What are you *doing* in here?!

TITO: (*Shrugging innocently.*) Nothing.

SAUNDERS: You haven't changed yet.

TITO: Change?

SAUNDERS: I told you to change! For God's sake, you'll ruin everything!

TITO: I'm a-sorry, eh? (*Trying to get him out.*) Thanks a-for coming.

SAUNDERS: Will you cut the phony accent! I'm not amused.

TITO: You done like it?

SAUNDERS: Look. I know you think this is great fun. You're Il Stupendo. Big
    star. Hot stuff —

TITO: Yeah.

SAUNDERS: But it's not the time to fool around! Just imagine what would hap-
    pen if anybody found out. My blood runs cold when I even — (*He stops
    in his tracks. He's staring at the floor — at Maggie's dress. He picks it up and
    holds it out, confirming that it is, indeed, a woman's dress. He looks at Tito.*)
    Is there a woman in here?

TITO: Yeah.

SAUNDERS: Are you out of your mind?

TITO: I'm not so sure.

SAUNDERS: You're really having a field day, aren't you?

TITO: (*Shrugging.*) Heh . . .

SAUNDERS: (*Lowering his voice.*) Can she hear us?

TITO: I dunno.

SAUNDERS: That explains the accent.

TITO: It does?

(*Saunders sidles over to the kitchenette.*)

SAUNDERS: (*Whispering.*) Is she in there?

TITO: No.

SAUNDERS: (*Looking around the room.*) Well, where is she?

TITO: The bathroom.

SAUNDERS: The bathroom?! Are you crazy?! What about the body?!

TITO: The body?

SAUNDERS: The body!

TITO: Like I said, she's in the bathroom.

SAUNDERS: Not that body. The other body.

TITO: Oh. (*Resigned.*) The closet.

SAUNDERS: The closet? You stuffed the body in the closet?

TITO: Is a big closet.

SAUNDERS: Look. I would be the first to admit that you deserve a little reward for all you've been through.

TITO: Thanks.

SAUNDERS: But it's not the time!

TITO: Okay.

SAUNDERS: Now first of all, I want you to get rid of the girl —

TITO: Which one?

SAUNDERS: There's more than one?

TITO: *(Sheepishly.)* Two.

SAUNDERS: You've got two girls in there?

TITO: Yeah.

SAUNDERS: I knew you had potential, but this is incredible.

TITO: Thanks.

SAUNDERS: Look. I'm impressed. All right? I'm very impressed. But get them the hell out of here!! Do you have any idea who's downstairs right now?

TITO: No.

SAUNDERS: The police! And they're asking questions!

TITO: *(Croaking.)* Police?

SAUNDERS: That's what I came up to tell you. They're looking for some madman who tried to break into the theater tonight. In costume!

TITO: Police?

(A knock at the sitting room/corridor door.)

SAUNDERS: Oh hell. That could be them. *(Lowering his voice.)* All right. Here's the story. You're still Tito. You came back from the theater and went straight to your room. *(During the following, Saunders leads Tito to the connecting door, to hide him in the bedroom.)* You haven't seen anything unusual, whatsoever. And whatever we do, we keep them away from the closet! *(He closes the connecting door, leaving Tito in the bedroom. Another knock at the door.)* Coming!

(He opens the door. Max, still dressed as Otello, rushes in.)

MAX: I've got to talk to you! *(He closes the door.)*

(Saunders is speechless and reels backward. Meanwhile, Tito, still in the bedroom, leans against the connecting wall, arm outstretched; Max does the same in the sitting room. They unknowingly create a mirror image.)

SAUNDERS: This is no time for jokes, you idiot!!!

MAX: Jokes?

SAUNDERS: Are you out of your mind?! What's the matter with you?!

MAX: What did *I* do?!

SAUNDERS: This whole thing could blow up any second!!

MAX: I know!

SAUNDERS: Well, who was at the door?!

MAX: What door?

SAUNDERS: That door! Who was knocking?!

MAX: Me.

SAUNDERS: Before that!

MAX: How should I know?

SAUNDERS: You were there!

MAX: Where?!

SAUNDERS: At the door!

MAX: What door?!

SAUNDERS: *That door!!! (Pause. They're at an impasse. At this point, Tito opens the bedroom/corridor door and exits, pulling the door closed quietly behind him. Saunders goes on reasonably, restraining himself.)* Max. A minute ago, you were standing here and I was talking to you. There was a knock at the door, and I said, "That may be the police"

MAX: It wasn't me.

SAUNDERS: I know that!

MAX: I mean, in here!

SAUNDERS: Max —

MAX: I was downstairs, looking for you! When I couldn't find you, I came back up!

SAUNDERS: You were looking for me?

MAX: That's what I want to tell you! He's gone.

SAUNDERS: Who?

MAX: Tito! He's gone!

SAUNDERS: Max! We all have to go sometime!

MAX: I mean he's not on the bed!! He disappeared!! Look. You told me to go change and you went downstairs. I walked in there and I tried not to look, but I couldn't help it, so I looked at the bed and he wasn't there.

SAUNDERS: He's in the closet.

MAX: Who told you that?

SAUNDERS: You — *(He freezes. He figures it out.)* Oh my God. He's alive.

MAX: Do you really think so?

SAUNDERS: I was standing here talking to him!!! *(He bolts to the connecting door*

and throws it open. He looks around the bedroom and sees that it's empty.)
He's gone.

MAX: But he's alive. That's terrific!

SAUNDERS: You moron! He could ruin everything! *(A knock at the sitting room/corridor door. Saunders and Max freeze. Saunders goes on, lowering his voice.)* It's either him or the police.

MAX: Oh great.

SAUNDERS: Whatever I say, just play along.
(Max sits on the sofa as Saunders walks to the corridor door and opens it. The Bellhop enters, carrying an ice bucket, a bottle of champagne, and two glasses.)

BELLHOP: Nightcap, anyone?

SAUNDERS: Oh no!!

BELLHOP: Mr. Merelli! Oh sir, I know how tired you must be and I won't take up much of your time, but I simply must tell you how magnificent you were tonight. You were wonderful!

MAX: Thanks.

BELLHOP: I'll never forget it as long as I live.

MAX: You liked it, eh?

BELLHOP: I adored every note.

MAX: What exactly did you like a-best?

SAUNDERS: *(To Max.)* Not now!!

BELLHOP: *(Dramatically.)* When you realized that she was innocent, but it was too late. *Oh, Desdemona. Morta. Morta. Morta.* It was so beautiful!

SAUNDERS: Who the hell ordered champagne?!

BELLHOP: He did.

MAX: I did?

SAUNDERS: You did?

BELLHOP: That's what they told me downstairs.

SAUNDERS: Oh yes of course. I remember now. *(To Max.)* The champagne.

MAX: Oh yeah. I forget, eh?

BELLHOP: And guess what? It's on the house, and *I* arranged it.

SAUNDERS: Well, that's very nice of you.

BELLHOP: I did it for *him.*

SAUNDERS: Well, now you've done it, so get out.

BELLHOP: *(Ignoring Saunders.)* Is there anything else I can do for you, Mr. Merelli?

MAX: I done think so. Thanks.

SAUNDERS: Out.

BELLHOP: Well, if you want anything, just pick up the phone. I'm on all night.

SAUNDERS: Out!!

BELLHOP: *(Unruffled, to Max.)* I'll see you later. *(He frowns.)* Good-bye, Henry. *(He exits, closing the door.)*

SAUNDERS: All right, now listen. Here's the plan. Number one, you change. And do it this time!

MAX: Yes, sir.

SAUNDERS: I'll go find Tito and explain everything. And then, if I have to, I'll pay him off.

(He goes to the corridor door.)

MAX: Sir? Since we're not doing the *Requiem,* can I do the *Carmen*?

SAUNDERS: Change!

MAX: Yes, sir.

(Saunders exits. Max walks into the bedroom, leaving the connecting door open, and heads straight for the bathroom. He walks into the bathroom and closes the door. Pause. A cry from Max, as the door swings open, Max holding the handle for dear life. Diana, still in her towel, yanks him back in and the door slams. Repeat. Bubbles each time. Silence for a moment; then the closet door opens and Maggie cautiously emerges. She wears Tito's trench coat over her underwear.)

MAGGIE: *(In a whisper.)* Tito? *(There's a yelp from the bathroom, and Maggie is startled by it. Then she realizes that he must be using the bathroom.)* Oh. *(She calls quietly.)* Sorry! *(She sighs with relief and goes into the sitting room, smiling happily. Then she notices the champagne.)* Oh, Tito! Champagne! *(She picks up one of the glasses admiringly. She notices a speck of dirt on it. She picks up the other glass, decides that both glasses need washing, and walks into the kitchenette, happily humming a popular tune. As Maggie exits, the bathroom door crashes open and Max reels out, breathing heavily. Diana follows him out still wearing her towel.)*

DIANA: Now, don't go 'way, I have a little surprise for you. I'll be right back. *(She exits into the bathroom and closes the door. Max catches his breath, then staggers into the sitting room, closing the connecting door behind him. Maggie, who's heard the door, enters from the kitchenette without the glasses.)*

MAGGIE: Darling. *(She shrugs the trench coat off her shoulders, and it falls to the floor.)* Alone at last. *(Max falls to his knees, speechless and exhausted.)* You poor thing, you look tired. You've had a rough day, haven't you? *(Max nods his head yes. Maggie goes to him.)* Now, don't you worry. I'm going to make it all better. *(She leads him to the sofa and pushes him on to it.)* You'll see.

(Max is flat on his back. Maggie's on top of him, kissing him passionately, which is when the bedroom/corridor door opens and Tito rushes in, closing the door quickly, but quietly. He's on the lam and breathing heavily. He runs to his suitcase, grabs it, and turns to go when Diana enters from the bathroom. She wears a nightie that is extremely sexy. Tito sees her, freezes, and drops the suitcase.)

DIANA: Well? Do you like it? *(Tito nods his head yes.)* I thought you might.

TITO: Heh . . .

DIANA: You poor thing, you look tired. You've had a rough day, haven't you? *(Tito nods his head yes. Diana goes to him.)* Now don't you worry. I'm going to make it all better. You'll see.

(She pushes him onto the bed and climbs on top of him, kissing him passionately.)

MAX: *(In the sitting room.)* Shall we turn off a-the lights?

DIANA: *(In the bedroom.)* I like it with the lights on.

MAGGIE: *(In the sitting room.)* If that's all right with you.

TITO: *(In the bedroom.)* It's a-fine with me.

(Both couples go at it again, with increasing passion. And as they continue, the lights fade to black. As the lights fade, music comes up: the final moment of the tenor/soprano duet "Da quel di che t'incontrai" from Donizetti's Linda di Chamounix. *It's a love song that begins with a lilt, then breaks into a gallop, building to a final cry of joy from the soprano.)*

SCENE TWO

Fifteen minutes later. When the duet is over, the lights come up. Both couples have just finished making love. Diana is propped up in bed; Maggie is sitting on the sofa. Tito and Max are both pulling their boots back on. Obviously, each couple is unaware of the other couple in the adjoining room.

MAGGIE: It was even better than I thought it would be. I guess that's because you're Italian.

MAX: I guess so, eh?

DIANA: I bet you don't feel tired anymore, do you?

(Tito sways from exhaustion. He's about to collapse.)

TITO: No . . . no . . .

DIANA: I must look awful. I think I'd better do some reconstruction. *(She leaves the bed and heads for the bathroom.)* I won't be long.

TITO: Take a-you time, eh?

(Diana exits into the bathroom and closes the door. Tito falls backward onto the bed in utter exhaustion.)

MAGGIE: I think I'd like some champagne now. Want some?

MAX: Why not, eh?

MAGGIE: It was so sweet of you to think of it. But then you think of everything, don't you?

MAX: It's the way I am, eh?

MAGGIE: You pop the cork, I'll dry the glasses. *(Sexy.)* Maybe it'll put us in the mood again.

MAX: Could be.

(She exits into the kitchenette. The moment she's gone, Max breaks into song — the "Toreador Song" from Carmen. *He dances to the sofa and begins opening the champagne.*

After a moment, Tito sits up in bed and listens. He hears the singing ,and it sounds close by. He cocks his head, to listen better, then looks toward the sitting room. As Max continues opening the bottle, Tito gets up from the bed and goes to the connecting door. He listens — then opens the door, cautiously and silently, to find out who's in there. Max is facing the opposite wall and doesn't see —or hear — the door open.

Tito takes a step into the sitting room and sees Max — or rather, he sees himself opening a bottle of champagne and singing. He freezes, speechless. He looks down at himself, then back at Max. He now realizes there's a fair possibility that he's lost his mind. And if he hasn't lost his mind, he doesn't want an explanation, he just wants out. Tito steps back into the bedroom, leaving the connecting door open. Then he runs to his suitcase, grabs it, and runs from the room, out the corridor door, closing it behind him.

As that door closes, the bathroom door opens and Diana enters the bedroom, still in her nightie. She sees that the bedroom is empty but notices that the connecting door is open. She walks to the door and sees Max — who is still opening the champagne. As Diana enters the sitting room from the bedroom, Maggie enters from the kitchenette, holding the glasses.)

DIANA: The champagne!

MAGGIE: *(Simultaneously.)* All set! *(Max is speechless. Maggie turns to Diana.)* What are you doing here?!

DIANA: I was about to ask you the same thing.

MAGGIE: This happens to be a private party.

DIANA: It certainly is, so scram.

MAGGIE: Tito, tell her to leave!

MAX: *(To Diana.)* A-leave!

DIANA: Tell *her* that, you idiot!

MAGGIE: Tito, what is she doing here?!

MAX: I-I-I-I-I-I-I —

MAGGIE: *(To Diana.)* How long have you been here?

DIANA: About a half hour.

MAGGIE: That's impossible. *I've* been here a half hour.

DIANA: Yes, I know. I was here when you arrived. He said he'd get rid of you as soon as possible.

MAGGIE: Tito. Did you know she was in there?

MAX: I-I-I-I-I —

MAGGIE: *(Pale.)* You did.

MAX: It's not a-what you think, eh?

MAGGIE: How could you do this?! After what you said to me?!

DIANA: Never trust a man in tights.

MAGGIE: You louse. *(Approaching him.)* You . . . you crumb.

DIANA: Just what I was thinking.

MAX: Hey! I gotta go now.

> *(He pushes them back onto the sofa and bolts away.)*

MAGGIE: Stop him! Don't let him out!

> *(Diana runs to the corridor door to block it.)*

MAX: Hey!

> *(He throws the champagne in the air and Maggie catches it, then he hands the vase of flowers to Diana and darts toward the bedroom.)*

DIANA: Get him! *(Max runs into the bedroom, pursued by both women.)* Block the door!

MAGGIE: Grab him!

DIANA: I'm trying!

MAGGIE: Stop him!

> *(Max rushes into the bathroom and closes the door. The women rush to the door and try to open it. Too late.)*

DIANA: It's locked!

> *(Maggie grabs the doorknob and rattles it violently.)*

MAGGIE: Come out of there, you-you rat!

DIANA: It's no use.

MAGGIE: Coward!!

DIANA: Save your breath. I know his type.

(Pause. Maggie sighs in frustration.)

MAGGIE: Now what do we do?

DIANA: I don't know about you, but I'm getting dressed.

MAGGIE: Good idea.

(Maggie glares at the bathroom door, then walks into the sitting room to retrieve her dress. Meanwhile, Diana looks around the room for her dress, then remembers she left it in the bathroom. She walks to the bathroom door.)

DIANA: Tito. My dress is in there. *(No response. Diana knocks on the door.)* Tito. I need my dress. I promise I won't hurt you. *(No response.)* GIVE ME THE GODDAMN DRESS OR I'LL KILL YOU!!! *(In a single action, the bathroom door opens, the dress flies out, the door slams shut and is locked again from the inside.)* Thank you, Tito.

(The women get dressed in silence, both in the bedroom.)

MAGGIE: I wouldn't have believed it was possible. He seemed so nice.

DIANA: He is nice. He's just a little tricky, that's all.

MAGGIE: Does this sort of thing happen very often?

DIANA: Yes and no. I've been two-timed before, but never with quite so much flair. I mean, you've got to hand it to him.

MAGGIE: I did. That's the problem.

DIANA: Hook? *(Diana turns and Maggie hooks up the back.)* Thank you.

MAGGIE: My pleasure.

(At this moment, the sitting room/corridor door opens, and Maria enters, carrying her vanity case. She leaves the door ajar.)

MARIA: One a-more chance, eh? One a-more chance and that's it!

(Maggie and Diana both hear Maria and look at each other, puzzled. Maria enters the sitting room.)

DIANA: Oh my God, he's got another one!

(Maria is startled, then glares suspiciously at Diana.)

MARIA: Who are you?!

DIANA: A friend of the family. Who are you?

MARIA: The family.

DIANA: Tito's wife?

MARIA: That's a-right.

DIANA: *(Calling.)* Maggie, dear. Guess who's here.

MARIA: I'm gonna keel 'im.

DIANA: We know just how you feel.

MAGGIE: *(As she enters the sitting room.)* Hi.

MARIA: You again.

DIANA: You've met before?

MAGGIE: Just once. In the closet.

DIANA: You realize of course that she's Tito's wife.

MAGGIE: Yeah. Only she isn't really his wife. Tito told me. She likes to pretend she is, and he plays along because he doesn't want to hurt her feelings.

MARIA: Tito tell you this?

MAGGIE: Of course.

MARIA: I'm gonna keel 'im. I swear before God, on everything that's a-holy, I'm gonna strangle him!

DIANA: She sounds like his wife.

MARIA: With my bare hands!!

DIANA: She's his wife.

MAGGIE: But he *said* . . . *(She realizes.)* Oh my God.

MARIA: Where is he? *(Maggie and Diana look at each other.)* Where is he?!!

MAGGIE/DIANA: *(Together.)* The bathroom.

> *(Maria stalks into the bedroom, toward the bathroom door. Diana and Maggie follow her.)*

DIANA: He locked himself in.

MAGGIE: He won't come out.

DIANA: We tried!

MAGGIE: You're sure you're his wife?!

> *(Maria growls in response. Then she tries the door, without success.)*

MARIA: Tito. It's Maria.

MAX: *(Offstage.)* Oh no!

MARIA: *(Banging on the door with her fist.)* Open the door right now 'cause I'm gonna keel you!! You hear me, you big a-pig! Open the door!!

> *(As Maria bangs and hollers, there's an eruption of overlapping voices as Tito runs in through the sitting room/corridor door pursued by Saunders, Julia, and the Bellhop.)*

TITO: Help!

SAUNDERS: Stop!

JULIA: Tito! Please!

TITO: Help!

BELLHOP: Leave him alone!

TITO: Help!

SAUNDERS: I just want to talk to you!

JULIA: Tito, you promised!

BELLHOP: Leave that man alone!

(Maria, Diana, and Maggie have by now entered the sitting room to see what's going on.)

MARIA: Tito!

TITO: Maria! *(He runs to her.)* Oh, Maria! Get me outa here! Please!

MARIA: *(Wheeling on Diana and Maggie.)* So! You make a-fun of me, eh?! You tell a-me lies!

SAUNDERS: What are you two doing here?

MAGGIE: Well —

DIANA: We were passing by, so we stopped in.

MAGGIE: To get his autograph.

BELLHOP: Did you get it?

MAGGIE: We sure did.

MARIA: *(To Tito.)* They told a-me you were locked in the bathroom.

JULIA: The bathroom?

MARIA: They make a-me think you were fooling around!

TITO: Maria? Me?!

DIANA: We didn't say that.

MAGGIE: Of course not.

DIANA: We were standing here, waiting for Tito —

MAGGIE: And-and-and somebody ran in there —

DIANA: Who sort of . . . looked like Tito.

MAGGIE: Right.

JULIA: Oh my God. It's the lunatic! It must be!

MAGGIE: Ahhhh-h-h-h!

MARIA: Luna-what?

JULIA: Lunatic. A madman. He's running around the city pretending he's your husband. And apparently he's violent. He actually hit a policeman!

TITO: No!

JULIA: Yes! We should call the police.

SAUNDERS: Julia —

JULIA: He could be dangerous, Henry!

SAUNDERS: Oh I doubt that —

BELLHOP: Well?! Let's see who it is!

SAUNDERS: Stay out of this!

MARIA: He's right, eh? I wanna see this a-lunatic. Maria want to see 'im!

(She walks into the bedroom, followed by the others, who speak simultaneously.)

SAUNDERS: I really wouldn't bother —

DIANA: It's hardly important —

MAGGIE: Who cares who it is!

JULIA: I still think we should call the police!

SAUNDERS: Julia!

MARIA: *(At the bathroom door, hollering.)* Hello?! Who's in there?! *(No response. Maria bangs on the door.)* Come outa there! You hear me?!

BELLHOP: This-is-the-police! Come-out-with-your-hands-up!

(They all look at him. He looks behind himself and shrugs.)

MARIA: I'm gonna give you three numbers! One! . . . Two! . .

(The door unlocks . . . then opens. Max emerges — himself again. His makeup is washed off, and he wears white tie and tails.)

MAX: Did I miss something?

BELLHOP: It's Max.

MAGGIE: *(Shocked, sitting down on the bed.)* Max?

SAUNDERS: Max! What a surprise!

MARIA: He doesn't even look a-like Tito!

MAX: Hi, Tito! You look great!

TITO: Max! My friend! They drive a-me crazy! You done know!

MAX: Gee, I'm sorry.

TITO: Maria, please! Take a-me home! Anyplace! Just get a-me outa here!!

MARIA: I take care, eh? Maria, she takes a-care.

TITO: *Bellezza.*

MARIA: *Carissimo.*

TITO: *Mia vongole.*

MARIA: Let's go!

JULIA: Wait! Tito!

MARIA: *(To Tito.)* We go to Greece, eh?

TITO: Greece. That's a-good. I take a rest.

JULIA: Tito, you promised!

MARIA: Leave him alone!

JULIA/SAUNDERS/BELLHOP: *(Together.)* Right!

(Julia, Saunders, and the Bellhop retreat into the sitting room, followed by Maria and Diana.)

MAX: Bye, Tito.

TITO: Max. Thanks a-for everything, eh?

MAX: Take care of yourself.

TITO: And done forget. You gotta say "I'm a-the best. I'm a-Max."

MAX/TITO: *(Together.)* "I sing good!"

MARIA: *(At the sitting room/corridor door.)* Tito! Let's a-go!

TITO: Maria. My love.

(Tito joins Maria at the door, and they exit.)

JULIA: Wait! *(She hurries to the door.)* Just five minutes, that's all I need! *(She exits, running. From offstage.)* Tito! Please!

(Pause.)

SAUNDERS: Well, I guess that's that. Everything seems to be in order now.

(Max and Maggie are next to each other. She looks at him in shock and confusion, realizing that she slept with him. He smiles, enjoying it.)

MAX: Yeah.

MAGGIE: Just . . . fine.

(Max and Maggie join the others in the sitting room. Saunders looks at Maggie — and suddenly recognizes her dress. He examines one of the sleeves.)

MAGGIE: *Is anything wrong?*

SAUNDERS: I'll speak to you later, young lady. You don't think I believe that story about the autograph, do you?

(The Bellhop has by now picked up a piece of paper from the coffee table.)

BELLHOP: *(Reading.)* "To Maggie. A very special person, and beautiful to look at. Merelli."

SAUNDERS: *(Snatching the paper.)* Let me see that!

BELLHOP: I wish I'd gotten one.

MAX: You still might catch him.

BELLHOP: Do you think so?!

MAX: It's worth a try.

BELLHOP: *(Bolting out of the room and down the corridor.)* Mister Merelli! Mister Merelli!!

MAGGIE: *(Taking her autograph from Saunders.)* I'll take that, thank you.

SAUNDERS: *(Puzzled.)* Yes, of course.

(During the following, Maggie stares at the paper, lost in thought.)

DIANA: Henry, is there any food left downstairs?

SAUNDERS: I should think so.

DIANA: Good. Let's go. For some reason, *(Looking at Max.)* I'm very hungry.

(She takes Saunders' arm. He beams.)

SAUNDERS: Oh. Well, what a lovely idea.

(They head for the door.)

MAX: Sir? Shall we say tomorrow morning? Ten o'clock. Your office.

SAUNDERS: Max —

MAX: You see, I've got some new ideas for next season.

SAUNDERS: Max!

MAX: *Carmen, La Boheme.* Then finish off with something lighter —

SAUNDERS: Like *Die Fledermaus?*

MAX: Good idea.

SAUNDERS: I'll see you in the morning. Ten-thirty.

MAX: Sir.

SAUNDERS: Max?!

MAX: Don't be late!

> *(Beat. Saunders is stunned. He exits, dazed. Diana pauses in the doorway, gives Max a look, then follows Saunders, closing the door behind her. Max and Maggie are alone. Pause.)*

MAGGIE: Well . . . at least I had a fling.

MAX: Yeah.

MAGGIE: Max. I . . . I really liked it.

MAX: Me too.

MAGGIE: And I'm really glad it was with you.

MAX: Me too.

MAGGIE: But you really took an awful chance, you know, wearing his costume and making all that fuss at the stage door. And hitting a policeman! If you hadn't gotten away, you might be in prison!

MAX: Maggie —

MAGGIE: The worst part is, you didn't even get to hear him sing. And he was so wonderful.

MAX: Was he?

MAGGIE: Oh, Max, he was unbelievable. When he first came out, a . . . a shock went through the audience. And then he sang and . . . I know it sounds silly, but I started to cry. I couldn't help it. I guess that's why he's Tito Merelli.

MAX: Yeah.

> *(Music begins playing: the final orchestral moment from Act I of* Otello. *Max hears it; Maggie doesn't.)*

MAGGIE: And even then I was thinking, God, where's Max? I want him to hear this. You know? I want to share this with him, and —

> *(Max kisses Maggie's palm and starts to sing. She is lulled by the music and closes her eyes.)*

MAX: *(Singing.) Gia la pleiade ardente al mar discende.*

Vien . . . Venere splende.

(As Max holds the final note, Maggie's eyes snap open and her jaw drops. She realizes at last.)

MAGGIE: Oh, *Max!!*

(She throws her arms around him and they kiss. Bells peal out loudly through the final orchestral swell as . . .)

(The curtain falls.)

END OF PLAY

CURTAIN CALL

In the London and New York productions, the play proper was followed by an elaborate curtain call of sorts — that is, the actors pantomimed the entire action of the play in eighty-five seconds to the music of the finale to Jacques Ibert's *Divertissement.* (*Divertissement* was written by Ibert in 1930 as incidental music for Labiche's farce, *Un Chapeau de Paille d'Italie.* The music is therefore not only the right length but also superbly frantic. It's also generally available on record.)

A scenario describing the action of the curtain call is set forth below. The action is divided into numbered paragraphs for the sake of convenience in rehearsal. However, the action is intended to flow continuously from beginning to end without a pause, with the actors literally running from one place to the next where necessary. It's also essential that the actors use extremely broad gestures so that the story emerges as clearly (and frantically) as possible.

To avoid confusion, it should be noted that in some instances, entrances and exits occur through different doors than they do in the play proper and that, in condensing the story to eighty-five seconds, some portions of the action have been consciously omitted. A few props will have to be preset before the curtain call can begin. However, the curtain call should explode into action as soon as possible after the play is ended.

Finally, the director should feel free to change the action of the curtain call, where necessary, to reflect any business that may have been added to the particular production. Thus, the curtain calls in London and New York differed slightly in detail.

SCENARIO

1. Max and Maggie are onstage in the sitting room. Maggie, on the pouf, swoons with pleasure (thereby cueing the start of the music). Max answers the phone and reacts to Saunders' yell; and Saunders walks in from the corridor.

2. Saunders points at Maggie, then at the door (telling her to leave). Maggie walks through the connecting door and straight into the closet.

3. Max and Saunders hear the phone. Max answers it, indicates that it's Tito, and hangs up. Saunders opens the sitting room/corridor door, and the Merellis walk in. Tito is still dressed as Otello from the end of the play, but he has his topcoat over his shoulders at the moment.

4. Tito and Maria sling their wraps at Max, as the Bellhop enters the bedroom from the corridor and throws his arms up, singing.

5. Max hands the wraps to the Bellhop at the connecting door. The Bellhop opens the closet door and throws the wraps in to Maggie. Then he exits into the corridor.

6. Meanwhile, Tito and Maria argue. Then Maria stalks into the bedroom and straight into the bathroom, slamming the door.

7. Saunders picks up the phone and screams. He slams down the phone and walks out.

8. Tito and Max "shake" themselves, then sing, arms out. Then each picks up a wine glass and stirs the other's drink with his finger.

9. Maria emerges from the bathroom, making her farewell gesture. Then she walks to the closet, opens the door, sees Maggie, and stifles a growl. Maria stalks out into the corridor, followed by Maggie.

10. Tito staggers into the bedroom, picks up the farewell note, screams, and collapses onto the bed. Max heads for the bedroom. As he passes the corridor door, Diana enters, gives Max a kiss and exits. Then Max enters the bedroom as Saunders enters the bedroom from the corridor.

11. Max points at Tito ("He's dead!"), and Saunders climbs onto the bed and starts shaking the corpse. Saunders then pulls the Otello wig from a hidden spot (perhaps the night table), throws it at Max, and points to the bathroom.

12. Max reacts with horror, then exits into the bathroom, as Saunders walks to the sitting room/corridor door and opens it. Julia and the Bellhop enter. Saunders grabs the Bellhop by the lapels, and Maggie rushes into the sitting room from the corridor, holding the rose.

13. Saunders, Maggie, Julia, and the Bellhop chase around the sofa, halt for the Bellhop's flash picture, then continue the chase, as Max enters (in the Otello wig) from the bathroom. He walks to the upstage "wall" dividing the two rooms, looks at the audience and shrugs, then steps through the wall.

14. Maggie hands Max the rose. He indicates that he'll do the opera, and everyone (except Max) registers elation.

15. Everyone in the sitting room exits into the corridor, as Tito gets up from the bed. He walks into the sitting room and sits on the sofa. Simultaneously, Max enters the bedroom from the corridor, discovers that Tito's gone, and runs back out the same door.

16. Julia walks into the sitting room from the corridor and frightens Tito. He ushers her back out into the corridor, then walks into the bedroom — as Max enters the sitting room from the corridor.

17. Immediately, Maggie enters the sitting room from the kitchenette, and Diana enters the bedroom from the bathroom. They push the men onto the sofa and bed, respectively.

18. Maggie goes back into the kitchenette, and Diana stands back to allow Tito to bound to his feet. As Max works on opening the champagne, Tito enters the sitting room, sees Max, reacts, then runs out the sitting room/corridor door.

19. Diana, hard on Tito's heels, enters the sitting room as Maggie reenters the sitting room from the kitchenette. They both discover Max at the same time, and all three react.

20. Maggie and Diana chase Max through the bedroom to the bathroom door. Max exits into the bathroom, closing the door before they can catch him. As soon as Max slams the door, Maria enters the bedroom from the corridor.

21. Maggie and Diana point to the bathroom. Maria bangs on the door as Tito, Saunders, Julia, and the Bellhop run into the sitting room and then into the bedroom, where they see the three women and stop.

22. Maria hits the bathroom door again, and Max strolls out of the bathroom (without his Otello wig). He gestures "What's the matter?" Shock from the others.

23. Everyone exits except Max and Maggie: Maria, Tito, and Saunders go through the sitting room and out the sitting room/corridor door, as Julia, the Bellhop, and Diana exit through the bedroom/corridor door. Max and Maggie simultaneously walk into the sitting room.

24. Max throw his arms up, singing. Maggie cries "Max!," and they kiss.
    (Blackout.)
    (Traditional curtain calls now follow.)

MOON OVER BUFFALO

Pictured (L–R): Philip Bosco (George Hay), Carol Burnett (Charlotte Hay)

ORIGINAL BROADWAY PRODUCTION

Moon Over Buffalo premiered on Broadway on October 1, 1995, at the Martin Beck Theatre. It was produced by Elizabeth Williams, Heidi Landesman, DLT Entertainment, Ltd., Hal Luftig, and Jujamcyn Theaters. The set designer was Heidi Landesman, the costumer designer was Bob Mackie, the lighting designer was Ken Billington, and the sound designer was Tony Meola. The fights were staged by B. H. Barry. General management was by 101 Productions, Ltd. The production supervisor was Steven Beckler, and the stage manager was Tom Capps. It was directed by Tom Moore with the following cast:

GEORGE . . . . .Philip Bosco
CHARLOTTE . . . . .Carol Burnett
ETHEL . . . . .Jane Connell
ROSALIND . . . . .Randy Graff
HOWARD . . . . .Andy Taylor
EILEEN . . . . .Kate Miller
PAUL . . . . .Dennis Ryan
RICHARD . . . . .James Valentine

Understudies: Richard Poe, Jane Sell Trese, Lannyl Stephens, and David Beach.

Replacement cast: Lynn Redgrave as Charlotte and Robert Goulet as George.

ORIGINAL LONDON PRODUCTION

The play was subsequently presented in London on October 15, 2001, under the title *Over the Moon* at The Old Vic by Bill Kenwright. The set and costume designer was Tim Goodchild, and the lighting designer was Brian Harris. It was directed by Ray Cooney with the following cast:

GEORGE . . . . .Frank Langella
CHARLOTTE . . . . .Joan Collins
ETHEL . . . . .Moira Lister
ROSALIND . . . . .Sarah Wateridge
HOWARD . . . . .Cameron Blakely
EILEEN . . . . .Emma Barton
PAUL . . . . .Robert Fitch
RICHARD . . . . .Paul Bentley

AUTHOR'S PREFACE

Moon Over Buffalo started with an article in a newspaper. One morning, coffee in hand, I was leafing through the *New York Times* and noticed an article about Trevor Howard and Celia Johnson, the two British actors who had played lovers in the movie *Brief Encounter* in 1945. Apparently they had not seen each other for many years, and their reunion was considered noteworthy by the press because their performances in the film were so beloved by the British public.

This got me thinking: two actors, romantically associated . . . What if they were married, beloved by the public for what they had done in the past but were now on their uppers and touring in rep? Perhaps they were touring in smaller and smaller towns, trying to revitalize their failing careers. Then, for no reason that I know of, I imagined them playing a scene onstage together: only it was not one scene, it was two scenes at the same time. One was the balcony scene from *Private Lives,* and the other was the boasting scene from *Cyrano de Bergerac.* And one of them was drunk.

I laughed out loud, which is always my marker as to whether I am on the right track, so I tried to think it through as a whole play. For the next several weeks, however, I could not get farther than that single scene, and I had no idea what it meant.

Eventually, I put the idea in a drawer — I just could not crack it — but a few months later that changed. I was having lunch in New York City with a man named Bob Montgomery. He was the dean of the entertainment lawyers in the city and a leading partner in one of the city's most prestigious firms. He was natty, soft-spoken, had a warm sense of humor, and he had taken a sort of fatherly interest in my career. Whenever I was in New York, I would call him up, and he would take me to lunch at the Four Seasons Restaurant at his regular table where he ate lunch with friends and clients virtually every day of the week. The manager and waiters treated him like royalty, and I always felt like a privileged major domo walking in behind him.

One day, as we were getting to the dessert course, I described in detail my lone idea for this new play. I remember holding my head in my hands and bewailing the fact that I could not for the life of me devise a story to go with the one scene that kept playing through my head. Bob waited until I was finished, and then said quietly, "Ken. Listen to me. Listen very carefully. Finish your overpriced plate of crème brulée, go home, sit down at your desk, and write me the whole play. Don't second-guess yourself. Don't dawdle. Don't whine.

Just bring me a play by this time next week. I don't care if it's good, I don't care if it's lousy. Just bring it to me. Now get the hell out of here."

So I went home, sat at my desk and wrote *Moon Over Buffalo* in a week.

It landed on Broadway a few months later starring Carol Burnett in her return to the theater after thirty years in television and the movies. It also starred Phil Bosco, Jane Connell, and Randy Graff, and it was directed by the fine director Tom Moore. The replacement cast in New York starred Lynn Redgrave and Robert Goulet; and in London, at the Old Vic, it starred Joan Collins and Frank Langella. Carol and Phil were both nominated for Tony Awards, for Best Actress and Best Actor.

One of my fondest recollections of the Broadway production of *Moon Over Buffalo* is the final preview in New York before opening night. Heidi Landesman had designed a crackerjack set that allowed the opening scene of the play to unfold on the full stage; then the floor raised up to form the ceiling of the greenroom where the rest of the play took place. It was nifty, fun, always set off a nice burst of applause, and we all loved it. However, just once during the run of the play — at this particular preview — the mechanism for moving the deck broke down. So there we were, ten minutes into the play, the action at a halt, and we did not know quite what to do. Then Tom got the brilliant idea of going to Carol and asking her to get out there in front of the curtain and chat with the audience while the crew tried to fix the deck. Needless to say, Carol was brilliant. To paraphrase Noël Coward, she could read the Albanian telephone directory and people would come and enjoy themselves. We had some celebrities in the audience that night, including Bernadette Peters and Dom DeLuis, and the audience had a simply rollicking time. So my hat is off forever to Tom and Carol. They saved the day.

An equally fond memory of *Moon Over Buffalo* is working with the sunshiny Moira Lister in the London production of the play at the Old Vic. The great farceur Ray Cooney was our director (he has written many stage hits of his own, of course, including *Run for Your Wife* and *Out of Order*). Ray had suggested Moira for the role of Ethel — they had worked together many times before — and Moira, although the picture of elegance and sophistication off the stage (in real life she was a vicomtesse), imbued the role of the whacky old mother with the kind of cutting, deadly humor that cannot be taught. For me one of the joys of working with Moira was that she had played opposite Noël Coward as his very last leading lady.

My thanks to the producers of *Moon Over Buffalo* on Broadway, including Elizabeth Williams, Rocco Landesman, Jack Viertel, and Hal Luftig. They were all supportive and great fun to be with. Thanks also to Bill Kenwright, who produced the play in London, and to Ray Cooney, who not only directed it there but also coproduced and cast the play, encouraged all of us, and became our friend. —*KL*

CHARACTERS

GEORGE, an actor

CHARLOTTE, an actress, George's wife

ROSALIND, a former actress, their daughter

ETHEL, a retired actress, Charlotte's mother

HOWARD, not an actor, Rosalind's boyfriend

PAUL, a stage manager, Rosalind's former boyfriend

EILEEN, an ingénue

RICHARD, George and Charlotte's lawyer

PLACE AND TIME

Onstage and backstage at the Erlanger Theater, Buffalo, New York, 1953.

ACT I

A midmorning in June

ACT II

Scene One: Two hours later

Scene Two: Immediately following

Scene Three: Two hours later

MOON OVER BUFFALO

ACT I

A fusillade of musket and cannon, the bloody cries of a pitched battle — and as the lights come up, we're at the Siege of Arras in 1640, at the outpost of the Company of Carbon de Castel-faloux. But we're not, really. We're on the stage of the Erlanger Theater in Buffalo, New York, during a rehearsal of Act IV of Cyrano de Bergerac. *The stage is full of smoke, noise, and tattered flags, and the actors are in silhouette. George and Charlotte Hay are playing Cyrano and Roxane, and the rest of the parts are played by members of their company.*

CONFUSED VOICES: "Retreat! For God's sake retreat!"

FIRST SOLDIER: "Sound the alarm!"

SECOND SOLDIER: "We are all dead!"

DE GUICHE: "Retreat!"

THIRD SOLDIER: "Retreat!"

THREE SOLDIERS: "Retreat!"

CYRANO (GEORGE): "No! Never! Not in this life!"

DE GUICHE: "You fool, we shall all die! It is ten to one against us!"

CYRANO (GEORGE): "Be damned your numbers! And damn you! I am Cyrano de Bergerac!"

THREE SOLDIERS: *(Weakly.)* "Yay."

GEORGE: Stop! Stop!!
(The music stops and we go to work lights.)

GEORGE: For the hundredth time, I want the cheer louder! The audience won't hear you! Let's try it again. "I am Cyrano de Bergerac!"

THREE SOLDIERS: *(Weakly.)* "Yay!"

GEORGE: *(Disgusted, turning away.)* I don't know why we even bother rehearsing . . . Louder!

THREE SOLDIERS: *"Yay!"*

GEORGE:: That's better. All right, let's run it.
(The music and lights restore to performance level.)

DE GUICHE: "You fool, we shall all die! It is ten to one against us!"

CYRANO(GEORGE:.) "Be damned your numbers! And damn you! I am Cyrano de Bergerac!"

THREE SOLDIERS: *(Weakly.)* "Yay."

DE GUICHE: "Popinjay!"

(De Guiche walks off in a huff. We hear the sound of a horse and carriage approaching.)

SECOND SOLDIER: "Halt, who goes there?!"

FIRST SOLDIER: "It's a coach!"

THIRD SOLDIER: "What?!"

FIRST SOLDIER: "In the camp?!"

(Off, the horse whinnies.)

SECOND SOLDIER: "Look! 'Tis Roxane!"

(Roxane enters with a basket of fruit, and the Soldiers cheer.)

THREE SOLDIERS: *(Weakly.)* "Yay!"

(George gives them a look.)

SECOND SOLDIER: "She brings supplies!"

FIRST SOLDIER: "Bread!"

SECOND SOLDIER: "And wine!"

THIRD SOLDIER: "And chicken!"

(Roxane exits.)

LE BRET (PAUL): "Cyrano! That was the Comte de Guiche you insulted! Stop trying to be the Three Musketeers in one!"

(During the following oration, Ethel, an actress in her seventies, enters from the wings. She's dressed in her everyday 1950s clothes and therefore looks incongruous.)

CYRANO (GEORGE): "What would you have me do?

Hanh?!

Seek for the patronage of some great man, And like a creeping vine on a tall tree crawl upward, where I cannot stand alone? No thank you!"

ETHEL: Oh my God, I've seen more talent at a dog show.

(Ethel joins in the speech with George. After a line or two, we hear only Ethel, and the "onstage" action fades away. Simultaneously, she makes her way to the greenroom of the Erlanger Theater. [For a staging suggestion, see Note on Staging at end of play.] The room is large, comfortable, and a bit shabby. It contains a chaise, a large pouf, and one or two easy chairs. It's decorated with theater posters and other theatrical bric-a-brac. Stage right is a door to the street; stage left, two doors to the backstage area, one of them up a short flight of steps. Up center is another door to the backstage area and also a door to a utility closet. The time is a midmorning in June 1953. When Ethel enters the room, she continues playing Cyrano, even as she potters around straightening things up.)

GEORGE/ETHEL: "Dedicate, as others do,

> Poems to pawnbrokers? Be a buffoon In the vile hope of teasing out a
> smile On some cold face?"

ETHEL: "Eat a toad

> For breakfast every morning?
> Wear out my belly grovelling in the dust? No thank you!
> But,"
>
> *(Rosalind enters from the street door, carrying a suitcase. She's bright and at-*
> *tractive, in her early thirties. She sees Ethel and smiles with affection. Ethel is*
> *facing the other way and can't see Rosalind. Also, as we'll soon realize, Ethel*
> *is quite deaf and is never aware of very much unless it's in front of her and*
> *shouting.)*

ETHEL: "To sing, to laugh, to dream,

> To walk in my own way and be alone,
> Free, with an eye to see things as they are."

ROZ: Grandma.

ETHEL: "To travel any road under the sun,"

ROZ: *Grandma!*

ETHEL: "Nor doubt if fame or fortune

ROZ: *Grandma!!*

ETHEL: *(Startled, then overjoyed.)* Oh! . . . Rosalind!

> Dearest girl! What a surprise! You're getting more beautiful every day. *(A*
> *big hug.)* You look adorable!

ROZ: So do you.

ETHEL: What?

ROZ: *(Louder.)* So do you! You look great!

ETHEL: I'm afraid you'll have to speak up, dear.

ROZ: *Grandma, can I get you your hearing aid?!*

ETHEL: *(Fondly.)* No thank you, dear, I'm not in the mood for lemonade. Oh,
> I miss you terribly. It isn't the same here without you.

ROZ: *I miss you too, Grandma. Hey! How is the tour going? Do you like Buffalo?*

ETHEL: No. I don't. It stinks. If it wasn't named for an animal, it would have
> nothing going for it.

ROZ: Grandma . . .

ETHEL: I don't mind so much for myself, really, but it's quite a comedown for
> your mother. She played Broadway, you know, in the forties. Then your
> father dragged her down to his level.

ROZ: Grandma!

ETHEL: Revivals of tired old plays. B-movies. You should have heard him doing Cyrano just now at the dress rehearsal. The man is a walking ham. They should stick cloves in him and serve him with pineapple.

ROZ: *Grandma, listen! I have a surprise. I'm getting married.*

ROZ: It isn't Paul.

ETHEL: The boy has spunk.

(It takes a moment to sink in, then Roz and Ethel squeal with delight, like schoolgirls, and hug each other.)

ETHEL: Oh, Rosalind, how wonderful! I've always said that you and Paul were made for each other.

ROZ: *Grandma, it's not Paul! Paul and I broke up!*

ETHEL: . . . It isn't Paul?

ROZ: *No!*

ETHEL: Well that's a mistake. *(Roz sighs; here it comes.)* You look ravishing on the stage together. You could do all the great couples . . .

ROZ: *Grandma, I'm not an actress anymore! I'm in advertising!*

ETHEL: Yes, I know, and it's revolting.

ROZ: *Don't you remember the talk we had at Christmas?!*

ETHEL: . . . No.

ROZ: *(Really pouring her heart out.)* Grandma, this is *your* life. And Mother and Dad's. And that's fine. I'm very proud of you. But I grew up with it. I want something different. Something that doesn't drive me crazy all the time. Does that make any sense?

ETHEL: *(Fondly.)* Rosalind, dearest, can I tell you something?

ROZ: Sure.

ETHEL: I haven't heard a single word you've said.

ROZ: . . . *Grandma, can I please get you your hearing aid!!!*

ETHEL: All right. Fine. *One glass . . ..* Now listen to me, young lady. The theater may be dying. The glamorous invalid may be crawling through the desert with but a single lung in its feeble chest, but it is still breathing and it is all we've got. It is our lifeline to humanity. Without it, we would all be Republicans. I'm very tired now, dear, and I'm going to lie down. *(At the door.)* It's wonderful having you back.

(She exits. Roz runs to the door and shouts.)

ROZ: *Grandma! I love you!*

(At which moment, we hear a knock at the street door.)

ROZ: Come in. *(Knock, knock, knock.).* Come in! *(Knock, knock, knock; angry.)* *Would you come in, please, the door's open!!*

(Howard enters. He's in his late twenties, very good-natured and quite good-looking. At the moment, he's rather frightened.)

HOWARD: . . . Sweetheart?

ROZ: Hi, honey. Come on in.

(They kiss.)

HOWARD: Are your parents here?

ROZ: I don't think so.

HOWARD: *(Relieved.)* Oh, good.

ROZ: Howard . . .

HOWARD: Well I'm sorry. You know how I feel about this. "Meeting the in-laws." It makes me nervous.

ROZ: You have nothing to worry about.

HOWARD: I'd be all right if they weren't such . . . big stars. The glamorous life . . .

ROZ: Howard, does this look glamorous? *(Indicating the room.)*

HOWARD: *(Looking around.)* . . . Well, yeah. It does.

ROZ: This is Buffalo, New York. It's like . . . Scranton without the charm.

HOWARD: I was born here, actually.

ROZ: Oh.

HOWARD: I like Scranton, too.

ROZ: Howard, the point is, it's not Broadway. And they're doing rep!

HOWARD: Right . . . What's "rep" again?

ROZ: More than one play. In repertory. They alternate. Right now it's *Private Lives* by Noël Coward and *Cyrano de Bergerac*. Only they've cut down *Cyrano* for a small company. They do it with five actors.

HOWARD: Aha. The sort of . . . one-nostril version.

(He laughs; then sighs with anxiety.)

ROZ: It's sort of sweet that you're nervous about meeting them.

HOWARD: Nervous? Look at me, I'm a wreck! Do they know that I'm in show business, too?

ROZ: Howard, you're not exactly in show business. I mean, they wouldn't think of it as show business.

HOWARD: Oh. *(Beat.)* I am on television.

ROZ: You're a weatherman.

HOWARD: Right. I mean, it's kind of acting, like your parents.

ROZ: Howard, they do Shakespeare. And Chekhov. You do precipitation.

HOWARD: *(Glum.)* Yeah, I know.

ROZ: Howard, I'm very proud of you. It's a wonderful job. We can settle down and have children . . .

HOWARD: I love children. I want to have six, at least.

ROZ: Let's start with one.

HOWARD: Okay.

ROZ: Now listen to me. I want you to be very, very nice to them. Tell them how much you admire their work.

HOWARD: Well I *do*! I mean, my God, when I was a kid, they were on the cover of *Life* magazine. "Shakespeare on Broadway . . ."

ROZ: "Look Out Barrymores, Here Come the Hays." They had it reproduced on their china.

HOWARD: Wow.

ROZ: Then they had two big flops in a row and went to Hollywood.

HOWARD: Yeah, I know. I saw every movie they ever made!

ROZ: Good.

HOWARD: *Sergeant Yukon, Apache Woman. (Suddenly.)* Oh my God! I forgot the bag!

ROZ: What bag?

HOWARD: I have a surprise for your father. When I was in New York last week, I read in the paper about an auction. They were selling off props and stuff from one of the big studios and . . . well, I bought one of your father's old costumes. I thought he'd like it.

ROZ: That is so sweet! Which one did you get?

HOWARD: General George S. Patton! Wait'll you see it! The trouble is, I don't have anything for your mother yet. I guess she wouldn't take cash . . . ?

ROZ: Howard. They will love you for who you are.

HOWARD: What if I freeze up?! I-I-I do that sometimes, when I'm nervous! I can't even remember my own . . . *name*.

ROZ: You'll be fine! I promise! *(A kiss.)* All right?

HOWARD: . . . All right.

ROZ: I'll see if they're in their dressing rooms.

HOWARD: I'll go with you.

ROZ: You stay here, in case they show up.

HOWARD: I'd rather go with you . . .

ROZ: Howard, stay! Nothing's going to happen in two minutes!

(She exits. Pause. He looks around the room. He spies a Cyrano hat on the table. He picks it up and puts it on. He preens. When he takes off the hat, a Cyrano nose drops out to the floor. He picks it up and looks at it with curiosity

— then suspicion. He moves it down toward his crotch . . . Is that what it is?! At this moment, George bursts through the center door, still wearing his Cyrano costume, nose, and makeup and brandishing a sword.)

GEORGE: CHYAA!

(Just as suddenly, Charlotte Hay bursts through the door at the top of the stairs. She's still dressed as Roxane, and she also has a sword.)

CHARLOTTE: CHYAA!

(George and Charlotte face off—then start fencing in the best Errol Flynn tradition. This is their daily exercise, as well as their fun.)

GEORGE: Aroint thee, villain!

CHARLOTTE: Stay back, thou knave and cutpurse!

GEORGE: Stand thy ground, I say, or thou shalt bleed from ear to ear like the vomiting stream at flood tide!

(More sword play. Howard watches with his mouth hanging open.)

CHARLOTTE: Dungheap!

GEORGE: Witch!

CHARLOTTE: Bull's pizzle!

(The next exchange brings the combatants nose to nose, their swords crossed — then suddenly Charlotte stamps on George's foot to get the advantage.)

GEORGE: Ow!

CHARLOTTE: Ha!

GEORGE: Villain!

(They're at it again. Then they both notice Howard for the first time and stop fighting.)

CHARLOTTE: What is this?

GEORGE: I know not, but 'tis passing strange.

HOWARD: *(Waves.)* Hi.

(Charlotte lunges at George, George counters, then grabs Howard around the neck in a hammerlock, with his sword at Howard's throat.)

CHARLOTTE: Ha!

GEORGE: Ha!

HOWARD: Argh!

GEORGE: Stay back, I say, or the lad shall die!

CHARLOTTE: Coward!

GEORGE: If thou dost move *one inch,* the lad shall spout blood like a fountain.

(Howard is terrified. He tries to chuckle, to be a good sport.)

HOWARD: *(To Charlotte.)* Don't move.

(Charlotte lunges —)

CHARLOTTE: Ha!

GEORGE: Ha!

 (— *and George discards Howard like a sack of potatoes. Howard careens off a chair. Then George and Charlotte go at it again and exit fighting.*)

CHARLOTTE: Hold up thy head, vile Scot!

GEORGE: I'll make a ghost of him that lets me!

 (*And they're gone. Howard gets to his feet, panting. After a beat, Roz enters at the top of the stairs.*)

ROZ: They're not in their dressing rooms.

HOWARD: I-I-I-I —

ROZ: Howard?

HOWARD: I have to go now.

 (*He heads for the street door.*)

ROZ: Where are you going?

HOWARD: I need a few minutes. I'll be back.

ROZ: Howard, what's wrong?

HOWARD: I have to think about this! You don't just-just-just rush into a relationship! It takes some thinking!!

 (*He exits.*)

ROZ: Howard! Are you crazy?! (*Exiting.*) Get back here!!

 (*She runs out. A moment later, George and Charlotte reenter in high spirits.*)

GEORGE: Do you know what I like most about the author of *Cyrano*? He's dead, so he can't argue with me. (*Charlotte laughs.*) Now listen, I have a new idea for tomorrow. When the carriage arrives, during the battle, and you step out, I want you to pause, curtsey to the soldiers — and I'm going to put a spotlight on your face to suggest that you have descended like an angel from the heavens.

CHARLOTTE: Oh, George, let's try it! Now!

GEORGE: All right.

CHARLOTTE: Clip-clop clip-clop clip-clop. Na-a-a-y. (*A whinny.*)

GEORGE: "Halt, who goes there?"

CHARLOTTE: "It's a coach!"

GEORGE: "What? In the camp?!"

CHARLOTTE: "Look! 'Tis Roxane!"

GEORGE: "Thank God!"

CHARLOTTE: (*Weakly.*) "Yay." (*She steps elegantly down the last two steps of the stairway.*) And I float down, out of the carriage, like an angel from heaven.

GEORGE: Spotlight!

CHARLOTTE: *(As Roxane.)* "Good morning, gentlemen."

GEORGE: "Roxane, on the King's service!"

CHARLOTTE: "Yes. In the service of my own king: Love."

GEORGE: That's it! It'll make the scene!

CHARLOTTE: "Cyrano. My best friend. I need your help."

GEORGE: *(As Cyrano, kneeling, taking her hand.)* "I am at your disposal, madam, now and forever."

(He kisses her hand and lays his cheek upon it.)

CHARLOTTE: *(Moved.)* When you do that, George, center stage, in front of a thousand people holding their breath, I wet myself. I can't help it.

GEORGE: Thank you, my darling.

CHARLOTTE: Kiss me. Now. Before the moment passes.

(She lifts his nose and kisses him on the lips. They start necking on the chaise — when Ethel enters from backstage.)

ETHEL: Don't mind me, I'm just the hired help.

GEORGE: Well, well, if it isn't the Hound of the Baskervilles.

(During the following, George and Charlotte remove their Cyrano clothes and put on their relaxing clothes. Charlotte, of course, looks stunning. Ethel gathers up their costumes to take them away.)

CHARLOTTE: *(To George.)* Don't start.

GEORGE: Oh, she can't hear a thing I'm saying. She hasn't heard a word in twenty years. *(To Ethel.)* Have you, Quasimodo?

CHARLOTTE: George, stop it.

GEORGE: Tell me, Ethel, have you frightened any little children lately? Offered them a ride on your broomstick?

CHARLOTTE: George . . .

GEORGE: I cannot believe, to this day, that *that* is your mother. Here you are, the greatest stage actress in a generation, and you were spawned by a troll?

CHARLOTTE: George, cut it out.

GEORGE: You must have been switched at birth. Somewhere out there is Ethel's real daughter, traveling with Ringling Brothers as the Wolf Woman of Borneo.

CHARLOTTE: *(As Ethel starts to exit heaped with the bundle of clothes.)* Thank you, Mother!

GEORGE: *Thank you, Mother!*

ETHEL: *(As she goes out the door.)* George, my hearing aid is in, now grow up!

(She exits, and George slams the door, hurting his back.)

GEORGE: *Ow!* God, my back! Am I getting old, Charlotte?

CHARLOTTE: No, dear, you're just falling apart.

GEORGE: *(Bitterly.)* No wonder they didn't want me for the Pimpernel movie.

CHARLOTTE: Us, dear, they didn't want us.

GEORGE: We were *this close,* Charlotte. I could taste it! George and Charlotte Hay in the new Frank Capra production, *The Twilight of the Scarlet Pimpernel.* It would have put us right back on top.

CHARLOTTE: There will be other movies.

GEORGE: Not like this one! We were perfect for it! *(Beat.)* No wonder Hollywood is such a cesspool. I mean, please. *Frank Capra* directs *The Twilight of the Scarlet Pimpernel*???

CHARLOTTE: I know. I agree with you.

GEORGE: Comedies. Fine. Christmas movies. But *The Scarlet Pimpernel*?!

CHARLOTTE: I didn't even get to meet him.

GEORGE: Nor did I. Nor do I care to, may he rot in hell.

CHARLOTTE: I can see it now. "Mr. Pimpernel Goes to Washington."

GEORGE: Exactly! Ow!

CHARLOTTE: Get down, George. I'll work on your back.
   (During the following, George sits next to the chaise, and Charlotte massages his neck and shoulders.)

GEORGE: You do realize they started filming yesterday. At this very moment, the cameras are rolling, and Ronald Colman is wearing *my tights.*

CHARLOTTE: *(Calmly, as the massage continues.)* Oh George, let them have their Ronald Colman and their Greer Garson. Who gives a damn.

GEORGE: You're right.

CHARLOTTE: I'm sure that Miss Garson will do a perfectly adequate job.

GEORGE: You're right.

CHARLOTTE: If that's what they want.

GEORGE: I agree entirely.

CHARLOTTE: . . . Stupid little bitch. *(George laughs.)* I met her once. Did you know that? *(With increasing bitterness.)* She was filming *Pride and Prejudice.* and I was next door filming *Apache Woman.* She was cutting the crusts off little tea sandwiches, and I was boiling a pig in a teepee.

GEORGE: Charlotte —

CHARLOTTE: She was making love to Laurence Olivier, and I was sacrificing a chicken with Chief Chunkachook. *(She starts chanting an Indian war chant, beating on his back with the edges of her hands.)* Hiya hiya hiya hiya . . .

GEORGE: *(Overlapping.)* Charlotte . . . Charlotte!

(She stops.)

CHARLOTTE: How's your back?

GEORGE: Better. But don't stop.

(The massage continues. George is relaxing. He's almost asleep.)

CHARLOTTE: George?

GEORGE: Hm?

CHARLOTTE: Can I ask you a question?

GEORGE: Mm.

CHARLOTTE: Did you sleep with Eileen?

(He sits up with a start.)

GEORGE: Charlotte! How can you say such a thing?!

CHARLOTTE: I've seen how you look at her.

GEORGE: She's a pretty girl. I'm not dead.

CHARLOTTE: Not yet. I know exactly when it happened, George. We were in the middle of that terrible fight.

GEORGE: And whose fault was that?

CHARLOTTE: It was your fault, dear. You called me the world's oldest living ingenue.

GEORGE: I merely mentioned that a woman in her fifties should not try to play Saint Joan. It's like watching Eleanor Roosevelt play Peter Pan.

CHARLOTTE: I happen to admire Eleanor Roosevelt.

GEORGE: So do I, but I don't want to watch her fly out the window.

CHARLOTTE: You're changing the subject.

GEORGE: For heaven's sake, Eileen barely knows I exist.

CHARLOTTE: Oh, please. When you walk into the room, she starts to glow. I could use her for a reading lamp.

GEORGE: You are off your rocker. It's extraordinary. It is unkind.

CHARLOTTE: George, I don't mind as long as you tell me the truth! Did you sleep with her or didn't you?! Yes or no?!

GEORGE: . . . *No!!!* All right?! The answer is no!!

CHARLOTTE: *(Skeptically.)* Really?

GEORGE: Oh, it's killing you about the film, isn't it.

CHARLOTTE: Don't be silly. That has nothing to do with it.

GEORGE: Scarlet Pimpernel, Scarlet Pimpernel.

CHARLOTTE: Oh, stop it.

GEORGE: *Greer Garson!*

CHARLOTTE: Don't be an idiot!

GEORGE: I'm sure it's slaying you to be stuck out here in Siberia while Miss Garson swans around the set in Hollywood like the Queen of Sheba.

CHARLOTTE: George —

GEORGE: I'm sure you had fantastical visions of being slobbered over by a legion of toadies, having your ears powdered.

CHARLOTTE: All right, George, I'm sorry!

GEORGE: *(The injured husband.) Well it's too late now, isn't it?! You have hurt my feelings!*

CHARLOTTE: . . . Oh stop it, I did not.

GEORGE: You did so.

CHARLOTTE: Did not.

GEORGE: *You did so!*

(Pause.)

CHARLOTTE: Well I know how to fix it.

GEORGE: *(Knowing what's coming.)* Charlotte, don't.

CHARLOTTE: It always works.

GEORGE: Not this time!

(She sits on his lap and starts to tickle him.)

CHARLOTTE: Tickle, tickle, tickle!

GEORGE: *(Laughing.)* Stop it!

CHARLOTTE: Tickle, tickle, tickle!

GEORGE: *(Laughing.)* Charlotte! I'm warning you — !

CHARLOTTE: Tickle, tickle, tickle, tickle, tickle, tickle, tickle — !

(They're having a wonderful, intimate time tickling and laughing, when Eileen walks in from the street. She's young and very beautiful. They see her and stop cold.)

GEORGE: Eileen!

CHARLOTTE: Good morning.

(Beat. Eileen bursts into tears and runs across the room and out the door to the dressing rooms.)

GEORGE: Eileen! Wait! Eileen!

(George stands up and hurries to the door — and Charlotte rolls off his lap to the floor. Then she stands up and looks at him with blood in her eye.)

GEORGE: Don't look at me like that.

CHARLOTTE: Fine. I'll go talk to her.

GEORGE: I'll do it! You have caused enough trouble for one morning. *(Exiting.)* Eileen!

(The moment he's gone, Paul enters from the street. He's in his thirties, good-looking in a rough-and-ready sort of way, and very likeable.)

CHARLOTTE: Hello, Paul.

PAUL: What's with Eileen? She walked right past me. I think she was crying.

CHARLOTTE: Well, she was born in Buffalo. Maybe she suddenly realized she's still here.

PAUL: Actually, she loves it here. She started out here in the theater, but what she really wants to do is television.

CHARLOTTE: Oh, please.

PAUL: She could do all right on TV. She's pretty. Wholesome.

CHARLOTTE: Wholesome isn't the word. She could give milk.

PAUL: . . . Charlotte. Have you talked to Roz lately?

CHARLOTTE: Last Sunday. I brought up your name, and she started screaming.

PAUL: Oh, great.

CHARLOTTE: I never understood why you two broke up.

PAUL: Oh, she wanted me to give up the theater so she could lead a "normal life." *(He shakes his head and laughs.)* Can you imagine anyone in your family being normal?!
(Charlotte starts to laugh — then stops and gives him a look. At which moment, Roz enters from the street.)

ROZ: Hi, Mother.

CHARLOTTE: Pumpkin! Sweetie! *(They hug.)* When did you get here?!

ROZ: A few minutes ago.

CHARLOTTE: We were just talking about you. This second!
(The following exchange is rapid and monotone, anger overlaid with social intercourse.)

ROZ: Hello Paul.

PAUL: Hi Roz.

ROZ: How's showbiz?

PAUL: Great I've never been happier.

ROZ: Well good for you I'm thrilled.

PAUL: Thanks.

ROZ: You're welcome.
(Pause.)

CHARLOTTE: . . . This is going well.

ROZ: I thought you were in New York.

PAUL: I came back to work for your parents.

ROZ: How nice.

PAUL: I'll check on Eileen.

(Paul exits.)

CHARLOTTE: Rosalind, why don't you two just get married and get it over with.

ROZ: I wish you would stop trying to run my life. It's my life, not your life!

CHARLOTTE: You're right. I'm sorry. You're right. *(Pause. The wounded mother.)* I'm only the one who gave birth to you.

ROZ: Mother . .

CHARLOTTE: Twelve pounds, fourteen ounces . . . They needed a forklift.

ROZ: Mother!

(George enters.)

GEORGE: She locked herself in, she . . . Rosalind! My baby!

ROZ: Daddy!

(She runs to him and they hug.)

GEORGE:: How's my little girl? . . . Charlotte, how is it possible that two such plain people as ourselves could produce an offspring as beautiful as this one?

CHARLOTTE: . . . She's not yours. I slept around.

GEORGE: Roz, have you come to your senses? You could step right back into the company.

ROZ: No thank you. That's not why I'm here. I have a surprise for everybody, but I lost it.

GEORGE: *(Calling through the door.)* Paul, get in here! Look who's arrived!

ROZ: Daddy! God. Don't you two ever stop? . . . Look, I'll see you later, I've got to go.

GEORGE: Roz . . .

(Roz exits and Paul enters.)

PAUL: . . . She's gone?

GEORGE: She heard your name and fled into the Forest of Arden. You do have a way with women, Paul.

PAUL: Thanks.

CHARLOTTE: And how is Little Miss Eileen?

PAUL: She wouldn't open the door for me either. I wonder what happened.

CHARLOTTE: She's in love with George.

GEORGE: Charlotte, would you please keep your menopausal hallucinations to yourself. The girl is obviously in some distress.

PAUL: I'll go try again.

GEORGE: Yes, do. You are the company manager.

PAUL: I'm also your second lead this week.

GEORGE: I beg your pardon?

PAUL: Webster quit this morning. He packed his bags and left.

GEORGE: He can't do that! I'll sue the untalented little weasel!

CHARLOTTE: Why on earth would he just leave?

PAUL: Because he wasn't paid for two weeks.

GEORGE: Well none of us has been paid for two weeks! What kind of feeble excuse is that?!

CHARLOTTE: Nobody told me about this.

GEORGE: Well Paul just told you, didn't he, the big blabbermouth.

PAUL: Sorry. By the way, have you talked to your agent this morning? He called twice.

GEORGE: I have an agent? Surely you jest. Didn't you read about it in *Scientific American?* The day my checks went down to four digits, he vanished from the face of the earth.

(Paul exits.)

CHARLOTTE: *(Gently.)* George . . . talk to me. Are we in trouble?

GEORGE: Oh, we'll make it. We'll survive. We always do. It's television that's killing us. Entertainment by the yard. It's putting us out of business.

CHARLOTTE: George . . .

GEORGE: What's the matter with these people? Don't they care anymore?! Don't they know the difference?!

(There's a knock on the street door.)

GEORGE: I'm not here. You haven't seen me.

CHARLOTTE: George!

GEORGE: If it's a native Buffalonian, offer it water and some long grass, maybe it'll go away.

(He exits. Knock, knock, knock.)

CHARLOTTE: I'm coming!

(She opens the door, and Howard is there.)

CHARLOTTE: Yes?

HOWARD: Hi.

CHARLOTTE: *(Annoyed.)* What do you want?

HOWARD: I-I-I just want to tell you before you say anything else, that I think you're the most wonderful actress that ever lived!

CHARLOTTE: *(Suddenly the soul of graciousness.)* Please, come in. I'm Charlotte Hay.

HOWARD: *(Extending his hand.)* Hi. I'm . . . I'm uh . . . I'm uh . . . *(He turns white. His worst nightmare is happening; he's forgotten his name.) Oh my God!*

(He buries his face in his hands — as Richard Maynard enters through the open street door. He is a loveable, good-looking man in his fifties, in a conservative suit and tie.)

RICHARD: Knock knock.

CHARLOTTE: Richard!

(She runs to him and embraces him.)

RICHARD: Hello, Charlotte.

CHARLOTTE: What a wonderful surprise!

RICHARD: *(To Howard, who has looked up.)* How do you do. Richard Maynard. You are . . . ?

CHARLOTTE: I wouldn't ask him that. Apparently it's a trick question.

HOWARD: Are you famous, too?!

RICHARD: No, but apparently I remind some people of Loretta Young.

HOWARD: Wow.

CHARLOTTE: Mr. Maynard is our lawyer and represents every major star in Hollywood.

RICHARD: Who's your favorite? Besides Charlotte, of course?

HOWARD: Esther Williams. Do you know her?!

RICHARD: *(Nods.)* I taught her to swim.

HOWARD: Wow!

CHARLOTTE: I'm awfully sorry, but do you think you could possibly come back another time?

HOWARD: Oh. Sure . . .

CHARLOTTE: *(Helping him out the door.)* It was stunning meeting you. Whoever you are.

HOWARD: *(As the door closes in his face.)* Wait! I remember! It's How . . . *(The door is closed.)*

CHARLOTTE: Richard, what are you doing here?!

RICHARD: Well, I was sitting in my office this morning, making a great deal of money, and I suddenly realized that I was terribly bored. So I thought, what can I do to cheer myself up. Well, I considered raising my billing rate, that usually works, but then I thought no, I would much rather take Charlotte to lunch.

CHARLOTTE: So you flew here all the way from New York City?

RICHARD: *(Nods.)* I was in a plane, of course.

CHARLOTTE: *(Hugging him.)* Oh, Richard, you're such a darling. I accept. In fact, I could use some cheering up myself.

RICHARD: What has the brute done this time?

CHARLOTTE: I'm not sure. Maybe it's nothing. Maybe I'm just tired.

RICHARD: Well of course you're tired! It's inhuman the way he drags you around from one city to another.

CHARLOTTE: On top of everything else, I just found out that we're not meeting our payroll.

RICHARD: Oh, I know that.

CHARLOTTE: You do?

RICHARD: It's quite serious. I've told George for months to start cutting down expenses.

CHARLOTTE: Is there anything *I* can do?

RICHARD: Well, you could do a movie. Or better yet, some television.

CHARLOTTE: We could try a different play. *Pygmalion* always makes money . . .

RICHARD: Charlotte. Halloo in there. It's 1953. The road is dead. The only stars left touring anymore, besides you two, are Cornell and the Lunts, and they have a combined age of one thousand four hundred and sixty-two.

CHARLOTTE: Well, what am I supposed to do?!

RICHARD: Well, for starters, you can marry me. I've got tons of money and no one to spend it on. Except a cat with a thyroid problem. He's getting very large. I had some friends in last night, they thought I'd bought a new sofa.

CHARLOTTE: Would you be serious.

RICHARD: I'm being serious. I'll have to move out soon.

CHARLOTTE: Richard!

RICHARD: *(Suddenly very serious.)* Charlotte, listen to me. *(Pause.)* I'm not very good at this. I cannot lie the way most men do and tell you that your cheeks remind me of damask. I don't know what the hell damask is. But you really do deserve better than this. Let me pamper you a little. We can take a cruise together. Anywhere you want in the entire world. Rochester. Schenectady . . .

(Charlotte laughs.)

CHARLOTTE: Oh, Richard, you make me very happy.

RICHARD: Good. You deserve it. And frankly, so do I. I'm tired of living alone.

CHARLOTTE: What about George?

RICHARD: No, I don't want to live with him.

CHARLOTTE: *(Laughing.)* Richard . . .

RICHARD: Oh, I do love you so much. You're all I think about anymore.

CHARLOTTE: Richard . . .

RICHARD: Charlotte . . .

(He's about to kiss her, when we hear Paul's urgent voice.)

PAUL: *(Off.)* George!!

(Richard and Charlotte move guiltily apart, as Paul hurries in.)

PAUL: Oh, hi. Hi.

RICHARD: How do you do. Richard Maynard, lawyer to the stars.

PAUL: Paul Singer, schlepper for two stars. Where's George?

CHARLOTTE: In his dressing room, I think.

PAUL: *(Worried.)* He's not there.

CHARLOTTE: Is something the matter?

PAUL: No! No . . .

CHARLOTTE: Paul . . .

PAUL: There's nothing the matter! I . . . I have a question.

(She stares right through him, but decides to leave it.)

CHARLOTTE: When you find him, tell him I'll be out for the morning. Richard is taking me to lunch.

PAUL: Right. Have a nice time.

RICHARD: We intend to. Thank you.

(Charlotte and Richard exit to the street. A moment later, Ethel hurries in from above carrying a pair of trousers and hurries down the stairs.)

PAUL: Ethel, have you seen George? *(She doesn't hear him.)* Ethel!

ETHEL: *What?!*

PAUL: *Where's George?*

ETHEL: He's right behind me!

(She hurries across the room as George enters from above in hot pursuit.)

GEORGE: Stop! Give me those Cyrano pants!

ETHEL: No! I have to let them out!

PAUL: George . . .

ETHEL: They are far too snug, you look ridiculous!

GEORGE: They're my pants!

ETHEL: Your backside looks like a watermelon!

GEORGE: Nobody asked you!

(He grabs the pants and they struggle over them.)

PAUL: George!

ETHEL: They need fixing!

GEORGE: Your ears need fixing!

    (Rrrrrip! They rip down the middle, at the crotch. George and Ethel are each left with a leg.)

ETHEL: Now look what you've done. *(She takes George's leg and heads for the door.)* No wonder this company is going down the toilet.

    (She exits. George screams with frustration.)

PAUL: George, I have some bad news.

GEORGE: What? Bad news in this company? The House of Usher Repertory Theater?

PAUL: I think you better sit down.

GEORGE: "Sit down"? Because I'll tremble? My knees will wobble uncontrollably? That is a stage convention, you idiot, out of the cheapest melodrama!

PAUL: George, Eileen is pregnant.

    (Beat. George's knees start to wobble, and he sits down.)

GEORGE: Oh my God.

PAUL: She says you slept together in Detroit, and now she's pregnant.

GEORGE: That's a lie!

PAUL: You didn't sleep with her?

GEORGE: . . . It was Cincinnati.

PAUL: I think that's irrelevant.

GEORGE: Holy Mother of God. Charlotte will kill me.

PAUL: I know.

GEORGE: She'll make my life a living hell! *More than usual! (He holds his head and groans.)* What can I do?

PAUL: . . . Run?

GEORGE: Think of something, you idiot! That's what you're paid for!

PAUL: All right, all right. Let me think . . . *(He makes it up as he goes along.)* Okay. Now listen . . . Eileen could have the baby . . . in the country. With a relative, like an aunt or something. And we won't tell Charlotte, ever! And . . . you could take trips every few months and . . . and visit them in the country and have picnics, and . . . *then,* when the baby is like . . . ten years old, you could cast her as the Page in *Much Ado About Nothing,* and you could put on shows together!

GEORGE: . . . I need help, not Mickey Rooney!

PAUL: Sorry. Look maybe you should talk to Eileen.

GEORGE: Eileen. Oh my God. The poor kid. I'd better go see her.

PAUL: You'll have to hurry. She has a doctor's appointment at noon.

GEORGE: Already?

PAUL: They have to do a test or something.

GEORGE: . . . What test?

(The following section goes rapidly.)

PAUL: I don't know.

GEORGE:: A pregnancy test?

PAUL: I have no idea.

GEORGE: So she might not be pregnant?

PAUL: She says she's positive.

GEORGE: But she only *thinks* she's pregnant?

PAUL: She's positive! She thinks.

GEORGE: *(Shaking Paul.) Christ Almighty,* is *she pregnant or isn't she?!*

PAUL: *I don't know, George, I didn't examine her!*

(Charlotte suddenly enters from the street, and the two men instantly assume a pose of studied nonchalance and freeze.)

CHARLOTTE: It's chilly out there. I'm getting a wrap, and then I'll be back around one.

GEORGE: Good. Great.

CHARLOTTE: By the way. Richard is here. He's taking me to lunch.

GEORGE: Bon appetit.

(Charlotte exits to the dressing rooms, slamming the door behind her.)

GEORGE: Oh my God. What if Eileen talks to her?

PAUL: I doubt that.

GEORGE: Go in there and keep them separated. I have to think.

PAUL: She's going to find out sooner or later.

GEORGE: *Would you do what I'm telling you!*

(Paul exits. George is alone.)

GEORGE: Damn damn damn. Piss piss piss. Balls balls balls.

(Eileen enters down the stairs. She's clearly been crying and is still on the verge of tears, but she tries very hard to smile through it.)

EILEEN: Hi, George.

GEORGE: Eileen!

EILEEN: I guess Paul told you.

GEORGE: He did. Yes. Eileen. What can I say? What can I *do*?

EILEEN: I think you did it already, George.

GEORGE: Eileen, I'm so sorry. We got carried away.

EILEEN: I was such a fool!

GEORGE: We were both fools.

EILEEN: *(Breaking down.)* And now we're having a little fool! Oh, George . . .

GEORGE: *(Comforting her — but also afraid of discovery.)* Eileen . . . shh . . .

EILEEN: I hope he looks just like you!

GEORGE: Oh, my God!

EILEEN: I can't do the matinee today. I'm sorry.

GEORGE: But you don't have an understudy.

EILEEN: Well, I can't do it! I'd still be at the doctor's anyway.

GEORGE: The doctor's. For a test . . . *(She nods.)* To confirm that you are

EILEEN: That's right.

GEORGE: So then you might not actually be

EILEEN: I'm pregnant, George. Believe me. I'm two weeks late, and I've been tossing my guts up every morning for three days. What do you think it is?!

GEORGE: . . . Bad oyster?

EILEEN: I'll see you later.

    (She starts to leave.)

GEORGE: Eileen. You, uh, didn't tell Charlotte, did you?

EILEEN: I haven't seen her.

GEORGE: Good!

    (He walks away . . .)

EILEEN: So I left her a note.

    (And he trips.)

GEORGE: . . . What?!

EILEEN: Well she has to know sometime! I mean, she's gonna figure it out when I start waddling around here like a duck! "Romeo, Romeo, Quack quack quack quack." Anyway, I scribbled it down on something. I think it was her copy of *Variety.*

GEORGE: *Variety?*

EILEEN: I've got to go now, George.

    (She exits.)

GEORGE: Holy Mother of God.

    (Paul enters.)

PAUL: George, I couldn't find Eileen anywhere.

GEORGE: Paul! Go to Charlotte's room, quick, and bring me her copy of *Variety!*

PAUL: George, there's a copy of *Variety* right here.

GEORGE: I don't want to read it, you idiot!!

    (Charlotte enters with a copy of Variety.)*

CHARLOTTE: *(All smiles.)* Hello, George. Hello, Paul.

PAUL/GEORGE: Hi.

CHARLOTTE: Paul, would you excuse us for a few minutes?

PAUL: Sure.

GEORGE: *(To Paul.)* Stay where you are!

CHARLOTTE: Leave the room, Paul.

PAUL: Yes, ma'am.

> *(He exits at a run.)*

CHARLOTTE: *(Still smiling.)* George, the strangest item appeared in this week's *Variety.*

GEORGE: Charlotte . . .

CHARLOTTE: I think you should read it, George. Out loud. You see, I might just be having a menopausal hallucination.

GEORGE: Charlotte

CHARLOTTE: Read it, dear. Near the top. I'm waiting.

GEORGE: *(Takes the paper; reads.)* . . . "Box Office Biggie Boffo in Burbs."

CHARLOTTE: Below that.

GEORGE: "Dear Charlotte. I'm carrying your husband's . . . piles. Files?"

CHARLOTTE: "Child!" "I'm carrying your husband's *child!*"

GEORGE: Right. "I thought you should know. Eileen."

> *(She takes back the paper.)*

CHARLOTTE: Well?

> *(He drops to his knees.)*

GEORGE: Charlotte, I am profoundly sorry! I made a grievous mistake. Can you forgive me?

> *(He bows his head.)*

CHARLOTTE: No, George! *(She whacks him with the paper.)* I *cannot* forgive you! *(Whack!)* You betrayed me! *(Whack!)* After thirty-five years! *(Whack, whack, whack, whack.)*

GEORGE: Ow! Ow! Ow! Ow!

> *(At this moment, Eileen enters from the street and hurries across the room.)*

EILEEN: Sorry. I left something upstairs.

> *(Charlotte resumes whacking George with the paper, and Eileen turns back.)*

EILEEN: Charlotte, I'm sorry. But you shouldn't blame George. It was all my fault. I guess I shouldn't have believed him when he said that next season *I* could play Roxane.

> *(Pause. Charlotte turns and looks at George.)*

EILEEN: Sorry.

> *(And Eileen exits to the dressing rooms.)*

CHARLOTTE: . . . Roxane? . . . *Roxane?!!*

GEORGE: Charlotte, listen. Please. It was right after a performance and I was filled with all that passion for *Cyrano.* I lost my head.

CHARLOTTE: You lied to me.

GEORGE: I didn't want to! You cornered me!

CHARLOTTE: Don't touch me.

GEORGE: Charlotte, I'm flesh and blood! Did you expect me to be celibate all my life?!

CHARLOTTE: Three days! You couldn't be celibate for *three days*?!
(She starts hitting him again, and he wrestles her down onto the chaise.)

GEORGE: Stop it . . . stop it . . . would you please . . . *(She's down on her back, and he's standing in front of her.)* All right?! Now will you stop it?!
(Beat. Then she kicks him hard in the groin. He gasps with pain. Then she stands up, straightens her dress, and heads for the door to her dressing room.)

CHARLOTTE: I'm leaving with Richard on the next plane.

GEORGE: *Wait! (She pauses.)* We have a matinee.

CHARLOTTE: *(The last straw.)* . . . Good-bye, George. I have to pack.

GEORGE: *Charlotte!*
(She exits, slamming the door, and Paul enters from backstage.)

PAUL: Well? How'd it go? *(George looks at him.)* Not well. *(George sits.)* George? *(No response.)* George, would you say something?

GEORGE: *(With great bitterness.)* I'm a hack. I was always a hack and now I'm a bigger hack. I have sunk to new depths of hackdom.

PAUL: George, come on. You can't give up. What about all your fans?

GEORGE: My fans? *(He laughs.)* Fine. I'll call one, you call the other.

PAUL: George, you made a mistake. Everybody makes mistakes. Let me talk to her. She'll listen to me.

GEORGE: It's too late, Horatio. Just cancel the performance for this afternoon. In fact, cancel the whole tour.

PAUL: You can't do that. You'll get sued.

GEORGE: Let the bastards sue me! Let them nail me to a cross! God knows I've suffered enough.
(The phone rings, and Paul grabs it.)

PAUL: Hello?! . . . *(Covering the receiver, to George.)* It's your agent from New York.

GEORGE: I'm not here.

PAUL: *(Into the phone.)* He's right here. *(To George.)* Would you talk to him! *(George snatches the phone.)*

GEORGE: Hello, Henry. How's the blood-sucking business? . . . All right, I'm
    listening! . . . Well of course I know they started filming yesterday. I have
    a little Ronald Colman doll that I'm sticking pins into . . . What? . . .
    You're joking.

    *(The tone of the conversation changes completely now; something incredibly
    wonderful has happened, and George becomes increasingly euphoric.)*

GEORGE: . . . Henry, if this is a joke, I'll kill you. Oh, my God! *I don't believe it!*

PAUL: What happened?

GEORGE: *(To Paul.)* Shh. *(Into the phone.)* Oh, my God, that's wonderful!
    Henry, I love you!

PAUL: George, what happened?

GEORGE: Would you shut up! *(Into the phone.)* . . . *Today?* . . . Yes, of course I'll
    be here . . . Right. I'll call you.

    (He hangs up.)

PAUL: Well?

GEORGE: *(Beside himself with excitement.)* We're back in business. *(Calling
    through the door.)* Charlotte, get in here!

PAUL: *What happened?!!*

GEORGE: Yesterday, on the set of *The Twilight of The Scarlet Pimpernel*, Ronald
    Colman made his first entrance . . . and fell down a flight of stairs and
    broke his legs.

PAUL: Oh my God.

GEORGE: As a consequence, the director of the film, Frank Capra, winner of
    two thousand Academy Awards, Mr. Hollywood himself, is flying here to
    watch the matinee.

PAUL: Frank Capra?

GEORGE: *Ha haaaa!*

    (Charlotte enters, carrying a suitcase, and heads straight for the street door.)

CHARLOTTE: Good-bye, George.

GEORGE: *(Intercepting her.)* Yes yes yes. I'm sorry.

CHARLOTTE: George!

GEORGE: Now listen. The most wonderful thing in the world has happened:
    Ronald Colman is crippled!

CHARLOTTE: What?

GEORGE: Henry just called. It seems that Mister Colman made a most dramatic
    entrance yesterday on the set of *The Scarlet Pimpernel* by careening head-
    first down a flight of steps. *(With great relish.)* I'll bet it was the tights that
    got him, apparently, in both of his legs. Not one. *(Ecstatic.)* Both!

CHARLOTTE: Henry told you this.

GEORGE: The studio is desperate! Every minute they delay is costing a fortune. So, what director do you think is on a plane this very second heading for Buffalo, New York? I'll give you a hint. *(Cheerleading.)* Give me a C. *C!* Give me an A. *A!* Give me a P. *P!*

CHARLOTTE: George . . .

GEORGE: I know what you're thinking, Charlotte. Where do you fit into all this. Well, if I do get the role, and it's beginning to look extremely likely, I will insist that you play Marguerite.

CHARLOTTE: I don't know what to say, George.

GEORGE: *(Bows his head.)* I know. I'm a saint.

CHARLOTTE: Except this is easily the most ridiculous lie you have ever told me.

GEORGE: . . . What?

CHARLOTTE: Good-bye, George. Take care of yourself.

(She picks up her suitcase and starts to exit.)

GEORGE/PAUL: *Stop! Wait!*

GEORGE: *(Incredulous.)* You don't believe me?

CHARLOTTE: Oh, George, please

GEORGE: Wait! Charlotte, you must believe me. Have I ever lied to you before?

(She staggers — then exits.)

CHARLOTTE: Good-bye, George.

(He runs after her.)

GEORGE: *(Off.)* Charlotte! Charlotte, please!

CHARLOTTE: *(Off.) I said good-bye!!!*

GEORGE: I'm going to kill myself. No! That's too easy.

(We hear a crash, off. Charlotte has hit George with the suitcase.)

GEORGE: *(Off.) Ooowww!!!*

(George reenters, limping badly.)

GEORGE: *Ahh! Ahh! Ahh!*

PAUL: George? . . . George?

CHARLOTTE: George . . .

GEORGE: There are fractures. I'm going to get very, very drunk, and *then* I'll kill myself.

(Ethel enters carrying George's Cyrano pants.)

ETHEL: There you are. Well I'm glad to say they're finished. No thanks to you. Now try them on. *(She throws the trousers onto George's lap. George stares at her blankly.)* Go ahead! I'll turn around. Puh. As if you're modest. That'll be the day.

(George looks at the pants — then winds them around his hands as if to strangle her.)

PAUL: George, give me the pants.

GEORGE: No.

PAUL: George!

GEORGE: They can give me the chair. It'll be worth it.

PAUL: *(Grabbing the pants.)* Now stop it!

GEORGE: Let me go!

(They struggle over the pants. Then, rrrrip! They rip the pants in half again.)

GEORGE: *Goddammit to hell!!!*

(George throws the pants to the ground and jumps up and down on them. Ethel turns around. The phone rings. And Roz enters from the street.)

ETHEL: I don't believe it.

ROZ: Daddy! What's wrong?!

PAUL: Roz!

ROZ: Paul?!

(Ring! George stalks out, heading for his dressing room.)

GEORGE: *(Exiting.) Ahhhhhh!*

ROZ: Daddy! Where are you going?!

PAUL: George!

ETHEL: He has finally gone completely insane!

(Ring!)

PAUL: *(Into the phone.)* Yes?! . . . Hold on. *(He runs to the door and calls off.)* George! It's Capra's New York office! What do I tell them?! George! *(No response.)*

ROZ: Paul, what's going on?

PAUL: That's a very good question. *(Into the phone.)* Hi. He's in a meeting. Could Mr. Capra come tomorrow?

ROZ: Frank Capra?

PAUL: *(Nods to Roz and continues on the phone.)* He's on his way to the airport. Right. *(He hangs up.)* . . . Holy God!

ROZ: Paul, what happened?!

PAUL: Come on, we have to stop him!

(Paul grabs Roz by the hand and pulls her out the door to the dressing rooms to find George.)

PAUL: George!

(They're gone — leaving Ethel alone onstage, sitting, sewing up the Cyrano

pants. An instant later, Charlotte hurries in from the street, followed by Richard. She's carrying a newspaper.)

RICHARD: Charlotte, what are you doing?!

CHARLOTTE: *(Calling.)* George . . . ! *George!*

RICHARD: You buy a newspaper and you go berserk.

CHARLOTTE: Read that.

RICHARD: "Earthquake in Guatemala. Thousands killed —"

CHARLOTTE: *(With scorn.)* Not that. *That.*

RICHARD: "Disaster at MGM. Colman on Crutches. Garson Walks Out."

CHARLOTTE: *(A maniacal gleam in her eye.)* She walked out. *(Then.)* Mother? *(No response.)* Mother?!

ETHEL: What?

CHARLOTTE: *Where's George?*

ETHEL: I hope he's getting a root canal.

CHARLOTTE: *(Heading through the door to the dressing rooms.)* Richard, come on.

RICHARD: I'd rather not.

CHARLOTTE: Richard!

RICHARD: Oh. Right. Coming.

CHARLOTTE: *(Off.)* George!

(They're gone — at which moment, Paul and Roz enter through another door.)

PAUL: George . . . ?

ROZ: Grandma. *(No response.)* Grandma!

ETHEL: What?!

ROZ: *Have you seen Daddy?*

ETHEL: Too many times. Your mother's looking for him too.

ROZ: Mother?

PAUL: Charlotte's back? Oh great! This is great! *Ethel, where did she go?*

ETHEL: *(Pointing.)* Through there. *(The door to the dressing rooms.)*

PAUL: Come on.

ROZ: *(Hurrying off after Paul.)* This is why I left the theater.

PAUL: Would you come on! . . . Charlotte!

(Paul and Roz exit — at which moment, Charlotte and Richard enter through another door.)

CHARLOTTE: George! . . . He has to be here someplace . . . *Mother?!*

ETHEL: *(Pointing.)* Through there. *(The door to the dressing rooms.)*

CHARLOTTE: Richard, come on!

RICHARD: I find this very tiresome.

CHARLOTTE: *(Off.)* George!

> *(They're gone — and Paul enters through another door.)*

PAUL: Roz . . . ?

ETHEL: *(Pointing.)* Through there. *(The door to the dressing rooms.)*

PAUL: Now I lost Roz.

> *(And Eileen enters from the top of the stairs.)*

PAUL: Eileen! Have you seen George!

EILEEN: *(Crying, heading for the street door.)* No, and I never want to see him again as long as I live!

> *(She's gone.)*

PAUL: Oh, hell. *(Exiting through the door to the dressing rooms.)* Roz?! George?! Charlotte?!

> *(He's gone — and Roz enters through another door.)*

ROZ: Paul?

ETHEL: *(Pointing.)* Through there. *(The door to the dressing rooms.)*
> *(Howard enters from the street.)*

HOWARD: Roz, I've been looking all over for you!

ROZ: Howard . . .

HOWARD: I'm ready, I can meet your parents.

ROZ: Not now, you can meet them later. *(She closes the door in his face and runs off, calling.)* Paul?! Daddy?! Mother?!
> *(She's gone — and George enters at the top of the stairs carrying a bottle of Scotch and an envelope.)*

GEORGE: Ethel!

ETHEL: What?!

GEORGE: When you see Rosalind, give her this letter.

ETHEL: I am not your personal slave.

GEORGE: Give it to her *or I'll have you killed!*

ETHEL: *(Taking it.)* Oh all right!

GEORGE: *(Exiting to the street.)* Where the hell is the Mafia when you need them.

> *(He's gone — and Paul and Roz hurry on through different doors.)*

PAUL/ROZ: George?!/Daddy?! *(They see each other.)* Roz!/Paul!

PAUL: Did you find him?

ROZ: No.

PAUL: He's got to be here somewhere!

ETHEL: Oh, Rosalind, this is for you. It's from Mr. Potatohead.

ROZ: *(She takes the letter and tears it open.)* "Dear Roz, Don't worry about me, I'll be back in a few days." *A few days?!*

PAUL: Oh my God!

(Charlotte and Richard enter.)

CHARLOTTE: Roz! I can't find your father

ROZ: Mother . . .

CHARLOTTE: Wait. I'll bet he's at the hotel.

PAUL: Charlotte . . .

CHARLOTTE: Paul, Paul, Paul. Guess what?! He was telling the truth! Capra is coming to the matinee!

ROZ/PAUL: Mother/Charlotte . . .

CHARLOTTE: Do you realize what this means?! *(From the depths of her being.)* No more Apache Woman. I'm going to be a *big star* . . . !

PAUL/ROZ: Charlotte!/Mother!

(Charlotte begins doing an Indian dance of joy.)

CHARLOTTE: Hiya hiya hiya hiya! Whoop whoop whoop whoop!

ROZ: *Mother!* Would you *listen! (Charlotte stops.)* Daddy left me a note. I think you should read it.

CHARLOTTE: Okay! *(Happily.)* "Dear Roz, Don't worry about me, I'll be back in a few days. Love, Daddy." Fine!

(She hands the letter back to Roz — and then it sinks in.)

CHARLOTTE: *(Screams — and falls back into the arms of Paul and Roz.)* Nooooooooooo!!!

(Quick fade to black.)

END OF ACT I

ACT II

SCENE ONE

The greenroom, about two hours later. Roz is sitting in front of a telephone and a phone book. Paul is pacing nervously, upset. They both look frazzled.

PAUL: I don't believe this . . . I don't believe it!

ROZ: Paul . . .

PAUL: How could your father just disappear? I mean, my God, Frank Capra?!

ROZ: Paul!

PAUL: Don't you have any ambition left? I mean, this could be it, for all of us!

ROZ: Don't you ever think about anything but acting?

PAUL: . . . Sure. Directing. I could direct. I've also written a play that happens to have a terrific part for you in it.

ROZ: Excuse me, but I have a life . . .

PAUL: *(Looks around.)* This isn't a life? Wait, I'm breathing. I think it's a life . . .

ROZ: Paul, not now! I want to find my father!

PAUL: Well, so do I! *(Pause.)* Are you sure we called *all* the bars?

ROZ: I'm positive. I checked them off.

PAUL: I still can't picture your father getting drunk. I've never seen him take a drink in all these years.

ROZ: He only drinks when he's under great stress. The night I went out on my first date, he drank an entire bottle of vermouth. Then he followed me around disguised as an Irishman. It was like being stalked by Eugene O'Neill.

(Charlotte drags in from the street.)

PAUL/ROZ: Well?!

CHARLOTTE: He's still not at the hotel. The manager has alerted the staff, and they'll call us if he shows up.

PAUL: I don't believe this!

CHARLOTTE: *You* don't believe it?!

ROZ: I believe it.

CHARLOTTE: How could he do this to me?!!

ROZ: It's not his fault.

CHARLOTTE: Of course it's his fault, Rosalind! Don't defend him!

ROZ: But *you* walked out on *him.*

CHARLOTTE: Which I wouldn't have done if he hadn't lied to me.

ROZ: Well you must have driven him to it.

CHARLOTTE: . . . *I* drove *him* to it?

ROZ: Well you must have.

CHARLOTTE: *(Staggered.)* This is what I get . . . for four days of the worst labor in the history of medicine? "I must have"?!

ROZ: Oh, Mother, don't get dramatic.

CHARLOTTE: Do you know how big your head was?!

(The phone rings. Paul grabs it.)

PAUL: Hello! . . . Yes it is . . . Great! *(To the others, excited.)* It's the Paramount Bar, on Delaney. They think George just walked in.

ROZ/CHARLOTTE: Great!/Thank God!

PAUL: *(Into the phone.)* Now listen, can you keep him there? . . . Oh. Hold on. *(To the others.)* He wants to know if there's a reward.

CHARLOTTE: Oh for God . . .

ROZ: Tell him two tickets to *Private Lives.*

PAUL: *(Into the phone.)* Two tickets to *Private Lives.*

ROZ: Well, fine!

PAUL: *(Into the phone.)* With dinner afterwards. *(Beat; to the others:)* He wants free parking.

ROZ: *(Grabbing the phone; a killer.)* Listen to me, you pinhead! You want a reward?! Well you keep him there for the next ten minutes, and I *won't* tear your heart out!! . . . *Fine!*

(She slams down the phone.)

CHARLOTTE: *(Shaking Roz's hand.)* Atta girl.

PAUL: I'll go.

CHARLOTTE: No. I know where Delaney is. I'll be right back.

(Charlotte exits to the street.)

ROZ: . . . Do you see what I mean?! About the theater?! I'm back here for three hours and I'm acting like a lunatic. I'll be in analysis till I'm a hundred.

PAUL: It won't help.

ROZ: Oh shut up.

(Pause.)

PAUL: So why did you come back?

ROZ: I came back . . . to see my parents. Is that a crime? And I didn't know you were here or I wouldn't have come.

PAUL: Well I'm sorry. Next time I'll put up a sign on the thruway. "Paul in Buffalo. Turn Back. Save Yourself."

ROZ: Okay. Just forget about it.

PAUL: Fine. That's fine with me.

ROZ: Well fine!

PAUL: . . . Let's run your lines and get it over with.

(He tosses her a script.)

ROZ: Don't bother. I've done *Private Lives* a hundred times. I know it backwards. And I don't see why I have to play Sibyl.

PAUL: Because Eileen took the day off. We don't know where she is. Why don't you blame me for that too?

ROZ: I'm not blaming you.

PAUL: I suppose I got her pregnant.

ROZ: I wouldn't be at all surprised.

PAUL: Fine.

ROZ: Well, fine!

PAUL: *(Opening the script.)* Two adjoining balconies. Posh hotel. South of France.

ROZ: I know the play!

PAUL: The lights come up.

ROZ: For the record, I hate this. I swore I'd never set foot on a stage again. I'm breaking a vow here.

PAUL: The lights come up.

(Roz glances at her script, then delivers her lines totally deadpan, straight out front, with an English accent.)

ROZ: "Elli Elli dear do come out it's so lovely."

PAUL: "Just a minute." Elyot comes out. Your father plays Elyot.

ROZ: No kidding. He always plays Elyot. He's been playing Elyot since I was five years old.

PAUL: He looks at the view. "Not so bad."

ROZ: *(Deadpan.)* "It's heavenly look at the lights of that yacht reflected in the water oh dear I'm so happy."

PAUL: "Are you?"

ROZ: "Aren't you?"

PAUL: "Of course I am. Tremendously happy."

ROZ: "Just to think here we are you and I married."

PAUL: "Yes, things have come to a pretty pass." *(He laughs as Elyot.)*

ROZ: "Don't laugh at me, you mustn't be blasé about honeymoons just because this is your second."

PAUL: "That's silly."

ROZ: "Have I annoyed you by saying that?"

PAUL: "Just a little."

ROZ: "Oh darling I'm so sorry kiss me."

(Beat. Paul looks at the script — a sort of double take to make sure the kiss is really there. It is. He kisses her — a peck, to get it over with.)

PAUL: "There."

ROZ: "Ummm, not so very enthusiastic. Again."

(Beat. He kisses her again.)

PAUL: "That better?"

ROZ: "Three times, please, I'm superstitious."

(Pause. He leans into her, and they kiss with conviction. Then with passion. They really get involved. In fact, they're both getting hotter by the second. He starts kissing her neck and her ears. She's panting for breath.)

ROZ: *(Hardly able to talk.)* This isn't in the script . . .

(They go at it again. The following lines come in gasps, between kisses.)

PAUL: I know. I'm ad-libbing.

ROZ: Oh, Paul . . . We have to rehearse . . . It's so important . . . to Mother and Dad . . .

PAUL: You're right . . . I agree . . . Take your clothes off.

(He starts to undress her.)

ROZ: Wait! Paul, there's something important I have to tell you.

PAUL: Tell me later, when you're naked.

ROZ: Okay.

(They drop their scripts and hit the floor — when the phone rings.)

ROZ: Oh, hell.

(It rings again. Paul answers it.)

PAUL: Hello? . . . Yes it is . . . Oh my God!

ROZ: What?

PAUL: Shhh! . . . Right. I'll be right there . . . Yes, of course we'll pay for the damage!

(He hangs up.)

ROZ: What happened?

PAUL: That was the manager of the hotel. Somebody walked into the dining room, climbed onto a buffet table, and started reciting *King Lear*.

ROZ: It's him.

PAUL: Let's go. We can get there faster if we go through the house.

(They exit hurriedly through the door to the backstage area. The stage is empty. Then the street door flies open, and George staggers in holding a bottle of whiskey. He's so drunk he can hardly stand up.)

GEORGE: *(Declaiming.)* "They seek him here,
They seek him there,
Those Frenchies seek him
Everywhere.
Is he in heaven?
Or is he in hell?
Ronald Colman
Tripped and fell!" *(Then.)*
I could have had that part. It was mine for the taking. Now they'll give it
to some no-talent has-been like . . . John Gielgud. I could play it better
than both of them with my legs tied behind my back. Legs, legs . . . ? Legs!
Of course! I almost forgot! I should write Ronald Colman a get-well card!
Must do it. *(He finds a pen and a piece of paper and starts writing.)*· "Dear
Ronnie. How are the old pins? Hm?" *(He laughs; then.)*
"What? Is Brutus sick? And will he steal out of his wholesome bed To dare
the vile contagion of the night?" Ah, Shakespeare! "To be or not to be." .
. . Big deal. The kid's depressed. We're all depressed! Dear Ronnie. Did
you ever play Hamlet, huh? Or Henry Five? Or Falstaff?! "If sack and sugar
be a fault, God help the wicked. If to be old and merry be a sin, then
many an old host I know is damned. No, my good lord; banish Peto, banish Bardolph, banish Poins — but for sweet Jack Falstaff, kind Jack Falstaff,
true Jack Falstaff, valiant Jack Falstaff, and therefore more valiant, being
as he is old Jack Falstaff, banish not him thy Harry's company, banish not
him thy Harry's company, banish plump Jack, and banish all the world."
That is writing, Ronnie. That is glory on the tongue, gold on the canvas.
It is not the movies, it is not television, it is the theater! The theater! *(His
histrionics have brought him to the call-board where he sees the performance
schedule. He reads it aloud.)* "Schedule of Performances . . . Matinee —
Private Lives." Wrong! *(He crosses it out and writes in.)* "*Cyrano.*" *(He looks
at his handiwork.)* Puh. She got it wrong again. Charlotte. Dear, sweet
Charlotte. She has the brain of a chicken. And yet, I'll miss her. The pitter
patter of her size twelves. The dainty whine of her voice, nagging at me
like an open cold sore. O, to return to that midnight hour when you gave
birth to our only child. I can still see you, flopping around on the table
like a tuna on a hook. I can still hear your dulcet voice, cutting through
the night like an air raid siren. *(Faintly, as if in the distance.)* "Please," she
cried, "please, give me the Demerol!" I can't even tell you now that I love
you. Too late. She's gone. Gone with the wind. *(Bitter.)* I would have been

excellent in that film. Ah, well. Good-bye, Charlotte. Take care of yourself. And it shall be written on his tombstone: *(Almost crying.)* "One mistake. He made one lousy, innocent mistake, and they kicked the shit out of him."

(He trips and collapses behind the sofa, or anywhere else he's hidden from view. Then Charlotte stalks in from the street and slams the door. She does not see George.)

CHARLOTTE: *(To herself; she wants to strangle him.)* George . . . George! . . . You never had good timing, George, but this is incredible! . . . Well. It's over now. Gone. Gone. Gone with the wind. *(Bitter.)* God, I would have been great in that film!

(Roz and Paul hurry in from the theater.)

ROZ: No luck at the bar?

CHARLOTTE: It wasn't him. It didn't even look like him!

PAUL: Well he may have been at the hotel a few minutes ago, but he's gone now.

(The telephone rings. Charlotte grabs it.)

CHARLOTTE: Yes? Yes, I'm *Charlotte* Hay, his wife. *(To Roz and Paul.)* It's the police. *(Into the phone.)* What? . . .

(She listens — and she turns white and sits down because her knees are weak. This is very serious.)

CHARLOTTE: Oh my God . . . Oh no . . . Yes, we'll be right there. *(She hangs up, stunned.)* A body just arrived at the morgue, and it fits your father's description. They want us to go take a look.

PAUL: Oh my God . . .

ROZ: Maybe it's not him. Let's go!

CHARLOTTE: Wait! Before we go, I . . . think we should say a prayer.

PAUL: A prayer?

CHARLOTTE: I'm not religious, you know that, but I think it would be appropriate.

ROZ/PAUL: Okay./All right.

CHARLOTTE: Let's hold hands.

(The three of them hold hands and bow their heads. Pause. Then.)

CHARLOTTE: Does anybody know a prayer?

ROZ: Not me.

PAUL: Huh-uh.

CHARLOTTE: Wait! . . . "God is great, God is good . . ."

(Roz and Paul join in.)

CHARLOTTE/ROZ/PAUL: "And we thank Him for our food . . ."

(At this point, we hear George join in, and then he rises up groggily from behind the sofa, holding his bottle. It takes a beat for the others to register George's voice.)

CHARLOTTE/ROZ/PAUL/GEORGE: "By His hand we all are fed . . ."

(They turn and see him, rising up like a ghost.)

GEORGE: "Thank you for our daily bread."

CHARLOTTE/ROZ/PAUL: *Yaaaaaaahhh!!!*

PAUL: George!

ROZ: Daddy!

CHARLOTTE: *(Joyously, throwing her arms around him.)* Oh, George, I knew you'd come home, I knew it! *(Reeling backward, aghast.)* Uch! George! You smell like a distillery!

GEORGE: That's odd. I haven't been to a distillery.

ROZ: Oh, Daddy.

CHARLOTTE: *(To Roz and Paul, ignoring George.)* All right, listen. We have a half hour till curtain.

PAUL: We can still make it!

CHARLOTTE: First, we'll have to sober him up. Give him coffee. Lots of coffee.

ROZ/PAUL: Right.

ROZ: There's plenty here, you know Grandma.

CHARLOTTE: Then we'll get him into a cold shower.

ROZ/PAUL: Right.

CHARLOTTE: I'll lay out his costume, then we'll shovel him into it.

ROZ/PAUL: Right.

(A loud snore. They look around and see George curled up on the sofa with his bottle.)

CHARLOTTE: George!

ROZ: Daddy!

CHARLOTTE: George, wake up! Oh, for God's sake.

(She shakes him.)

GEORGE: Huh? What?

CHARLOTTE: *Wake up!!*

(He opens his eyes and sees Charlotte, as if for the first time.)

GEORGE: Oh my God, Charlotte, you're back!

CHARLOTTE: Of course I'm back. I've *been* back.

GEORGE: *(On his knees, hugging her legs.)* I'm sorry, Charlotte. I made a mistake.

CHARLOTTE: We'll talk about that later.

GEORGE: You'll never forgive me, I can tell.

(He starts to cry.)

CHARLOTTE: George, I forgive you.

GEORGE: No, you don't.

CHARLOTTE: I forgive you, George!

GEORGE: You're just saying that . . .

CHARLOTTE: (Shaking him.) George, stop it! We have a performance in thirty minutes!

GEORGE: . . . A performance? Well, we'd better get moving.

(He stands up — and promptly falls backward. Paul and Roz catch him.)

CHARLOTTE: Oh, hell.

PAUL: I've got him.

ROZ: Come on, Daddy, let's go!

GEORGE: (As if seeing her for the first time.) Rosalind! My baby! What are you doing here?!

ROZ: I'm playing Sibyl to your Elyot in the matinee.

GEORGE: . . . Matinee? What matinee?

CHARLOTTE: I just told you!

GEORGE: (As if seeing Charlotte for the first time.) Oh my God, Charlotte, you're back!

CHARLOTTE: Would you please get him upstairs!

(As they help George up the stairs, Ethel enters down the stairs carrying George's Cyrano pants.)

ETHEL: That is the last time I fix his filthy trousers! . . . What's wrong with him?

CHARLOTTE: He's drunk.

ETHEL: So what? He always stunk.

(George tries to wallop her, but Paul and Roz stop him. Then the three of them exit.)

CHARLOTTE: (Handing Ethel the bottle of whiskey.) Here. Get rid of this.

ETHEL: What?

CHARLOTTE: Pour it out! And make some more coffee!

ETHEL: We have a matinee, you know. You should be in costume.

CHARLOTTE: Thank you, Mother!

(Charlotte exits. Ethel is now alone in the room, holding the bottle of whiskey.)

ETHEL: Now why does she want Irish coffee?

(She walks to the coffee pot and pours all the remaining whiskey from the bottle — most of a bottle's worth — into the coffee pot, which fills the pot to *the brim. The coffee pot is glass, so we can see that the combination of coffee and whiskey still looks like coffee.)*

ETHEL: I suppose they're having guests at the intermission. Now in my day, we served strawberries and champagne. Puh. It's only called civilization. Why bother?

(She puts down the coffee pot — and sees the performance schedule on the call board and reads from it.)

ETHEL: "Schedule of Performances . . . "Matinee *Cyrano*"? I thought it was *Private Lives.*

(At this moment, there's a knock on the door; Ethel, of course, doesn't hear it.)

ETHEL: Good thing I saw this. They'd think I was round the bend.

(As she potters across the room, Howard comes in from the street, carrying a program. He sees Ethel, who has her back to him, and approaches her.)

HOWARD: Hello? *(She doesn't hear him.)* . . . Hello? . . . *(He walks around her.)* . . . Hi.

ETHEL: *Ah!* You startled me.

HOWARD: Oh, sorry. I'm a friend of Roz. You must be Roz's grandmother. She talks a lot about you.

ETHEL: Young man, I cannot hear a word you're saying.

HOWARD: *I'm a friend of Roz!*

ETHEL: Well, how nice to meet you.

HOWARD: *She left me a note at the hotel! It's very exciting, isn't it?!*

ETHEL: What's exciting?

HOWARD: About Frank Capra.

ETHEL: What?

HOWARD: *Frank Capra!*

ETHEL: Oh. How nice.

(Charlotte and Paul rush in from the door at the top of the stairs. Paul is carrying George's shirt. From where they are, they can't see Howard.)

CHARLOTTE: How could you lose him?!

PAUL: I'm sorry! I left him in the hall to turn on the shower!

CHARLOTTE: *Mother, have you seen George?!*

ETHEL: You took him up the stairs.

CHARLOTTE: *Since then!* . . . Oh, God.

PAUL: Look, I'll try backstage again. You check downstairs.

CHARLOTTE: Right.

(Paul exits and Charlotte hurries down the stairs — and sees Howard for the first time.)

HOWARD: . . . Hi. I'm back.

CHARLOTTE: *(Hustling him to the door.)* Look, I'm sorry, but we're busy now. We have a show in twenty minutes.

HOWARD: 1 know. 1 bought a program.

CHARLOTTE: . . . Oh, all right! *(She snatches the program from him, takes a pen from his pocket, and signs the program.)* "Best wishes, Charlotte Hay." How's that?

HOWARD: I-I-I don't think you understand . . .

CHARLOTTE: No, I don't think *you* understand. We're very busy now, so good-bye!

(And she pushes Howard out the door and slams it.)

CHARLOTTE: These people! They walk right in as if they own the place.

ETHEL: You didn't have to be rude to him.

CHARLOTTE: Mother, stay out of this.

(Charlotte is heading off.)

ETHEL: I used to know a man named Capra. I wonder if he's related . . . ?

(Charlotte stops cold.)

CHARLOTTE: . . . Capra?

ETHEL: What?

CHARLOTTE: *Capra?!*

ETHEL: What about him?

CHARLOTTE: *Why did you say Capra?!*

ETHEL: I didn't say it. He said it. He introduced himself. Frank Capra. It sounds extremely familiar.

CHARLOTTE: *(It sinks in, and she clutches her breast.)* Oh my God! *(Shaking Ethel.)* Mother, why didn't you tell me?!! *(She rushes out the street door.)* Wait a second! Please! Wait!

ETHEL: *(As she heads backstage.)* It's like living in an asylum on the guard's day off.

(Ethel exits; then Charlotte reappears, leading a bewildered, reluctant Howard into the room.)

CHARLOTTE: I am so *sorry.* I could just beat myself with a stick! Please, come in.

HOWARD: . . . You're sure? I could wait outside. It's a nice day, which is pretty much what I predicted.

CHARLOTTE: Oh no no no no! Oh, God. You must think I'm completely mad.

HOWARD: Mmmno.

CHARLOTTE: My mother should have said something. The older lady who was standing here. I'm afraid she's just a teensy bit hard of hearing.

HOWARD: "Grandma."

CHARLOTTE: Hm?

HOWARD: Maybe I should call her "Grandma." Heh heh. Or "Granny"!

(He chuckles about this.)

CHARLOTTE: . . . Why not?! Granny it is! So. Perhaps we should start over. *(Extending her hand, with enormous charm.)* I'm Charlotte Hay.

HOWARD: Hi . . .

CHARLOTTE: Now before you say another word, I just want to tell you what a *huge fan* I am of your work.

HOWARD: . . . Gee, thanks.

CHARLOTTE: *It Happened One Night!*

HOWARD: . . . Well, actually it happens every night at six and eleven.

CHARLOTTE: *It's a Wonderful Life.* Wow.

HOWARD: Gee, you have such a good attitude.

(Absentmindedly, he picks up a paperweight from the table and plays with it.)

CHARLOTTE: *You Can't Take It with You.*

(He quickly puts it down.)

HOWARD: I'm not! I-I-I —

CHARLOTTE: And you're such a young man to have accomplished so much. I had no idea.

HOWARD: Thanks. A lot of people think it's easy. Like there's nothing to it.

CHARLOTTE: Oh, come now

HOWARD: They do! They think it's all just a matter of barometric pressure.

(He laughs at this; Charlotte joins in — trying to figure it out.)

CHARLOTTE: I'm sure the pressure must be intense these days.

HOWARD: It's pretty bad. But there's a cold front moving up from Atlanta, so that should give us some relief.

CHARLOTTE: . . . Really? Well. Can I get you some coffee?

HOWARD: Mmmmmno. No thanks.

CHARLOTTE: A drink drink?

HOWARD: I never drink.

CHARLOTTE: Nor do I. Nor does George, my husband. The minute we start to work, there is no such thing in the world as liquor.

(At which point, George bursts in through the backstage door with a new

bottle of whiskey in his hand, reeling with drunkenness. He wears an under-shirt and trousers.)

GEORGE: "Once more unto the breach, dear friends, once more!
   Or close the wall up with our English dead!"
   (He collapses in a heap on the floor. Silence. Charlotte just looks at him, at a complete loss. Then she starts clapping furiously.)

CHARLOTTE: Bravo! Brav-o!!

HOWARD: *(Starts clapping too, trying to be a good sport.)* Bravo!

CHARLOTTE: *(Confidentially.)* He's been working on this concept for months. Henry the Fifth, the-the-the . . . Pickled Prince. [Or "Plastered Planta-genet."]

HOWARD: He's very convincing. *(Calling to George, who is still out cold on the floor.)* That's very good!

CHARLOTTE: Shhh! Please. He's concentrating.

HOWARD: Sorry.

CHARLOTTE: Oh my God, just look at the time. We really must get you to your seat. But we will see you after the performance. Do you promise?

HOWARD: Sure.

CHARLOTTE: *(Escorting him out.)* And let me say again what an absolute thrill it is to have you here. We're extremely honored.

HOWARD: . . . I have to say, you people are much friendlier than I expected.
   (He exits, and Charlotte waves with an ingratiating smile.)

CHARLOTTE: Bye-bye! *(She closes the door; to George.)* You drunken lout!
   (Paul enters.)

PAUL: You found him!

CHARLOTTE: No, *he* found *me* while I was talking to Capra!

PAUL: Oh my God. Do you think he realized that George is . . .

CHARLOTTE: No, he thought the theater was built on Lake Chivas Regal.

PAUL: Maybe he didn't notice.

CHARLOTTE: Notice? Notice?! If you lit a match in here, the whole room would blow up!
   (George starts snoring.)

CHARLOTTE: *(Shaking him.)* Would you please wake up?!

GEORGE: Oh my God, Charlotte, you're back!
   (Charlotte screams with frustration.)

PAUL: Listen, we'll dress him here. You get his costume. I'll give him some coffee.

GEORGE: I hate coffee.

PAUL: George, please!

>*(Charlotte exits up the stairs as Paul pours George a mug of coffee.)*

GEORGE: I don't need coffee! I'm fine now!

PAUL: *(Handing George the coffee.)* Just drink it! We have to be onstage doing *Private Lives* in fifteen minutes.

GEORGE: *Cyrano.*

PAUL: *Private Lives.*

GEORGE: The matinee is *Cyrano.* Look at the schedule.

PAUL: George . . .

GEORGE: I just read it!

PAUL: You did not! Look!! *(He snatches the schedule from the call board and reads it.)* "Saturday matinee . . . *Cyrano*"? Who wrote this in?

>*(George looks at the schedule.)*

GEORGE: No idea.

PAUL: They must have changed the schedule.

>*(By this time George has tasted the coffee. He looks at it closely, then looks around at the coffee pot.)*

GEORGE: I must say, I have completely underestimated coffee. It is an excellent drink.

PAUL: Is this your Cyrano shirt?

GEORGE: It is indeed.

PAUL: Well put it on. Hurry up.

GEORGE: I have to finish my coffee.

PAUL: *George, we have less than fifteen minutes!!*

GEORGE: Oh, all right.

>*(Charlotte hurries in with George's* Private Lives *costume. She sees Paul trying to get George into his ruffled Cyrano shirt and stops cold.)*

CHARLOTTE: Paul, what are you doing? That's his Cyrano shirt!

PAUL: I know that!

>*(During the following, George sits in his undershirt and happily pulls off his trousers, one leg at a time. He has boxer shorts on underneath. Thus, when he's done, he's in his underwear, and his trousers are lying on the floor.)*

CHARLOTTE: We're doing *Private Lives*!

PAUL: We're doing *Cyrano*! Look! *(He hands her the schedule.)* It was changed.

CHARLOTTE: That's George's handwriting.

PAUL: Are you sure?

CHARLOTTE: Of course I'm sure!

PAUL: Why would he change it?

CHARLOTTE: *Who knows why George does anything?!!*
   (There's a knock at the door. Knock, knock, knock.)
CHARLOTTE: Oh, God. This is a nightmare! *(Knock, knock, knock.) Who is it?!*
HOWARD: *(Off.)* Uh, hi. It's me!
CHARLOTTE: It's Frank Capra!
GEORGE: *(Heading for the door.)* Ah, tell him to come in. I'd love to meet him.
CHARLOTTE: *(Grabbing George.)* No! *(Calling off.) One second! (To Paul.)* Hide
   George.
PAUL: Hide him?
CHARLOTTE: *Hide him!*
GEORGE: *(Jumping up and down with childish frustration.)* Why can't I meet
   him?!!
CHARLOTTE: Because you don't have any clothes on!!
   (Paul opens a door that hasn't been opened before — the closet.)
PAUL: George, in the closet. Quick.
   (Knock, knock, knock.)
CHARLOTTE: *(Throwing them George's* Private Lives *costume.)* Just a minute!
   Coming! *(To Paul.)* And put this on him! *(Knock, knock, knock.)* Coming!
   *(George and Paul disappear into the closet as Charlotte opens the door to the
   street. Howard is standing there holding a garment bag with a ribbon on it.)*
CHARLOTTE: *(All smiles.)* Hello again.
HOWARD: Hi. I-I-I'm sorry to bother you
CHARLOTTE: Bother us? You could never bother us!
HOWARD: Gee, that-that's . . .
CHARLOTTE: I was just saying to my husband *(She sees the trousers on the floor.)*,
   who was here not a minute ago, I was just remarking how much I love
   your work. I could watch it all day.
HOWARD: No kidding. Hey! Wait wait wait! Stand here. Watch this. *(He takes
   a breath.)* "The barometer is falling rapidly, and we might just see some
   flurries by this afternoon." *(Charlotte stares at him blankly.)* "So-o-o stay
   warm, wear those woollies and God bless."
   (He smiles broadly. It was a good performance.)
CHARLOTTE: . . . *Really?*
   *(At this moment, the closet door flies open, and George and Paul come out,
   struggling. George, in his underwear, is trying to get out of the closet, and Paul
   is pulling him back in.)*
GEORGE: *Take your hands off me! I want to meet him!*

PAUL: *George, stop it right now!*

> *(They disappear back into the closet, banging the door closed behind them. Beat. Charlotte is about to speak . . .)*

CHARLOTTE: So . . .

> *(when George and Paul come barrelling out of the closet again.)*

GEORGE: *I want some more coffee!*

PAUL: *George, put your pants on now!!*

> *(As Paul pulls George back into the closet, George manages to grab Howard and pulls him along with them. Bang! The door slams shut, and all three of them are gone. Charlotte, who didn't see him disappear, looks around for the missing Howard. Then the door opens for an instant, and Howard comes hurtling out. Bang! The door slams shut again. Charlotte acts as if nothing unusual has happened.)*

CHARLOTTE: So. What can we do for you?

HOWARD: *(Completely bewildered; holds up the garment bag.)* Hm? Oh. Well, I-I-I have a present for Mr. Hay.

CHARLOTTE: . . . You bought him a suit?

HOWARD: Yeah. No! It's one of his old costumes. General George S. Patton. It came with the helmet and the gun and everything. Hey! I could try it on and surprise him!

CHARLOTTE: *No! (She looks at her watch.)* Oh, dear, just look at the time. *(She ushers him out the door.)* Now don't forget, you come right back here after the show.

HOWARD: If I can wait that long.

CHARLOTTE: *Try.* Just . . . *try.*

HOWARD: Okay. Uh, good luck . . . "Mom."

> *(He kisses Charlotte on the cheek, chuckles nervously, and exits.)*

CHARLOTTE: . . . "Mom"? . . .

> *(George and Paul come flying out the door, struggling.)*

GEORGE: *I want one more cup!*

PAUL: *George!*

GEORGE: *One cup!*

> *(They fall on the pouf.)*

PAUL: *George, stop it!*

CHARLOTTE: George, would you please cooperate!

PAUL: *Lift your leg!*

> *(Paul is on top of George, trying to pull George's* Private Lives *pants on over*

his backside. George's legs, with Paul between them, are flailing wildly. At this moment, Richard walks in from the street.)

RICHARD: I thought I better tell you . . .

(He sees George and Paul — and reels backward in horror. He had no idea. George and Paul — gay???)

RICHARD: Good God! You found him! Where was he?!

CHARLOTTE: He just came out of the closet.

RICHARD: Well, I can see that. I had no idea.

CHARLOTTE: Not that closet. *That* closet!

RICHARD: Oh. Anyway, I thought I should tell you, there's a rumor that Capra's in the audience .

GEORGE: *(Seeing Richard for the first time.)* Richard?

RICHARD: How are you, old boy?

GEORGE: Paul. Come here. I would like you to meet one of my oldest and dearest friends, Richard Maynard, lawyer, trusted advisor, and low-down sneaking *wife stealer!*

(George springs at Richard and starts to strangle him.)

CHARLOTTE/PAUL: *George! Stop it!*

RICHARD: *Aargh!*

GEORGE: *You leave my wife alone, do you hear me?!!!*

CHARLOTTE: *George!*

RICHARD: *She doesn't love you anymore!*

GEORGE: *Liar! Take it back!*

CHARLOTTE/PAUL: *George!*

(Charlotte and Paul pull George off Richard.)

RICHARD: The man's insane!

CHARLOTTE: Richard, I think you should go.

RICHARD: Gladly . . . And Charlotte: you really do deserve better than this.

(George springs at him with a cry of anger; but Richard exits and closes the door before George can reach him.)

CHARLOTTE: *(To Paul.)* I don't understand it. He's getting drunker.

PAUL: Me neither.

CHARLOTTE: *(Pointing at the coffee pot.)* More coffee!

GEORGE: Oh, good.

(Ethel enters from backstage wearing the costume of a sixteenth-century duenna. Simultaneously, Roz hurries in from above. She's wearing a smart evening dress of the 1920s. The two costumes could not possibly be in greater contrast.)

ETHEL: Well, *I'm* all ready.

ROZ: *(Simultaneously.)* I can take over now.

> *(Charlotte, in the middle, sees them, staggers backward, and screams.)*

ETHEL: Rosalind, you're in the wrong costume.

ROZ: No, you are.

ETHEL: What?

ROZ: *You* are! We're doing *Private Lives.*

ETHEL: No, dear, *Cyrano.* Look at the schedule.

CHARLOTTE: Mother . . .

ROZ: *(Reading the schedule.)* Look. She's right. It's *Cyrano.*

CHARLOTTE: It is not *Cyrano*! *(Right in Ethel's face.)* We are doing *Private Lives, Private Lives, PRIVATE LIVES!!!*

> *(Silence. Slowly, Ethel turns with wounded dignity, walks, head high, to the door to the backstage area, and with a final, dignified, reproachful look at Charlotte, she exits, closing the door. Beat. Then Charlotte, Roz, and Paul look around and realize that George is gone. During the argument about which play they were doing, he walked out [carrying the coffee pot and his mug] without anyone noticing.)*

PAUL: Oh my God. Where's George?!

ROZ: He was right here!

CHARLOTTE: *(Sinking onto the sofa.)* Oh, no . . .

PAUL: Now wait. We still have seven minutes.

CHARLOTTE: *(Lying stricken on the chaise.)* Forget it. Forget it, forget it. It's over.

PAUL: *(Controlling himself.)* It's not over. He can't be far. This is no time to panic, we can still do the show, so *don't panic!!!* . . . Sorry.

ROZ: Now listen. Mother, go put your costume on. Paul, you take the first floor, I'll take the second. And Mother, check the stage before you change. We'll meet back here in five minutes.

ALL THREE: Right.

> *(As they run out, Charlotte gets hit in the forehead by the door. She staggers with dizziness — then exits, straight-backed, trying to keep her balance and her dignity. The stage is empty for a moment. Then the door at the top of the stairs opens, and George walks in, carrying the coffee pot in one hand and his mug in the other. He's half wearing his* Private Lives *costume — that is, he's wearing the black trousers that Paul pulled onto him earlier and a starched but askew white tux shirt.)*

GEORGE: *(Thoughtfully, sniffing at his mug.)* Beans. It's the quality of the beans.

(He falls down the stairs, almost killing himself. At this moment, Eileen hurries in from the street.)

EILEEN: Oh, George! Thank God you're here!

GEORGE: Eileen!

EILEEN: George, listen! Something awful has happened! I went to see the doctor a few minutes ago, to get the results . . .

GEORGE: And and?!

EILEEN: Yes, I'm pregnant. I told you that.

GEORGE: *(Starts to cry.)* Oh, no . . .

EILEEN: Just listen! As I was coming out, I bumped into my brother and . . . I don't know why, but I told him about the baby, and he got *really upset.* He threatened to kill you.

(Pause.)

GEORGE: Your brother?

EILEEN: Yes.

GEORGE: Your brother the hairdresser?

EILEEN: Yes!

(He starts to laugh uproariously.)

GEORGE: I'm sorry. It strikes me as funny, that's all.

EILEEN: George, listen . . .

GEORGE: *(Laughing.)* What does he plan to do? Put me under a hot dryer? *(Really yucking it up.)* Wrap my curlers too tight?!

EILEEN: George, you don't understand.

GEORGE: Stick my head in a basin and shampoo me to death?!

(He howls with laughter.)

EILEEN: George, he was in the marines during the war! He lifts weights! He could break you in half!

GEORGE: . . . You're joking.

EILEEN: He landed at Guadalcanal. He went home to get his gun!

GEORGE: What should I do?!

EILEEN: I don't know. Just . . . be careful. If you see him, run.

GEORGE: How will I know it's him?

EILEEN: He'll be the one in uniform pointing the *gun* at you! Take care of yourself.

(She exits quickly. George is stunned.)

GEORGE: One lousy mistake and I'm a dead man. Wait! *(He rushes to the telephone.)* Hello? Get me the airport. Now!

(Holding the phone, he peers cautiously out the door. Paul enters and sees him.)

PAUL: George!

GEORGE: *(Throwing the phone — which Paul catches.)Yaaaahhh!!!*

PAUL: George, we have less than five minutes!

GEORGE: Paul, he's after me.

PAUL: Who's after you?

GEORGE: Eileen's brother! He's out for revenge!

PAUL: What are you talking about?!

GEORGE: He knows about Eileen!

PAUL: What?

GEORGE: You know. *(He gestures intercourse.)* He's sworn to kill me.

PAUL: Oh, George, you're hallucinating. *(Knocking at the street door: knock, knock, knock!)* Coming!

GEORGE: *No! Don't answer it!*

(Paul opens the door — and Howard bounds in wearing Patton's uniform and helmet, brandishing Patton's service revolver.)

HOWARD: *(Triumphantly.)* Hahaaa! Gotcha!

GEORGE: *(Running for cover.) Aaaaaahhhhhhh!!!*

HOWARD: George Hay . . . ?

GEORGE: Yes. *No!* I look a little like him. . .

HOWARD: Oh, come on. You are so. Well? What do you think? Do I look *tough*?!

GEORGE: *(A squeak.)* Yes.

HOWARD: Hey! Look at this baby! *(The gun.)* Blam blam blam blam!!

GEORGE: *(Falling to his knees and weeping.)* No, please! I beg of you! Please! Don't do it!

HOWARD: Gee, I-I just wanted to let you have it.

GEORGE: I know that! And I am so sorry!

HOWARD: "Sorry"?

GEORGE: I realize that she is young and innocent, and of course you love her greatly.

HOWARD: Who? . . . Roz?

(Beat. Paul and George look up.)

GEORGE: "Roz"?

PAUL: Roz?!

GEORGE: *(Suddenly angry, the father protecting his young.)* What has my daughter got to do with this?!

PAUL: Yeah!

HOWARD: Well, I-I-I-I think she's a very . . . desirable young woman.

PAUL: Who the hell do you think you are?!

HOWARD: *(Looks at his uniform.)* . . . General Patton?

GEORGE: *(Spitting out the words, advancing on Howard.)* You listen to me, you piece of slime! If you ever touch one hair on my daughter's head, I will hunt you down like a dog and pull your heart out through your mouth!!!

HOWARD: *(Waving the gun in terror.)* Stop! Stay back! I know how to use this! I saw the movie!

(Howard closes his eyes, turns his head, and shoots — bang! — and a lamp on the wall next to George explodes. For a beat, George just looks at what's left of the lamp, then he screams and starts chasing Howard around the room.)

GEORGE: You idiot!

HOWARD: I'm sorry!

GEORGE: Paul, get him!

PAUL: I'm trying!

GEORGE: Drop the gun, you maniac!

HOWARD: I didn't mean it!

PAUL: *(Grabbing Howard around the waist.)* Gotcha!

HOWARD: *Ahh!*

PAUL: Now what do I do with him?!!

GEORGE: *(Patting his pockets, looking for something.)* Wait a second! Stuff this hanky . . . *(Out of a pocket, he pulls a handkerchief, which was wrapped around a Cyrano nose. The nose falls to the floor, and George picks it up. He holds the nose about crotch high [Howard's crotch] to see what it is. Unfortunately, under the circumstances, it resembles a sexual device.)* So that's where it was.

HOWARD: *Ahh! Ahh! Ahh! Ahh!*

(And he faints, leaving Paul with a limp, unconscious body in his arms. Howard's head lolls from side to side like an old eggplant. Paul starts dragging Howard across the room like a sack of potatoes.)

GEORGE: Get him into the closet! Here! Stuff this in his mouth! *(The handkerchief.)* And tie him up!

PAUL: Why don't *you* do it?

GEORGE: *Because I'm the star!!*

(Paul drags Howard into the closet — as Charlotte appears at the top of the stairs in a robe with a towel on her head.)

CHARLOTTE: George!

(George turns, startled, and slams the closet door.)

CHARLOTTE: What are you doing?!

GEORGE: Nothing.

CHARLOTTE: Where's Paul?!

GEORGE: I haven't seen him.

(And Paul races out of the closet and slams the door.)

CHARLOTTE: Paul! You're not even in costume!

PAUL: *(With instant nonchalance.)* I know.

(And Roz runs in, still in her Private Lives *costume.)*

ROZ: Daddy! Oh thank God! Can he do the show?!

GEORGE: Of course I can do it! Just give me a moment.

CHARLOTTE: George, you don't have a moment, you have the second line in the play!

GEORGE: I do?

CHARLOTTE: Hurry up! The curtain is going up in three minutes!

(Charlotte exits, and Roz turns to George.)

ROZ: Daddy, we have the opening scene together. *(In character.)* "Elli, Elli dear, do come out, it's so lovely." Then you come out, onto the balcony, and you say —

GEORGE: "Not so bad."

ROZ: *(Touchdown!)* That's it! Now come on!

GEORGE: Right!

(Roz and Paul run out, with George right behind them. As he passes his mug of coffee, however, he stops short and quickly takes a sip.)

GEORGE: It must be Colombian.

(Blackout.)

SCENE TWO

The stage of the theater, as seen by the audience. A few seconds later. As the lights come up, the Act I set for Private Lives *is still getting into position.*

As described by Coward, "The scene is the terrace of a hotel in France. There are two French windows at the back opening onto two separate suites. The terrace space is divided by a line of small trees in tubs. For our purposes, the set should be extremely simple — and rather worn and tacky. [For a staging suggestion, see Note on Staging at end of the play.]

For a moment, the stage is empty. "There is an orchestra playing not very far off." Then Roz, playing Sibyl Chase, steps out onto the terrace. She looks very chic, à la 1920s. "She comes downstage, stretches her arms wide with a little sigh of satisfaction, and regards the view with an ecstatic expression."

ROZ: Elli, Elli dear, do come out. It's so lovely.

(She giggles happily. Pause. No one comes out. She looks worried, then catches herself. She smiles and gives a silvery laugh for the benefit of the audience.)

ROZ: . . . Oh do come out, Elli. It really is so . . . lovely out here. Just . . . wonderfully, beautifully . . . lovely.

(Silence. Nothing happens.)

ROZ: . . . Ell-i! Elli, can you hear me, darling? I do wish you'd join me so we could look at all this loveliness together. *(Roz laughs gaily. Still nothing happens.)*

ROZ: . . . *Elli, would you please get the hell out here!!*

(Silence.)

ROZ: . . . Well. That man . . . I suppose he's still getting into his smoking jacket. Perhaps he had to put it out first. *(She laughs that silvery laugh; pause.)* . . . Smoking . . . jacket. *(Pause.)* Well. I suppose I can just . . . stand here and look at the lights of that yacht reflected in the water. My God, I'd like to be on that boat . . . And if you were here, Elli, you would probably just . . . burst through that door, full of . . . *joie de vivre,* and-and *je ne sais quoi,* and . . . *que sera sera,* and say something terribly witty, like . . . "Not so bad!" *(She laughs gaily at his witty remark.)* And I would say . . . you mustn't be blasé about honeymoons, darling, just because this is your second. And you'd get very annoyed, and then I'd apologize and ask you to kiss me. Three times, because I'm superstitious. *(She laughs gaily, then glances into the wings and calls.)* Elli?! If you're not coming out, darling, perhaps we should all just go home!

(She starts to exit.)

GEORGE: *(Off.) I'm coming!*

(And she reenters.)

ROZ: Oh, thank God I mean my God I'm a happy girl . . . Now let's see, where was I . . . ?

(During the following, George strolls drunkenly, with confidence, out onto the balcony dressed as Cyrano, complete with large nose, long flowing hair, rouge, moustache, leather knee boots, sword, etc. His costume and makeup are badly askew, and he's clearly drunker than ever.)

ROZ: I asked you to come out and see how lovely it is, to which you would no doubt reply, "Not so bad," and then I would turn, and gaze out, over the balcony, feeling tremendously happy, and say . . . *(She sees him and screams.) Aaaahhhh!*

GEORGE: *(Looking around to see what scared her.)* What's the matter? What happened?

ROZ: Elli . . . Elli, darling! How wonderful! You-you-you-you-you remembered, about the *costume party*!

GEORGE: I did?

ROZ: But what are you doing in your costume *now*, darling?

GEORGE: *(Taking this as his cue.)* "What would you have me do?! Hanh?! Seek for the patronage of some great man, And like a creeping vine on a tall tree crawl upward where I cannot stand alone?! No thank you!"

ROZ: *(Laughing gaily.)* No. Thank *you*, Elli —

GEORGE: "But to sing, to laugh, to dream . . ."

ROZ: *All right, Elli, that's enough!!!* . . . I mean, it's wonderful that you remembered about the party, and-and now that you're *in* your costume, there's simply no reason we cannot just . . . stand here as if you *weren't* in your costume and chatter on about anything we please. For example: just look at the lights of that yacht reflected in the water. Oh dear, I'm so happy. Aren't you? I mean, just to think, here we are, you and I, married.
(No response. George has fallen asleep standing up. His head lolls on his chest and he starts to snore loudly. Roz is stunned.)

ROZ: Elli? . . . Elli? . . . *ELLI!!!*
(She stamps on his foot.)

GEORGE: *Owwww!!!*

ROZ: You mustn't be blasé about honeymoons, Elli, just because this is your second.

GEORGE: Ow! Ow! Ow! Ow!

ROZ: Have I annoyed you by saying that?

GEORGE: Saying *what*?!

ROZ: *(Giving him every signal she can think of.)* About our honeymoon, darling! Here in the south of France. At this beautiful hotel, with the two balconies, where we can lead such *private lives*.

GEORGE: . . . *Private Lives*?

ROZ: That's right, dear. *Private Lives*!

GEORGE: *(Looks around at the set and finally gets it.)* . . . Holy shit!

ROZ: *(Gaily, mortified.)* Elli! Darling! Such language!

GEORGE: I'm in the wrong costume!
(And he starts to pull it off.)

ROZ: *No!* Elli, it's *fine*! You were at a *costume party*!

GEORGE: Wait! Stay here! I'll be right back!

(He exits into the wings.)

ROZ: Elli, no! Don't leave me! . . . *Elli!!*

(And she runs off after him, leaving the stage empty. Pause. Then we hear Charlotte in the wings.)

CHARLOTTE: *(Off.)* Paul! Quick! Get the hell out there!

(Paul comes barrelling out of the wings, obviously pushed by Charlotte. He's playing Victor Prynne, Amanda's handsome new husband. He's wearing a tuxedo and a false moustache. He sees the audience and quickly stands up very straight and smiles broadly.)

PAUL: *(Calling.)* . . . "Mandy!"

CHARLOTTE: *(Off.)* "What?"

PAUL: "Come outside, darling, the view is wonderful."

(Charlotte enters as Amanda Prynne. As Coward describes her, "She is quite exquisite with a gay face and a perfect figure.")

CHARLOTTE: "Oh, Victor, Victor darling, I'm still damp from the bath. I shall catch pneumonia, that's what I shall catch."

PAUL: "God!"

CHARLOTTE: "I beg your pardon?"

PAUL: "You look wonderful."

CHARLOTTE: "Thank you, Victor darling."

PAUL: "Like a beautiful advertisement for something."

CHARLOTTE: "Nothing peculiar, I hope."

PAUL: "I can hardly believe it's true. You and I, here alone together, married!"

(They're starting to kiss, when George reels onto the stage, bellowing, with Roz running after him.)

GEORGE: *Where the hell is my dressing room! I can't find the frigging dressing room!*

ROZ: Daddy! *(Then she sees the audience.)* . . . Elyot! *(George staggers off, and Roz runs after him.)* Elyot, come back here!!

(And they're gone. Charlotte and Paul watch George and Roz go off, then turn around very slowly back to the audience.)

CHARLOTTE: I knew we should have gone to a better hotel.

(Paul, as Victor, laughs immoderately; then:)

CHARLOTTE: It's your turn.

PAUL: ". . . Tell me, darling, is it true that you love me more than you loved Elyot?"

CHARLOTTE: "I don't remember. It's such a long time ago, Paul."

(They both react to the wrong name.)

CHARLOTTE: "Victor! . . . Paul-Victor, to use your full name. Wait! I have an idea, Paul-Victor. I think we should leave here immediately and go straight to Paris!"

(They start to exit at a run, when George enters coming toward them, trying to pull his fly up.)

GEORGE: *Would you look at this! I can't get the frigging zipper down! What if I had to pee?! Huh?!*

ROZ: *(Running on after him.)* Daddy!

CHARLOTTE: Oh I give up.

PAUL: What?

CHARLOTTE: I give up!

PAUL: Amanda, darling!

CHARLOTTE: Oh, be quiet.

PAUL: I beg your pardon?

CHARLOTTE: I said *be quiet!*

GEORGE: *(Turning at the sound of Charlotte's voice.)* . . . Oh my God, Charlotte, you're back!

ROZ: *(Valiantly trying to stay in character.)* "Charlotte"? That isn't "Charlotte," dear. Could that be Amanda your first wife?

PAUL: *(The same.)* Then you must be Sibyl, Elyot's second wife.

ROZ: Which means that you're Victor, Amanda's second husband —

CHARLOTTE: *Would you all just shut up!* Can't you see they haven't the slightest idea what's going on?! *(Pointing to the audience.)* They think we're insane up here!

ROZ: *(Not one to give up.)* Do you mean up here on the balcony?

PAUL: I love it up here. Just look at the lights of that yacht reflected in the water.

(At which point, Ethel enters, dressed to the nines as a 1920s dowager, complete with tiara.)

ETHEL: *(Very grand, very British.)* Excuse me, but I'm looking for my son, Elyot, who has a tendency to dress up like Cyrano de Bergerac.

CHARLOTTE: Oh, God . . .

ETHEL: You know the English. He used to dress up like Roxane.

CHARLOTTE: Mother!

ETHEL: *(Deaf.)* What?

CHARLOTTE: *Mother, what are you doing?*

ETHEL: *(Confidentially.)* I thought I should try to straighten things out, if it's not too late.

CHARLOTTE: *(Hysterical.)* Of course it's too late! They all know!

ETHEL: *(Deaf.)* What?!

CHARLOTTE: *(Pointing to the audience.)* I said *everybody knows*!!!

GEORGE: *(As Cyrano.)* . . . "Nose"? . . . Did you say "*nose*"?

ROZ: Daddy! Elyot!

GEORGE: "Magnificent, My nose! You pug, you knob, you button head."

CHARLOTTE: *(Finally cracking, she screams and runs at George, wanting to choke the life out of him.)* Aaaahhh!!!

GEORGE: "Genial, courteous, intellectual, virile, courageous — as I am —"

CHARLOTTE: *Shut up shut up shut up shut up shut up!*

> *(As Charlotte tries to strangle him, George grabs her hair and unintentionally pulls off her 1920s wig. Underneath, she wears a stocking cap with a little knot on top. After a moment, she realizes what's happened and screams. At which point, Howard, who has escaped from the closet, enters hopping. He's hopping because he's tied up with a rope. However, his lungs work fine, and as he hops across the stage, he screams.)*

HOWARD: *Help!! Police!! Call the police!!*

> *(Charlotte pulls her wig back on as best she can and beams at the audience, as Howard hops onto the balcony.)*

ROZ: *(Rushing to him.)* Howard! Darling! What happened?!

PAUL: "Darling"? What do you mean "darling"?

ROZ: Who did this to you?!

HOWARD: He did it! Him!

ROZ: Paul?!

PAUL: Why the hell did you call him "darling"?!

ROZ: Because he's my fiancé!

CHARLOTTE: Oh my God! She's marrying *Frank Capra*!!

GEORGE: *(Waving his sword with a grand flourish.)*

> "Hark, how the steel rings musical!
> Mark how my point floats, light as the foam,
> Ready to drive you back to the wall —"

> *(Acting his heart out, George climbs onto the front of the balcony.)*

CHARLOTTE: *George! Stop!*

ROZ: *Daddy!*

CHARLOTTE: George!

PAUL: *George!*

ROZ: *Daddeeeee!*

GEORGE: "Then, as I end the refrain, thrust home!"

> *(On his final thrust, there's a blackout, and we hear him fall into the orchestra pit with a crash. In the transition to Scene Three, as the scenery changes, pan-*

demonium breaks loose. In silhouette, we see Howard hopping around in circles and then off, while everyone else onstage reacts to George's fall.)

ROZ: Call a doctor! Is there a doctor in the house?!

PAUL: Call an ambulance!

CHARLOTTE: *(Into the pit.)* George, can you hear me?!

ROZ: He's moving! Daddy!

PAUL: *(To Roz.)* Would you call the ambulance?!

ROZ: All right!

PAUL: I'll go underneath!

(Roz and Paul exit in different directions. Charlotte is reaching into the pit.)

CHARLOTTE: George, take my hand!

(We see George's hand reaching desperately out of the pit. Charlotte just manages to get a hold of it.)

CHARLOTTE: Reach! Farther! A little farther!

(They almost make it . . . but don't — and George hits the bottom of the pit with another crash.)

CHARLOTTE: *(Calling into the pit.)* Stay where you are! Don't move!

(Charlotte hurries off. Ethel follows her.)

ETHEL: *(To George, as she exits.)* You're right where you belong. In the pit.

(And they're gone. By now, the greenroom has reappeared. Order sets in, along with a depressing sense of peace.)

SCENE THREE

The greenroom, about two hours later. The stage is empty for a moment; then we hear voices from outside.

ROZ: *(Off.)* Careful, Daddy.

PAUL: *(Off.)* Watch your step.

ROZ: *(Off.)* Careful!

(The street door opens, and George enters, followed by Roz and Paul. George is still wearing his Cyrano costume, but he's using a cane and looks like he's been through a war. His head is bandaged, and wisps of hair are sticking out from under the gauze. He is not a happy man. In fact, all three of them are pretty low. Pause.)

GEORGE: I have never been so depressed in my whole life.

ROZ: Oh, Daddy

GEORGE: I'd commit suicide, but nobody would notice.

(George sits heavily on the sofa.)

ROZ: You know what the worst part is? As awful as it was, I actually enjoyed being onstage again.

PAUL: I knew you would.

ROZ: Oh be quiet.

GEORGE: What happened after I fell off the stage? Dare I ask?

PAUL: Well, for a second, after you hit the ground, there was dead silence. Then the audience burst into applause. They thought it was part of the show.

ROZ: Then Mother and I started screaming for a doctor, and some man hurried down the aisle. We asked him what kind of doctor he was, and he said he was a veterinarian.

PAUL: That got a big laugh.

ROZ: Then the ambulance arrived.

PAUL: Then the police arrived.

ROZ: Then Howard had to be sedated.

PAUL: Then we all went to the hospital.

ROZ: And that's about it.

(Pause.)

GEORGE: "Howard"?

ROZ: My fiancé. The one you gagged and locked in the closet.

GEORGE: Ah. And how is your mother taking all this excitement?

(Paul and Roz glance at each other.)

PAUL: . . . She's leaving with Richard this afternoon.

ROZ: I'm sorry, Daddy.

(Long pause. They all look miserable. Then George begins to chuckle. Something about this day from hell strikes him as being funny. He starts to laugh out loud. He stops himself. Then bursts out laughing again. He can't help it.)

PAUL: . . . Why does the word "straitjacket" come to mind?

ROZ: Daddy, what's wrong?

GEORGE: Can you imagine the look on Capra's face when I walked out onstage as Cyrano?! He came all the way from New York for that!

(He howls with laughter; Roz and Paul start laughing, too; it's infectious.)

GEORGE: *He must have thought we were out of our minds!!*

(All three of them are laughing now. Then Charlotte walks in from backstage, carrying an overnight bag. They see her and stop laughing.)

CHARLOTTE: I'm leaving you, George.

GEORGE: *(Very sober.)* Yes, I know.

(Beat. Then George, Roz, and Paul burst out laughing. They can't help it. Charlotte, offended, heads for the door to the street.)

GEORGE: Charlotte, wait! I want to talk to you!

CHARLOTTE: There's nothing to talk about.

GEORGE: Of course there is! Please. Just five minutes.

PAUL: *(To Roz, taking her arm.)* Come on. Let's go.

ROZ: Don't touch me.

PAUL: Sorry.

ROZ: *(To Charlotte.)* Don't hurt him, Mother. He has stitches.

(Paul and Roz exit.)

CHARLOTTE: I'll give you one minute, George.

GEORGE: Charlotte, I know how disappointed you are about the movie. And so am I. But is it really that important?

(She looks at her watch.)

CHARLOTTE: Forty-five seconds.

GEORGE: Oh, stop it. You can't just leave. And you certainly can't go off with Richard. You would die prematurely. He would bore you to death.

CHARLOTTE: At least he's stable. Mentally.

GEORGE: What good is that if you're bored, for God's sake!

CHARLOTTE: Fifteen seconds.

GEORGE: Would you stop that!

CHARLOTTE: George, I'm sorry, but I have to go

GEORGE: Think, woman! Think for a minute! Use your brain! Think of all the fun we have together. Rambling from town to town like minor royalty. Signing autographs, doing interviews. My God, you'll be laughing about my entrance as Cyrano for months! And think of the joy you give to thousands of people every week. As Amanda and Roxane. Lady Bracknell and Eliza Doolittle. You're an actress, Charlotte. It's in your veins. If you were caught in the spotlight of a runaway train, you'd break into a time step. It's a gift to be that reckless and insane. There are people out there in the darkness who are living through you. Dreaming of what they can be through your voice. Are you really going to turn your back on them because you lost a measly role in a film?

CHARLOTTE: . . . You give me a pain, George.

GEORGE: I know I do. I'm sorry. I can't help it. But I do love you, Charlotte. I haven't the faintest idea why. But the thought of living without you terrifies me.

(Long pause. Charlotte just looks at him. Then her face crinkles up, and she

starts to cry. She looks and sounds like a sweet little girl who is crying because she can't have all the candy in the window. This is the real Charlotte breaking through at last.)

CHARLOTTE: I wanted to be a movie star!

(She sobs on George's shoulder.)

GEORGE: *(Comforting her.)* I know you did.

CHARLOTTE: I wanted to be rich and famous. I wanted everybody to admire me!

GEORGE: I admire you.

CHARLOTTE: Oh, George, we were so *close!* We almost made it. After all these years!

GEORGE: There will be other movies.

CHARLOTTE: No there won't. That was our last chance and you know it. Oh . . . crap!

GEORGE: Perhaps we're not meant to be movie stars. Isn't it nice to know our limitations?

CHARLOTTE: No. I hate it.

GEORGE: I find it rather comforting, now that I think about it.

CHARLOTTE: I don't. I despise it. And I hate getting older. I'm starting to look like Ed Sullivan.

GEORGE: You're as beautiful now as the day we met. No. I take it back. You're more beautiful.

CHARLOTTE: You have glaucoma.

GEORGE: *(Shakes his head.)* Cataracts.

(They kiss. As they're kissing, Richard enters from the street and sees them.)

RICHARD: Oh. I take it this means we're not running off together.

CHARLOTTE: Oh, Richard. I'm so sorry. You must think I'm hateful.

RICHARD: No, no.

CHARLOTTE: Can you *ever* forgive me?

RICHARD: Well . . .

CHARLOTTE: You know I love you, but just in a different way.

RICHARD: I like his way better.

(At this moment, Roz enters, chased by Paul.)

ROZ: Paul, stop it!

PAUL: You're in love with me and you know it!

ROZ: I am not!

(By which time, Howard has entered through the street door.)

HOWARD: Roz . . . ?

ROZ: Howard, darling, how are you feeling?

HOWARD: Well, I'm-I'm better, I think, but —

GEORGE: Young man, I owe you a profound apology.

HOWARD: That's okay, I just . . .

CHARLOTTE: He thought you were someone else entirely.

ROZ: I still think it's unforgivable.

PAUL: It was a mistake! *(To Howard.)* Did I say I was sorry?

HOWARD: *Would you all just be quiet!!! (Silence.)* I'd like to say something.

CHARLOTTE: Please do.

GEORGE: Absolutely.

> *(George and Charlotte sit quietly.)*

HOWARD: Roz. I can't go through with it.

ROZ: Howard.

HOWARD: It's too much pressure! I mean, I'm sure it's just me, but . . . I've never been gagged and locked in a closet before.

ROZ: It was a mistake.

HOWARD: I know, but . . . well something else happened. I met this girl, and we went to the cafeteria, for some jello, and then it just "happened." It was like magic. We sort of knew.

> *(At this moment, Eileen enters through the street door.)*

EILEEN: Howard, honey. The cab is waiting. We'll miss the train.

HOWARD: Okay, right. I'll be right there.

> *(Shocked silence. They all gape at Howard and Eileen.)*

GEORGE: Eileen?

EILEEN: *(To Howard.)* You didn't tell them yet, did you?

HOWARD: I was just, you know, starting.

ROZ: Howard?

HOWARD: Well . . . this is a funny story . . . We, uh, we met at the hospital. I mean, we didn't "meet" there, we went steady in high school. Here in Buffalo. Anyway, we started talking, and it was like, oh my God, she's so *normal*! *(Eileen takes his hand.)* So.

EILEEN: Couldn't you just eat him up?

HOWARD: And hey, you know what the best part is? *(To Eileen.)* You tell 'em.

EILEEN: Go ahead.

HOWARD: Well . . . she wants to start a family *right away*!

> *(Everyone is stunned. Eileen looks sheepish. Howard looks proud.)*

GEORGE: . . . What a good idea!

CHARLOTTE: George!

GEORGE: No, wait. Just listen. *(The patriarch, putting his arms around them.)* Children. My children. Eileen. Horace.

HOWARD: Howard.

GEORGE: Howard. Speaking for myself and Mrs. Hay, perhaps you would do us the honor of making us the godparents of your firstborn.

CHARLOTTE: And remember: the first one is always early.

(Charlotte carefully avoids everyone's eyes.)

HOWARD: Gee.

EILEEN: I'd like that George, I really would.

GEORGE: So would I.

(From the street, we hear a taxi honking its horn impatiently.)

HOWARD: Oh my gosh, we've got to run. Bye-bye.

(Good-byes all around.)

HOWARD: *(Shaking Roz's hand.)* I'm sorry.

ROZ: *(Glum, but trying.)* That's all right. Have a safe trip.

HOWARD: Oh we'll be fine. There's a low-pressure area over the whole Northeast . . . so we should be seeing sunny skies right through the weekend!

(Howard and Eileen exit, wonderfully in love. Pause. Roz has never felt quite this discouraged before.)

ROZ: . . . I guess I shouldn't have come back.

PAUL: *(Bitter.)* And you wouldn't have if you'd known I was here. You said it four times.

(Paul starts to put on his sports coat and leave, as George looks up.)

GEORGE: Roz?

ROZ: Daddy, stay out of this.

GEORGE: Rosalind . . . I told you last week on the phone that Paul was here.

ROZ: Did you? I guess I forgot.

PAUL: You "forgot"?

ROZ: Yeah, I forgot! I have a lousy memory! Okay?!

PAUL: *(He gets it.)* . . . Hey. Come here.

ROZ: No. *(He walks to her, but she backs away.)* Paul!

PAUL: I think our first play together should be *Much Ado About Nothing.*

ROZ: *(Overlapping.)* Paul, stay away from me

PAUL: And then *She Stoops to Conquer,* and *Arms and the Man.*

(He picks her up . . .)

ROZ: *(Overlapping.)* Paul! Put me down! Paul, stop it!

(. . . and kisses her. She throws her arms around him.)

ROZ: Oh, Paul . . .

CHARLOTTE: *(Touched, she takes George's hand.)* Oh, George . . .

RICHARD: I find this totally revolting.

GEORGE: Family. My dearest family. I would like to make an announcement.

(Ethel enters from backstage.)

ETHEL: That wasn't a matinee, it was a national disaster.

CHARLOTTE: Mother.

ETHEL: What?

CHARLOTTE: *George* is *making one of his speeches.*

ETHEL: How exciting. Call the UN.

GEORGE: . . . There comes a moment in every man's life when it is time to step aside and pass the torch on to the younger generation. This, I believe, is such a season for George and Charlotte Hay. *(To Roz and Paul.)* To the two of you we hereby present Romeo and his Juliet, Hamlet and Ophelia, Beatrice and her Benedick, those younger roles that your mother and I have now outgrown.

CHARLOTTE: Speak for yourself, dear.

GEORGE: In the words of the man from Stratford:
"This rough magic
I here abjure; and when I have required
Some heavenly music (which even now I do)
I'll break my staff,
Bury it certain fathoms in the earth,
And deeper than did ever plummet sound
I'll drown my book."

(The phone rings, and Ethel, who is next to it, picks it up.)

ETHEL: Greenroom, hams to go . . . What? . . . *What?* . . . "Frank"? . . . Frank who?! . . . *(She listens hard, then shakes her head with disgust.)* I can't hear a word he's saying.

(And she starts to hang up the phone . . .)

EVERYONE ELSE: *No!!!*

(Charlotte, who is closest to Ethel, snatches the receiver from her.)

CHARLOTTE: Hello?! . . . Yes it is . . . *(All charm.)* Well, how do you do . . . Yes, he is . . . I see . . . Well, that's lovely. *(Caressing the phone.)* . . Right . . . Right . . . Uh-huh . . . Good-bye.

(She hangs up. She's so excited, she can hardly speak.)

CHARLOTTE: . . . Frank Capra. He said his plane was delayed, and he did not see the matinee. But he's in Buffalo now, at his hotel, and he plans to attend tonight's performance.

(Shocked silence.)

GEORGE: . . . Oh my God.

PAUL: *(Murmurs.)* Tonight . . . ?

ROZ: *(Taking his hand.)* Oh, Paul.

(Silence. Then.)

RICHARD: I really hate to ask you this . . . but which play are you doing?

CHARLOTTE: *Private Lives.*

GEORGE: No, *Cyrano*!

ROZ: . . . *Oh, no!*

(Everyone starts talking at once, the lines overlapping, as the curtain falls.)

GEORGE: *Cyrano!* Of course it's *Cyrano*!

CHARLOTTE: *Private Lives* is better for both of us!

PAUL: It has to be *Cyrano*!

ROZ: *Private Lives!* I have nothing in *Cyrano*!

ETHEL: I wonder who "Frank" is.

RICHARD: Definitely *Private Lives.*

(They continue arguing, as the curtain falls.)

END OF PLAY

NOTE ON STAGING

On Broadway, we had a fairly complex set, so that the "onstage" *Cyrano* scene at the opening of the play was played several feet above the actual stage. Ethel entered on the higher level; then she walked through a hole in the upper floor and down a flight of stairs to the greenroom. Simultaneously, the raked floor of the upper stage rotated upward to form the ceiling of the greenroom. This is obviously too expensive for most productions, and the transition from stage to greenroom can more easily be accomplished in a number of ways.

One way is to have the battle onstage occur behind a scrim. Smoke and lighting will disguise the fact that we're actually on the greenroom set. Then, as Ethel leaves the "stage," simply raise the scrim and alter the lighting to reveal the greenroom.

Another way is to cover the greenroom furniture with drop cloths. Have Ethel walk off into the wings after her first line. Then, after the drop cloths have been removed, she can walk back on through one of the doors to the greenroom reciting her lines from *Cyrano*.

The change of set to *Private Lives* at the opening of Act II, Scene Two can also be accomplished easily. All that is needed are some plastic shrubs in pots to separate the terraces and a simple railing to mark the edge of the terrace. If possible, a drop curtain at the back to hide the greenroom and indicate the hotel would be helpful. This is essentially what we did on Broadway.

LEADING LADIES

Pictured (L–R): Brent Barrett (Leo), Chris Duva (Jack)

ORIGINAL PRODUCTION

Leading Ladies had its world premiere on October 15, 2004, at the Alley Theatre, Houston: Gregory Boyd, artistic director, in association with the Cleveland Playhouse; Peter Hackett, artistic director; Dean R. Gladden, managing director. The scenic designer was Neil Patel, the costume designer was Judith Dolan, the lighting designer was Davie Weiner, the sound designer was John Gromada, and the associate sound designer was Ryan Rumery. The choreographer was Michael Tapley, the stage manager was Terry Crenshaw, and the assistant stage manager was Amy Liljegren. It was directed by Ken Ludwig with the following cast:

MEG	Erin Dilly
LEO	Brent Barrett
JACK	Christopher Duva
AUDREY	Lacey Kohl
DUNCAN	Mark Jacoby
FLORENCE	Jane Connell
DOC	Dan Lauria
BUTCH	Tim McGeever

AUTHOR'S PREFACE

The genesis of *Leading Ladies* was simple. The Broadway production of *The Adventures of Tom Sawyer* had just opened, and I did not have an idea yet for my next play. When I am in this position, I frequently wander to my bookshelf, pick up a book that evokes a good memory, and try to think very, very hard. On this particular day, I picked up *The Adventures of Huckleberry Finn*, and Mark Twain whispered to me and gave me a plot.

As you will recall, in the novel there are two characters known as the Duke and the King. They are con men posing as English royalty who are also, they say, Shakespearean actors. In one of their scams, they pose as two long-lost Englishmen who turn up in a small town to claim the inheritance of their "brother's" estate — and if they succeed in their scheme, they will end up cheating the "brother's" niece out of her money. I borrowed this story for the plot of *Leading Ladies*, then, about halfway through the writing, decided on the gender switch. From that moment on, I thought of the play as *Some Like It Hot* meets *The Beaux' Stratagem*.

Gender switching has, of course, a venerable tradition in the theater. First, there were the boy actors of Shakespeare's day who played all the women's roles as a matter of law and custom. Not surprisingly, the women that they played often pulled on a pair of trousers and played young men as part of the plot — hence Viola in *Twelfth Night* playing Caesario and Rosalind in *As You Like It* playing Ganymede. This tradition of "trouser roles" then became a staple of plays and operas for centuries, from Farquhar's *The Recruiting Officer* to Mozart's *The Marriage of Figaro* to J.M. Barrie's *Peter Pan*.*

More to the point in this case are the plays where male characters put on dresses and pretend to be women. This, too, has a long theatrical history but occurs less frequently. Shakespeare does it once, when Falstaff dresses as the Old Woman of Brentford in *The Merry Wives of Windsor,* and Ben Jonson does it in *Epicoene*. David Garrick, the most famous actor of the eighteenth century, was renowned for playing one such role, Sir John Brute, in *The Provoked Wife* by John Vanbrugh. And in the twentieth century, the custom is touched upon in Thornton Wilder's *The Matchmaker* and Tom Stoppard's *On the Razzle*

---

*There are actually two "trouser role" traditions. In one of the them, as in *The Recruiting Officer*, a female character impersonates a male character within the context of the play. In the other tradition, as in *The Marriage of Figaro* and *Peter Pan*, a female *actor* plays a male character for the entire duration of the play or opera.

(both derived from the same source). Most familiar of all of course is Brandon Thomas's *Charley's Aunt*, which has been popular on the stage for over a hundred years. Putting pencil to paper on *Leading Ladies,* I was very aware of *Charley's Aunt*, but I also knew that aside from that aunt (and from those Prohibition floozies Josephine and Geraldine in the film *Some Like It Hot*), the field was pretty clear, so I held my breath and plunged in headfirst.

• • •

The premiere of *Leading Ladies* was coproduced by the Alley Theatre in Houston, Texas, and the Cleveland Play House, and we had a sterling cast headed by the wonderful Brent Barrett. Among the cast was Jane Connell, who for many years was one of my chief muses.

Jane Connell made her name in *New Faces of 1956* and starred as the original Agnes Gooch in the musical *Mame*. Along with Carol Burnett and Jan Maxwell, she is one of the greatest natural comedians I have ever met. (Ironically, Carol starred as Princess Winnifred on Broadway in the musical *Once Upon a Mattress,* and Jane starred in the same role in the West End in London.) Jane came into my life playing Julia in the Broadway production of *Lend Me A Tenor.* She then played Mrs. Child on Broadway in *Crazy For You;* then the Widow Douglas on Broadway in *The Adventures of Tom Sawyer* (where she knocked the audience for a loop in her second-act duet with Huck Finn, played endearingly by Jim Poulos); then I wrote the role of Florence in *Leading Ladies* for her.

While we were in rehearsal for *Leading Ladies* in Houston, Jane stumbled over one of her lines and, upset with herself, pulled me aside and told me that because of her age and her ageing memory, this would be the last play she would ever do. "It's been a great honor and God bless you," she said definitively, and bustled back to rehearsal. From then on she started using individual note cards for each of her lines. She worried endlessly that she would forget a line and hurt a scene; but needless to say, by opening night she stole the show. She never *ever* missed a laugh once she had figured out how to get it. When the run of the show ended, she returned to her wonderful family in New York, and a few months later I learned that she had had a stroke. As of this writing, her husband, the fine actor Gordon Connell, tells me that Jane is full of life and on the mend. My mission is now clear, which is to write a new play for her.

• • •

Of the plays in this volume, *Leading Ladies* is the only one I directed in its world premiere, and I enjoyed it immensely. My thanks to Gregory Boyd for making the suggestion and to the Alley Theatre and the Cleveland Play House for making it possible. Greg has been artistic director at the Alley for many years, and the Alley values him for the jewel that he is. My thanks also to the wonderfully creative Peter Hackett, who was the artistic director at the Cleveland Play House at the time of the production. —*KL*

CHARACTERS

MEG, a local heiress
LEO, an actor
JACK, an actor
AUDREY, Meg's friend
DUNCAN, Meg's fiancé, a minister
FLORENCE, Meg's aunt
DOC, Florence's doctor
BUTCH, Doc's son

PLACE AND TIME

The play, essentially, has one set, and the majority of the action takes place in the large, handsome living room of the biggest house in York, Pennsylvania, in 1958. The room has large French doors up right leading out to a garden. We can see the patio and shrubbery through the glass. Double doors down left lead to the vestibule, a hall, and the front door. Double doors down right lead to the kitchen and additional rooms. There is a grand staircase that leads, at the top, to a bedroom door and a landing that leads off left. Under the staircase, up center, is an open doorway that leads to additional rooms. As we'll find out, all these rooms are interconnected offstage. It's a grand house with a second staircase that we can't see.

Scene two of the first act is set in the Shrewsbury, Pennsylvania, Moose Lodge — an area of stage in front of a curtain. Scene three of the first act is set inside a train, and all we see are two seats and an aisle.

ACT I
Scene One: Florence's living room
Scene Two: The Moose Lodge, an hour and a half later
Scene Three: A train car, the next morning
Scene Four: A telephone call, an hour later
Scene Five: The living room, that evening

ACT II
Scene One: The living room, three days later, late afternoon
Scene Two: The living room, ten days later, midmorning
Scene Three: The living room, ten days later, evening

LEADING LADIES

ACT I

SCENE ONE

The handsome, spacious living room of a beautiful, well-appointed house in York, Pennsylvania, in the spring of 1958.

York is a quiet town in an area of gently rolling hills in southern Pennsylvania known as the Amish country. York was once, briefly, the capital of the United States, during the American Revolution, when the Articles of Confederation were kept here after Congress left Philadelphia under threat of invasion. So it's old country, proud country, settled by the English and the Germans, the latter bringing with them a plain-spoken, plain-dressed brand of religion that has been here ever since. The food here is rich and deep, the farmland outside town is magnificent, and the people have a great tradition of music. The point of all this is that York is filled with good, wise people, many of whom are happy to be just where they are — but some of whom would love to see the world just over the horizon.

As the lights come up, Meg Snider, dressed to go out for the evening, enters at the top of the stairs. She looks around and sees no one below; then she hurries down the stairs to the French doors that open out to the garden. As she makes the turn at the bottom corner of the banister, she swoops around in a grand arc, full of joy and anticipation.

Meg is a local girl in her early thirties. She's vivacious, with enormous warmth and a great sense of humor. She also has the fresh, unstudied beauty that most women would kill for. Meg, however, is that second kind of Yorker. She knows there's a big world outside York, but she hasn't seen much of it yet. She harbors a world of dreams and sleeps on them every night. They keep her alive, but she doesn't know it.

MEG: Duncan? . . . Duncan?!

DUNCAN: *(Off.)* Coming!

MEG: Oh, Duncan, please hurry up! It's five-thirty! And it takes at least forty-five minutes to get to Shrewsbury. And the show starts at seven!

(Duncan Wooley enters, fixing his clerical collar. He's the local minister and

substantially older than Meg. He's a good man at heart, but rather fussy, set in his ways, a bit scatterbrained, and lives in his own world.)

DUNCAN: Meg, I'm moving as fast as I can. I normally don't go out in the evenings. You know that. I can't get organized. I-I can't find things . . .

MEG: I'm sorry, Duncan, but —

DUNCAN: I hope you're not going to rush me after we get married.

MEG: Of course not, but I —

DUNCAN: It's not as if I don't want to get married. But I don't like rushing. It's almost . . . un-Christian the way you do it.

MEG: Is it? I'm sorry.

DUNCAN: Kiss kiss?

MEG: Kiss kiss.

(They kiss lightly.)

But Duncan, we can't be late for this!

DUNCAN: If you want the truth, I don't particularly want to go anyway.

MEG: How can you say that?! It's Shakespeare! "Scenes from Shakespeare"! How often do we get a chance like this, living in York, Pennsylvania?

DUNCAN: Not very often, thank the Lord.

MEG: Duncan!

DUNCAN: Who's in this again?

MEG: It stars these two really wonderful actors from England. Leo Clark and Jack Gable. I saw them do a show like this in Philadelphia about two years ago. Don't you remember? I told you about it.

DUNCAN: Did you?

MEG: Oh, they were so wonderful! And to hear that language just . . . rolling over you in wave after wave. Oh. I think I love the theater more than anything in the whole world.

DUNCAN: Nonsense.

MEG: I do!

DUNCAN: Meg. Theater *can* be wonderful of course. At times. When it's something like the York County Bell-Ringers Annual Easter Pageant. Or *The Messiah* when they bring real sheep onstage. But there's something rather . . . troubling about professional theater. The people in it are so . . . theatrical.

MEG: Duncan —

DUNCAN: So loose and flamboyant.

MEG: That's not how I —

DUNCAN: Now take these actors of yours. What are they called again?

MEG: Clark and Gable.

DUNCAN: Right.

MEG: They're fantastic.

DUNCAN: Meg, they're playing at the Shrewsbury Moose Lodge. They can't be *that* "fantastic."

MEG: Well they must have had an open date on their touring schedule, but —

DUNCAN: You know, the church has never looked very kindly upon play-going as a phenomenon, as a way of —

MEG: Duncan, please! Can we go now?! It's late! And you promised!

DUNCAN: All right, all right! I'll start the car.

(He starts to exit, then walks right back to Meg.)

DUNCAN: Problem.

MEG: What?

DUNCAN: Big problem.

MEG: What is it?

DUNCAN: We don't have a car.

MEG: What do you mean?

DUNCAN: *(Defensively.)* Well, I drove straight here from visiting some of my congregants, who are ill, and as I was getting out of the car, Mr. Morton walked by and told me that *his* car had broken down and he needed to buy groceries for his family — and take his wife to see her mother — and I said use my car, as long as you bring it back at the proper time.

MEG: So?

DUNCAN: I told him I didn't need it till eight. I just remembered.

MEG: Oh, Duncan!

DUNCAN: I'm sorry, my dear. It slipped my mind.

MEG: How could you do this?!

DUNCAN: I'm very sorry.

MEG: Now we'll miss it! I can't believe it! Oh *damn*!

DUNCAN: *(Scandalized.)* Meg!

MEG: Well I'm upset! I wanted to see Leo Clark!

DUNCAN: An actor.

MEG: Yes! Exactly!

DUNCAN: Now, now, we can still have fun. We can meet up with old friends and have dinner and chat. Ooh this could be good. I'll call the Kunkles. See if they're busy.

(He starts dialing.)

MEG: Duncan, the Kunkles are a hundred years old!

DUNCAN: Only Grandma Kunkle. And when she's awake, she's a riot. *HELLO?! IS THAT GRANDMA KUNKLE?!!*

MEG: Oh, Duncan . . .

(Meg sighs with frustration and collapses on the sofa.)

SCENE TWO

We hear a recording of "Happy Days Are Here Again" and a raucous crowd having a good time. We're in an auditorium in Shrewsbury, Pennsylvania, that night. Doctor Myers comes down the aisle, shaking hands with his friends and slapping their backs. He's the Chief Moose — a crusty, likeable curmudgeon, a country doctor who takes no guff from anybody. He wears the distinctive red fez of the Moose. He bounds onto the stage and starts the meeting.

DOC MYERS: Ladies and gentlemen . . . *Ladies and gentlemen!* Thank you and welcome to the June 1958 general meeting of the Loyal Order of the Moose, Shrewsbury Pennsylvania Lodge Number Eighty-four! *Awhoo!!* *("Awhoo" is the sound of the Moose. When Doc Myers does the call, the other Moose in the lodge call back to him.)*

DOC MYERS: We hope you're having a heck of a good time tonight, and that you're all looking forward to the very special buffet spread we have waiting for you tonight across the hall — prepared exclusively by Pyemyers Pastries and Pigtrotters. Their motto is: "We go the whole hog and use the whole hog." Thank you, Carl Pyemyer and family. Now tonight, I have the honor of presenting what you might call a "departure" from our usual monthly entertainment. In April, we gave you "Hee Haw Hocum," a night of ferocious fiddling and hillbilly hilarity that, as you'll remember, raised the roof and brought the house down. Then in May, we saw the one and only "Mister Presto," whose amazing feats of prestidigatorial perfection brought us standing to our feet. (Personally, I will never forget how he manipulated his eggs and made that sausage of his appear out of nowhere.) Well folks, tonight we're plowing some new ground and bringing you some very special entertainment, entitled, believe it or not, "Scenes from Shakespeare," starring two actors who hail from London, England, coming to us direct from their last engagement at the Elks of Scranton, please give a Moose Lodge welcome to *Leo Clark and Jack Gable*! *Awhoo!!*

(Awhoo!! As Doc exits, the curtain flies, the lights change — and we're on a battlefield in England in the 1400s. Trumpets sound! Banners wave! We hear the sounds of war and we see a flimsy castle in the distance! These effects, unfortunately, are a bit down-at-heel. This is, after all, a tour of one-nighters, not the RSC. So the banners are a bit ragged, the music a bit tinny, and the one piece of scenery, the castle, can be folded for traveling.

Henry the Fifth, played by Leo Clark, rushes on in full battle gear, waving his sword and rallying his troops. Leo is in his early forties and has a British accent.)

KING HARRY: *Once more unto the breach, dear friends, once more!*
    Or close the wall up with our English dead.
    In peace there's nothing so becomes a man
    As modest stillness and humility,
    But when the blast of war blows in our ears,
    Then imitate the action of the tiger!!

(Hotspur, Henry's mighty nemesis, played by Jack Gable, rushes on, out of breath and fresh from fighting. Note: The boys have conflated two different plays here, and I can only assure you that they're ashamed of it. Note also: "Ha!" denotes a thrust of the sword and its accompanying shout of valor.)

HOTSPUR: Hold up thy head, vile Scot!
    Thou art Harry Monmouth.

KING HARRY: And thou art Hotspur, the rebel lord who comes
    To take my throne.

HOTSPUR: A plague on both your houses! *Ha! Ha!*

KING HARRY: Stay back I say!

HOTSPUR: I will not yield, for now is the winter of thy discontent!

KING HARRY: And yet tomorrow and tomorrow and tomorrow
    Creeps in this petty pace from day to day
    To the last syllable of recorded time!
    Ha! Ha! Ha!
    (They fight, furiously, a pitched battle of swords and bucklers. It is rather thrilling.)

HOTSPUR: A horse, a horse, my kingdom for a horse!
    (Harry's final thrust skewers poor Hotspur.)

HOTSPUR: Oh, Harry, thou hast robbed me of my youth!
    (Hotspur dies.)

KING HARRY: . . . To be or not to be, that is the question.
    Whether tis nobler in the mind to suffer

The slings and arrows of outrageous fortune,

Or to take arms against a . . .

(Leo notices something in the audience. People are walking out, including one Moose named Frank, who is clattering out of the second row and up the aisle. We can tell that Frank is a Moose from the fez he wears. [Frank is doubled by the actor who plays Butch.] Leo has skipped a beat, but tries to go on, just a little louder.)

KING HARRY: *Whether tis nobler in the mind to suffer the slings and arrows of* where the hell are they going? They're walking out!

JACK: *(Opening an eye.)* They're heading to the buffet across the hall.

LEO: Hey! *Hey! Come back here! What's the matter with you people! We are giving a performance up here!*

MOOSE FRANK: *(From the aisle.)* It's boring! Go back where you came from!

LEO: Oh, really?! Well why don't *you* go back where *you* came from?!! *Huh?!*

MOOSE FRANK: This *is* where I came from, you idiot. I live here!

LEO: "Idiot"? He called me an "idiot"!

JACK: Leo —

LEO: *You're the idiot! You! That's right, you!*

MOOSE FRANK: *(Pulling his coat off.) Want to make something of it, buddy?!*

LEO: *(Climbing off the stage.) By God, I'll knock your block off!*

JACK: *(Grabbing him.)* Leo! Leo, stop! STOP IT!

(To Moose Frank:) He's sorry. Go. Eat. Have a good time. Leo, let's go.

LEO: *Ohhh, CRAP! Crap, crap, crap!!!*

JACK: *(Shaking his head.)* "Tomorrow and tomorrow and tomorrow . . . ?"

LEO: *(Rounding on the audience again.) What's the matter with you people?! Haven't you ever heard of* culture?! Huh?! Or civilization?!!

JACK: Leo!

LEO: Next time we'll bring a *stripper*!

(From the back of the auditorium, the men cheer.)

MEN: *(Off.)* YAY!

(As the boys exit, the lights fade quickly, and we hear the voice of a train conductor.)

CONDUCTOR: *All aboard! Pennsylvania Line, East Coast Local, stopping at Loganville, New Salem, York, Goldsboro, Harrisburg, and points North. Please watch your step entering the train. East Coast Local, all aboard!*

SCENE THREE

The lights come up inside an empty train car the next morning, as Jack and Leo enter carrying their suitcases.

LEO: Morons! They were complete and utter morons!

JACK: Leo —

LEO: What ever happened to *respect*?! Hmm? And-and-and *courtesy*?! I mean, didn't they even *look* at our flyers?! I put them in the lobby. With our best reviews! "Mesmerizing."

JACK: The *Mecklenberg Ledger.*

LEO: "Fascinating."

JACK: The *Beaver Falls Dispatch.*

LEO: *(Glares at Jack.)* "A powerhouse night of theater." The *New York Times.*

JACK: You made that one up.

LEO: Yes, I know, but it was on the flyer!

JACK: Leo, do you really want to do Shakespeare all your life?

LEO: Yes! I spent three years at the Royal Academy of Dramatic Art.

JACK: You told me you went there to meet women.

LEO: I did, but then I got interested. God, just look at us! It's been *ten years,* and we're still at the bottom. *Rock bottom!* I can feel my arse scraping on the little stones . . .

JACK: Do you know what I want? I mean really want? *(He's deadly serious now.)* Neighbors. A house. People who care if I open the front door in the morning.

LEO: Well . . . of course . . . But Jack we can still make it! As actors! All we need is a break! *(Suddenly galvanized, turning on a dime.)* And we're in luck. Finally! This morning I read in *Variety* that MGM is doing a movie version of *Julius Caesar.* In Los Angeles. They have James Mason as Brutus, John Gielgud as Cassius, and they're looking for more *Shakespearean actors.* This is made for us. I mean, how many Shakespearean actors do they have in America? Six? Now, how much do we have in the kitty? For the flight — as of right now?

JACK: Leo, we can't afford it.

LEO: Don't be negative! Just tell me. How much have we saved?

JACK: You don't want to know.

LEO: A thousand? Eight hundred. Six. Five? How much?!

JACK: Nothing.

LEO: No really.

JACK: We don't have a dime.

LEO: *(In shock.)* But — but — what about last night? Our show for the moose people?

JACK: They wouldn't pay us.

LEO: What?!

JACK: I went right up to the Great Yak. He said six of his members resigned at the buffet. One more soliloquy, he would have lost the herd.

LEO: Those . . . *cheaters!* Those-those-those *crooks.*

JACK: Maybe we should do a whole play next time, like we used to.

LEO: Oh, oh, oh that's a great idea! *Except we have no actors, it's just the two of us!* We have *seven costumes!* From *different plays!* In a pinch we could put on "One Gentleman of Verona"! "The Taming of the Merry *Wife* of Windsor"!

JACK: All right, all right . . .

LEO: "Much Ado About Hamlet"!

JACK: All right!

LEO: I just . . . I . . . I mean it's . . . it's just . . .

(He's in despair. Real despair. Jack feels awful for him.)

JACK: Would you like some breakfast? Maybe they have a café car.

LEO: *(Bitterly.)* We can't afford it. Remember?

JACK: I lied. I have a dollar left. It's on me.

(Jack exits. Leo is alone and despondent. After a moment, he notices a local newspaper on the train seat across the aisle. The York *Dispatch. He picks it up and glances at the front page. Then something catches his eye and he reads more carefully. The more he reads, the more absorbed he becomes. The story continues on the inside, and when he opens the paper, we see the headline on the front page: "Oh Max, Oh Steve!" Jack reenters.)*

JACK: I can't believe it! They want a dollar-fifty for two eggs!

LEO: Jack, take a look at this.

JACK: It's highway robbery!

LEO: It's important. Look. "Oh Max, Oh Steve." "Dying Woman Seeks Loved Ones. Large Fortune at Stake." Listen! "Millionairess Florence Snider of York, Pennsylvania, is reported to be searching desperately for her sister's children, Max and Steve, to whom she intends to leave the bulk of her fortune."

JACK: I think I have some extra change some place . . .

LEO: "Miss Snider last saw Max and Steve when, as children, they sailed for
    England with their mother. She corresponded for a time, but then lost all
    contact —"

JACK: Would you get to the point, I'm hungry!

LEO: The boys went to *England*. They left here as *children*. Listen: "Repeated
    telegrams and advertisements in America and England have failed to get
    a response." She can't find them! And apart from a niece named . . . Meg
    who lives with her in York, she wants to leave them her money.

JACK: So what?

LEO: *So what?!* Jack, what are we? You and I. Are we Polish?

JACK: No.

LEO: Hungarian?

JACK: No.

LEO: Lithuanian?

JACK: No.

LEO: *We're English! We have English accents!* And look at us! We could be broth-
    ers. We even look alike.
    *(He holds Jack around the shoulders, and they look out at the audience. They
    look nothing at all alike, of course.)*
    You could be Steve and I could be Max.

JACK: Us? Her nephews?

LEO: Bingo.

JACK: But we're not her nephews. It's a lie.

LEO: Not necessarily. Do you know *all* your relations?

JACK: Oh, stop it. I can't pretend to be somebody else. Besides which, it's illegal.
    They could put us in jail!

LEO: Jack, Florence Snider has tried for months to reach her nephews and she
    can't find them. So we wouldn't be hurting anybody. Do you think that
    I would hurt anybody?

JACK: What about the niece? Meg.

LEO: The hell with her. She'll get plenty. Look, it says the estate is estimated at
    three million dollars. So instead of three million, she gets one million.
    And you get a million and I get a million.

JACK: A million dollars?

LEO: *(Emotionally.)* We could start over. Try again . . . from the beginning . . .
    become something . . .

JACK: Leo . . .

LEO: Jack, *please*.

JACK: But she could have seen pictures of her nephews! In the past couple of months!

LEO: I've thought of that, so we don't show up until she kicks the bucket.

JACK: Dead?

LEO: No, Jack, a little wooden bucket that she kicks on its side . . . *Yes of course dead!* We wait nearby and keep our ears to the ground. The minute she goes, we send a telegram.

JACK: It won't work.

LEO: Yes it will.

JACK: No it won't! We don't know anything about Max and Steve! How old they are. When they left. Their mother's name. Their father's name. We'd have to know somebody from *York, Pennsylvania!*

(At this moment, Audrey skates in on roller skates. She's wearing a brightly colored uniform with a matching hat. She also carries some text books and a towel. She's about twenty, extremely well built and extremely sweet and good-natured. She's a knockout.)

AUDREY: *Wheeee!*

(As she skates in, she can't stop herself and careens right into Jack, who catches her.)

AUDREY: Oh, thanks!

(For Jack, it's love at first sight.)

Hi. I bet you're wondering why I'm dressed up like this.

JACK: It's very cheerful.

AUDREY: It's my first day at the Tastee Bite. See? "Tastee Bite."

(She points to her chest, and her tight sweater has the words "Tastee Bite" across the front.)

LEO: The first E gets a bit lost in the middle.

AUDREY: I took the training course yesterday and I passed with flying colors. They said I had the best potential of anybody they interviewed since they opened their doors to the public!

JACK: When did they open?

AUDREY: Monday.

JACK: Good show.

AUDREY: They have faith in me and that counts for a lot. Right?

LEO: Absolutely.

AUDREY: To tell you the truth, I got the job just to make some money. I want to go to college. Ergo, the books. Ergo means therefore. I mean, I know it's a commute and all, living in York, but I figure it's worth it if it helps get me through college.

LEO: . . . You live in York?

AUDREY: Yeah.

LEO: York, Pennsylvania?

AUDREY: Yeah.

LEO: You wouldn't know a Miss Florence Snider by any chance?

AUDREY: Are you kidding me? When I worked for a doctor, she came to the office like every day.

LEO: Do you know when she last saw "Max" and "Steve"?

AUDREY: 1920.

LEO: How old they were?

AUDREY: Six and four.

LEO: Their mother's name?

AUDREY: Jennie.

LEO: Father's?

AUDREY: Irv.

LEO: *Yes!*

JACK: Oh, no.

AUDREY: I remember when she used to come to the office, everything with her was a big deal. If she had a headache, it was a migraine, she had a slight fever, she was burning up. She was always exaggerating.

LEO: And how's she doing?

AUDREY: She's dead. She died this morning.

JACK: Oh, crap!

AUDREY: I know. It's awful.

LEO: What about Max and Steve? Has anyone heard from them?

AUDREY: Nope, not a word. The funny thing is, she didn't even have a picture of them. I asked her. She was real broken up about it. She said she thought that the older one, that was Max, she thought that Max was in the theater.

LEO: In the theater . . . !

JACK: Oh, God.

LEO: Ha! Fate! Providence! *"If it be now, 'tis not to come; if it be not to come, it will be now; if it be not now, yet it will come. The readiness is all!"*

AUDREY: Yeah . . . Anyway, I feel bad for her. I found her very congenial. That means nice. One day she comes in and I'm helping her up the stairs and she says, "I'm gonna remember you in my will," and I say, "Do it with money" — teasing her, you know? And she says "You should live so long," which I thought was nice, her wanting me to live a long time.

LEO: Is there anything else she ever said about Max and Steve? Anything distinctive about them? A scar, a limp . . .

AUDREY: Nope. Not really. Just average normal people. She said that Steve was deaf and dumb, but that's about all.

LEO: Deaf and dumb?

AUDREY: Yeah. It's congenital. Not to be confused with congenial. Can I leave my stuff here? I gotta practice my skating. See, to work at this place you've got to roller skate from table to table. I still need some practice, but I've got a plan. The aisles. See? They're nice and straight. And they're numerous, which means there's a lot of them, and they're contiguous, which means that one comes right after the other in a straight line, like two worms sucking each other's lips. My name's Audrey.

JACK: Jack. Jack Gable. Like Clark Gable without the cleft in the chin.

AUDREY: Hey, You're cute. I'll see ya later!

(She skates off.)

JACK: She thinks I'm cute . . .

LEO: Fine, you're cute. And you'll be deaf and dumb and I'll do all the talking.

JACK: Oh, stop it.

LEO: Why not? It's perfect!

JACK: I can't be deaf and dumb, I-I-I don't know any sign language.

LEO: So you'll make it up! It's easy!

JACK: It is not!

LEO: Of course it is! Try it! Just try it! Say . . . "yes."

(Reluctantly, Jack holds his hands out facing each other, fingers up and extended, the hands parallel.)

Say "no."

(Jack crosses his hands.)

"Maybe."

(Wavy hand.)

"I'm hungry."

(Points to his mouth with his tongue out.)

"I'm thirsty."

(Swigs, using his thumb as a bottle.)

"I have an idea."

(Finger up with a big smile.)

All right, good.

(Still signing, Jack gives a silent thumbs-up.)

Stop it.

(Jack signs "stop it" by putting his palms face down and tossing them to the sides, the way an umpire indicates "safe" in baseball.)

Stop doing that, Jack.

(Jack does the "stop it" sign and points to himself.)

It isn't funny!

(Jack does the "stop it" sign, then imitates laughing.)

JACK: Oh. Sorry. I'm sure it's not real sign language.

LEO: We'll tell them it's a new system. Signing for the simple. We'll say you can't hear a thing. You read lips, but only mine. Now the problem is that Audrey lives in York, and she heard you talking just now. So you'll have to wear a beard or something to play Steve. So she doesn't recognize you.

JACK: I look terrible in a beard!

LEO: That's not the point! Now what have we got?

(He rummages through Jack's costume bag and pulls out a beard.)

LEO: Try this.

JACK: No.

LEO: Just try it!

JACK: It looks fake.

(Jack tries on the beard.)

LEO: Try it with this hat.

(Leo pulls out Jack's Polonius head covering, and Jack pulls it on.)

That's better. Now what about these glasses.

(Leo pulls out a pair of glasses, and Jack puts them on.)

Good.

(At which moment, Audrey skates back in. Jack is petrified; Leo recovers quickly.)

AUDREY: *(Off, then on.)* Whee! Hi. Sorry. I forgot my towel . . .

(She sees Jack and is startled.)

Hey! Did he have a beard just now?

LEO: Who? Him? I-I don't think you've met him.

AUDREY: I haven't?

LEO: No. Oh, oh, of course. You met Jack, an old friend. This is my brother Steve.

AUDREY: "Steve"? No kidding. Hi. How are ya?

LEO: I'm afraid he can't hear what you're saying. He's deaf and dumb.

AUDREY: Deaf and d — ! Holy cow! That's incredible! Usually I never even *hear* about anybody being deaf and dumb, now it comes up twice. Talk about a coincidence!

LEO: Ah, but is it? You see, this *is* Steve. And I'm his brother.

AUDREY: I know. It's amazing. Two deaf people named Steve.

LEO: Two . . . ?

AUDREY: Yeah. Don't you remember? Max and Steve. The two girls we talked about. Like I told you, the younger one is deaf and dumb.

LEO: "Two *girls*"?

AUDREY: Yeah.

LEO: But . . . Max and Steve are men, aren't they?

AUDREY: No. Oh oh *oh*! I get it! I bet you got mixed up because of their names, right? But they're not men, they're girls! Their real names are Maxine and Stephanie.

JACK: "Maxine and Stephanie"? Oh that's great, that is just *great*!

AUDREY: Hey, he just talked.

LEO: Amazing are you absolutely sure they're girls?

AUDREY: Sure. I talked to Miss Snider like a hundred times about them.

LEO: It didn't say they were girls in the paper.

AUDREY: I'll bet you just missed it. Most people don't read carefully.

JACK: Quite right, here it is. It says girls. Right here. Look. "Girls"!

AUDREY: You know, he talks very well for a beginner. Well, if you'll excuse me, I'm gonna go practice my skating.

> *(To Jack.)*

> CONGRATULATIONS. YOU'RE MAKING TERRIFIC PROGRESS.

JACK: Thank you.

> *(She skates away.)*

LEO: God damn it. *God damn it!* We were *so close*! I could *taste it*! With two million dollars, we could have made our own Shakespeare movie!

JACK: At least I can talk now.

LEO: *GOOOODDDDAAMMMMITT!*

> *(In a rage, Leo throws one of the suitcases on the floor — and it springs open, sending costumes spilling everywhere.)*

> Oh, great. Just look at this. Costumes, to remind me of our latest defeat.

JACK: I'll help, I'll help.

> *(As they begin gathering up the costumes, Leo holds up a wig and a dress and looks at them quizzically. Meanwhile, Jack is holding a gown up to himself.)*

> Ha. Remember this one? Juliet. We had that knockout actress, and I used

to say, "Pardon me, but would you like to climb up *my* balcony . . . ?" Ha. And look at this. *The Taming of the Shrew.* "If I be waspish, best beware my sting."

(He holds the dress in front of him and models it, chuckling. Then he notices Leo. Leo's mind is grinding away. He's getting a maniacal look in his eyes. He stares at the dress in his own hands, then looks back at Jack.)

LEO: *"If it be now, 'tis not to come; if it be not to come, it will be now —"*

JACK: No.

LEO: Yes.

JACK: *No!*

LEO: We can do it! It'll work! I'll be Maxine, you'll be Stephanie.

JACK: Wrong! I will not dress up as a woman. *Ever.* I don't do that.

LEO: For a million dollars? The question is, which dress do you wear.

(Leo starts rummaging through the suitcase, tossing costumes in all directions.)

JACK: No. Hey. *Would you stop it?! Hey cut that out! Right now! Just stop it!*

LEO: Ooh, ooh, ooh, I think *I'd* look good in this one. Cleopatra, Queen of the Nile.

JACK: You'd look ridiculous!

LEO: Now what about you . . . ?

JACK: I am not doing this. Do you hear me? *Are you listening?!*

LEO: What about this? It has a plunging neckline —

JACK: They wouldn't believe me! I'm not a good actor!

LEO: You get very good reviews.

JACK: *Because you write them!*

LEO: *(Holding up a diaphanous number.)* Ooh, ooh, ooh, look at this. It's perfect. Titania, Queen of the Fairies.

JACK: I can't wear that! It has *wings* on it!

LEO: We'll cut them off.

JACK: *No!*

LEO: Jack, don't you remember the good old days. We said we could do anything. And we believed it! You played Richard the Third with that big hump on your back, and you hobbled around the stage like some deranged homunculus. You played Romeo and bounded gracefully onto Juliet's balcony. You brought the house down.

JACK: I brought the balcony down.

LEO: Just that one night.

JACK: But Leo, those were all men! I can't play a woman!

LEO: Why not?

JACK: Because I'm a chap, a bloke, a *guy*!

LEO: Jack! Who do you think played the women's roles in Shakespeare's time? Huh?

JACK: Chaps?

LEO: Exactly. And how did they do it?

JACK: Small brassieres?

LEO: They did it with conviction. With sheer talent. Because they were actors, like you and me. And if this works, we can be *successful* actors. We can start over. Go to Los Angeles. Get another chance. Jack, it's the role of a lifetime. Will you meet the challenge? Will you rise to the occasion? *Will you fulfill your destiny and save your best friend from a life of crushing disappointment and defeat? Yes or no?!*

JACK: *NO!*

LEO: I'll take that as a yes. Now we'll get off at the next stop, send them a telegram, get into our costumes, get back on the train, and then it's on to *York, Pennsylvania! Ha ha!*
(*Blackout.*)

SCENE FOUR

We hear a telephone ring and the lights come up on Duncan and Meg, in separate places, on the phone with each other. Meg has placed the call, and Duncan is answering it. Meg is bright-eyed with excitement and can't wait to tell Duncan her news.

DUNCAN: Hello. Evangelical United Brethren Church of York. Reverend Wooley speaking.

MEG: Duncan, it's me! Guess what?! A telegram just arrived and guess who it's from. And don't say Grandma Kunkle.

DUNCAN: Winston Churchill.

MEG: Wrong. It's from *Max and Steve*!

DUNCAN: Max and Steve?

MEG: Yes! Isn't it wonderful! I have cousins! They arrive today at five-thirty. And I've never even met them. Isn't it exciting?!

DUNCAN: Yes it is, my goodness, but . . . You do realize this means you'll have to split your inheritance.

MEG: Well of course.

DUNCAN: Instead of three million, you'll only get one million.

MEG: A million dollars is enough for ten lifetimes. And you always say yourself that money isn't important.

DUNCAN: Well it isn't. Per se. But one can do so much good with three million dollars. I could set up a foundation. And run it from a nice new office. I'd interview charities that ask me for grant money. They'd take me to lunch and try to woo me . . .

MEG: Or we could give it all away in one big lump and just go on living the way things are.

DUNCAN: Now that's ridiculous! It would be vain and boastful.

MEG: Oh, Duncan. You were counting on all three million, weren't you.

DUNCAN: Yes, I was. But not for myself. For the foundation.

MEG: And for that little house on Nantucket.

DUNCAN: Well we'd have to run it out of some place.

MEG: They arrive on the six o'clock train.

DUNCAN: Very fortuitous, their arriving this week. And then one has to ask if it's entirely by chance.

MEG: What do you mean?

DUNCAN: Have you ever thought that they might be frauds.

MEG: Oh, stop it.

DUNCAN: Why not? I mean it's a very convenient time to arrive. They will get two million dollars.

MEG: Would you please forget about the money.

DUNCAN: I am not thinking about the money! I told you that. But maybe they're not . . .

MEG/DUNCAN: as Christian as we are.

MEG: Duncan, you're becoming awfully intolerant.

DUNCAN: Nonsense.

MEG: You know what God thinks of intolerant people.

DUNCAN: Meg —

MEG: One minute you're brushing your teeth, then whammo, you're a pillar of salt.

DUNCAN: Meg!

MEG: With greedy people it's even worse.

DUNCAN: I am not greedy! . . . Look. We'll all be very happy to meet your cousins. That's all that matters.

MEG: You will be here when they arrive, won't you? I want to meet them on the platform.

DUNCAN: I'll try. But we have a Boy Scout meeting here at five and I'm handing out the merit badges. It's very exciting. One of the boys is making Eagle, and we have two Hawks and a Pigeon, so I'd better go now and get ready.

MEG: All right, see you later.

DUNCAN: Kiss kiss.

(They hang up.)

SCENE FIVE

The action shifts to the living room of Florence Snider's house, a half hour later. Doctor Myers and his son Butch are hanging a banner that reads: "Welcome Max and Steve." Butch, early twenties, is a little slow on the uptake, but earnest and sincere, with a good heart. He played football in high school. Doc and Butch argue a lot and adore each other.

DOC: Butch, I want you to listen to me and keep an open mind! All right?! Are we clear on this?!

BUTCH: Yes, Father.

DOC: The point I'm making is: It's just as easy to go to bed with a rich girl as it . . .

BUTCH/DOC: *(Simultaneously.)* is a poor one.

BUTCH: Father!

DOC: The two women coming off that train will be rich as Croesus. Marry one and you'll be set for life.

BUTCH: But I'm in love with Audrey!

DOC: Butch! Sow your oats, by all means. Plow the field, till the soil, water the fruit, but marry for cash.

BUTCH: Oh, Father . . .

DOC: Look at me, Butch. I'm not joking! I married for love. Biggest mistake I ever made in my whole life. You could have had Meg, for God's sake! Before she got engaged to our anal retentive minister.

BUTCH: Father, Meg is my best friend!

DOC: People do stay friends after they're married, Butch. I read about them in a book once!

(Meg enters, hurrying down the stairs, and Doc stomps off to the other side of the room. Meg has smartened up for the arrival of her cousins and wears a twinset.)

BUTCH: Hey, Meg.

MEG: What's eating him?

BUTCH: He doesn't like Audrey. He thinks I should marry a girl with deeper pockets, like one of your cousins coming off the train.

(Meg sighs. Here we go again.)

MEG: Butch, are you in love with Audrey?

BUTCH: I think so.

MEG: How does she make you feel?

BUTCH: Happy.

MEG: And how do you make her feel?

BUTCH: Happy.

MEG: And what do you want to do about it?

BUTCH: Sleep with her.

MEG: What else do you want to do about it?

BUTCH: Marry her.

MEG: Well what are you waiting for, a comet?!

(Duncan enters from the front hall.)

DUNCAN: Well, well, well. Greetings all.

DOC: Well look who's here. It's the Reverend Do-gooder.

DUNCAN: And good afternoon to you, Doctor Death. Killed any patients yet today?

DOC: No, but I did enjoy your sermon on Sunday. Best sleep I've had in weeks. *Awhooo!*

(The call of the Moose.)

MEG: Would you two stop it. Duncan, we've got to hurry. We're going to be late.

DUNCAN: You're rushing me again, my dear. Now please. Nothing profits from haste.

MEG: Yes, Duncan, but did I tell you that Maxine is *in* the theater? She's an actress!

DUNCAN: Yes, you did, though personally I can't imagine why anyone would voluntarily put on a silly costume, stand up in front of a lot of people, and pontificate about something that most of the audience has absolutely no interest in.

BUTCH: . . . You're a minister. Don't *you* do that?

MEG: Wait. Oh, no. I forgot the flowers. Oh, darn it! I'll be right back!

(She dashes up the stairs and disappears into her room.)

DUNCAN: Haste, haste . . .

DOC/DUNCAN: *(Together.)* Nothing profits from haste.

DOC: You told us that, you jackass.

(At this moment, Audrey hurries in from the garden, wild with excitement.)

AUDREY: *Hey! Hey! Everybody, guess what, guess what?!*

BUTCH: Hey, Audrey. How was your first day?

AUDREY: Great, Butch, thanks, but listen —

BUTCH: I love you with roller skates. They really set off your eyes.

AUDREY: Thanks, now *listen! Guess who's coming?!*

BUTCH: Maxine and Stephanie.

AUDREY: How did you know?

DOC: We got a telegram this afternoon.

DUNCAN: They're due any time now.

AUDREY: "Due any time"? *They're outside!! I just met 'em and they're comin' up the path!!* And let me tell you, English girls are a whole other thing. These are not your ordinary women. I'll bring 'em in!

(Calling.) Hey! This way! Come on, don't be shy.

(Leo and Jack enter, dressed as women. Leo wears the dress of Cleopatra of the Nile. Jack's Titania dress still has wings on it. Leo, as Maxine, is chic and flamboyant. Jack, as Stephanie, is shy and demure. Butch, Duncan, and Doc stare gaping at them, their mouths hanging open. Audrey looks proud. Of course, whenever Leo speaks as Maxine, he uses a feminine, high-pitched voice.)

LEO: Hello, hello, hello, my darlings! Oh! How wonderful to arrive at long last into the bosom of my own dear family.

"Oh! This blessed plot, this earth, this realm, this York, P-A."

(Leo beams. Jack looks terrified.)

BUTCH: Are you really Maxine and Stephanie?

LEO: No, I'm just Maxine. This is Stephanie.

(He holds Jack's fingers to his lips.)

Stephanie, say hello to the nice people.

(Jack bows upstage in both directions, giving us a clear view of the back of his dress — which still has two fairy wings sticking out. At this moment, Meg hurries down the stairs, carrying flowers.)

MEG: Oh, I'm sorry! I'm sorry I'm late, I'm *AH!*

(The sight of them startles her. To Audrey:)

Is this . . . ?

(Audrey nods.)

. . . Here. These flowers are for you. I'm your cousin Margaret.

(Leo stops dead. He's dumbstruck. She's the most beautiful girl he's ever seen.)

LEO: How . . . how . . . how do you do? Auntie Florence never told us you were so . . . beautiful.

(Leo stares at her, unable to move. Meg wants to embrace them, but hesitates . . . then, with a cry of happiness, she gives in to her affectionate nature and gives them each a hug. The very touch of her makes Leo dizzy.)

MEG: Oh, I am so happy to meet you! Let me introduce you to my friends. This is our Pastor, Reverend Wooley.

DUNCAN: How do you do.

LEO: Ah, I see that you're a man of the cloth. I find that so inspiring, so *je ne sais quoi*. Do you speak French?

DUNCAN: No.

LEO: Anyone?

(Everyone murmurs no.)

Ah, *que jamais tout de suite a Sorbonne a la frommage et bon soir.* Next.

MEG: This is Doctor Myers, who has taken such wonderful care of Aunt Florence.

LEO: How good of you to bother.

DOC: If you ever need an operation, just call me. I do plastic surgery on the side.

LEO: But I don't need it on my side, it's my face that . . . Oh, ha! Next.

MEG: This is Butch. And Audrey.

BUTCH: She's my girlfriend. We're going to be married soon!

DOC: Over my dead body.

LEO: And wouldn't that make an unusual ceremony. "Do you take this woman, standing on this dead body, to be your . . . Ha!"

AUDREY: *(Putting Jack's fingers to her lips.)* WELCOME TO OUR METROPOLIS! THAT MEANS CITY!

(Jack hugs her warmly, rocking back and forth.)

AUDREY: Aww . . .

LEO: How sweet.

(Jack does it again.)

Such an affectionate little thing . . .

(Again.)

That's enough! . . . Now could you possibly take us to see dear Auntie Florence?

MEG: Well . . .

LEO: *What? Oh, no!* I can see it in your face. We aren't too late, are we?

MEG: Maxine . . .

LEO: *Oh, no, no, no!*

MEG: Maxine . . .

LEO: I can't believe it! After all this time! Stephanie! Stephanie, listen to me!
>   (Fingers to lips.)
>   *We're too late! Auntie Florence is dead!*
>   (Jack opens his mouth and screams in complete silence. He looks like Edvard Munch's The Scream, but rocking back and forth, arms up.)

MEG: Maxine! You're not too late! *She isn't dead!*
>   (Leo and Jack stop cold. They look at each other in horror.)

LEO: . . . Not dead?

MEG: No. She's hanging on. And she wants to see you.

LEO: But-but-but —

AUDREY: Butch, this morning you told me she was dead!

BUTCH: That's what Father said.

DOC: She had no pulse! Then she got better! What do you want from me?!
>   (Leo and Jack start sneaking away.)

MEG: Maxine? Where are you going?

LEO: The news. It's overwhelming. We thought a little stroll might help us recover . . .
>   (A voice from offstage is heard, and Leo and Jack freeze.)

FLORENCE: (Off.) *Are they here?! Where are they?! I want to see them!*
>   (Aunt Florence enters. She's very old, extremely crusty, and her eyesight is terrible.)

MEG: Aunt Florence! You should be in bed!

FLORENCE: (All sweetness.) Don't be ridiculous. I have two little nieces to meet. Where are they? . . . (Tough and angry!) WHERE ARE THEY?!

MEG: Right over here.

FLORENCE: Maxine? Stephanie?

LEO: Yes?
>   (Florence scrutinizes them; a tense moment.)

FLORENCE: (Crying.) . . . They're so beautiful! Maxine, my darling, it's really you . . .

LEO: Auntie Florence, dear Auntie Florence . . . You look so wealthy . . . healthy! So *rich* in color. So *loaded* with charm. *"Age cannot wither her, nor custom stale her infinite variety."*

FLORENCE: That must be Stephanie.

LEO: No, it's Shakespeare. Wait. Stephanie doesn't know yet. She thinks you're dead. *(Fingers to lips.)* Stephanie. Brace yourself. This is your Auntie Florence.

(Jack does a toreador flourish. Then he does some signing that clearly says "Let's get the hell out of here.")

LEO: Yes, I agree. As soon as possible. She says it can't be Auntie Florence, you look so young.

FLORENCE: Oh, the sweet baby!

(She pulls Jack fiercely to her bosom.)

DOC: Florence, you should be in bed.

FLORENCE: Oh be quiet, murderer. You said I was dead. I could have been buried alive.

DOC: I made a mistake. It happens. You don't make mistakes?

FLORENCE: Not like that I don't.

DOC: What about your stock tips? Huh?! *They all stunk!*

FLORENCE: *That's different! They don't kill people!*

DOC: *They all went straight down the toilet!*

FLORENCE: *IT'S NOT THE SAME THING!*

(And with that, Aunt Florence grabs her chest and starts to gasp.)

FLORENCE: Argh!

MEG: Aunt Florence!

FLORENCE: Argh!

BUTCH: I've got her! I've got her!

AUDREY: Florence!

DOC: Oh, damn. Get her inside.

MEG: Maxine, we'll be right back. She should be fine, don't worry.

LEO: Can I help?

MEG: No, it's okay, really. We put a bedroom on the ground floor. I'll be right back!

(Everyone helps Florence off, leaving Leo and Jack alone.)

JACK: All right, now let's get the hell out of here!

LEO: Wait. Wait. Wait! Not yet! I think we should stay.

JACK: Stay? Are you crazy?!

LEO: Jack, this whole thing could still work. I mean, why not?

JACK: Because she's still alive. And she's *really mean*!

LEO: But she can't last much longer. She must be a thousand years old.

JACK: She could linger. Old people do that, they linger out of spite.

LEO: I say we give it a couple of weeks.

JACK: *A couple of weeks?!*

LEO: Shh!

JACK: *Are you crazy?!* Look at me! I have *wings* on! I feel like I'm in "Charley's Aunt Meets the Fairy Queen!" And where the hell did this "Maxine" creature come from?!

LEO: *(Worried.)* I have no idea.

JACK: She's from another planet. She's possessing you. It's like *The Invasion of the Body Snatchers*!

LEO: Look, how about this. We take it a day at a time. We spend the night, and if they get suspicious, we reconsider.

JACK: No.

LEO: It's worth it, Jack.

JACK: No!

LEO: Two million dollars!

JACK: *No!*

LEO: Jack!

> *(Meg reenters.)*

> be nimble, Jack be quick, Jack jump over Hello, you're back, you're back!

MEG: Am I interrupting?

LEO: No, no, no, no, no, no! You're just in time. *(Hand to lips:)* Yes, Stephanie, of course you can take a stroll. Why don't you get one of those *train schedules* from the station. Then we'll know what time the little trainies leave from here to go to other places. It might come in handy if we're ever in a hurry. Who knows?

> *(Leo laughs gaily. Jack signs "All right, but I don't like it!" and exits.)*

LEO: Now how is dear Auntie Florence doing?

MEG: I'm afraid it doesn't look very good. It's been like this for months. But at least you made it before anything happened. She got to see you after all these years. That means a great deal to all of us.

LEO: Thank you.

MEG: But . . . oh I don't know how to put this . . . could you tell me just one thing? About yourself.

LEO: *(Worried.)* Yes, I-I suppose so . . .

MEG: It doesn't really matter at all, and I don't mean to pry.

LEO: No, please. Go ahead.

MEG: Well . . . is it true that you're really . . . in the theater?

LEO: The thea . . . Oh, oh, oh yes! Yes, I am. Absolutely.

MEG: Oh, I think that's so wonderful! My happiest memory in the world is when my father took me to Philadelphia to see my first Shakespeare. It was *Twelfth Night*, my favorite.

LEO: *(Stunned.)* . . . My senior project at the Royal Academy was *Twelfth Night*.

MEG: The Royal Academy of Dramatic Art? In London? Oh God, you're my hero!

LEO: I am?

MEG: Can I tell you a secret? If I could do anything in the whole world, I mean if somehow things changed like magic, overnight, all I'd ever want to do is be an actress. I'd want to recite Shakespeare every night and let those words just tumble out of me like a waterfall. I'd want to play Rosalind and Juliet and Cleopatra. Do you specialize in anything?

LEO: Specialize?

MEG: You know, comedy, tragedy . . . ?

LEO: Oh, I do a bit of everything. Comedy. Tragedy. Comical-tragedy. "Tragical-comical-historical-pastoral, scene individual or poem unlimited." I did a command performance of *Twelfth Night* not long ago for the Queen of England.

MEG: What did you play?

LEO: The Duke Orsino! . . . 'sssss lady love, the fair Olivia.

MEG: Oh my God, I'd give anything to have seen you in it. Do some for me. Would you? Just a little?

LEO: Now?

MEG: Yes!

LEO: Oh I couldn't.

MEG: Please!

LEO: You embarrass me.

MEG: A few lines. Please! I know it all by heart. I'll do Viola's lines. She's my favorite character in all the plays. "What I am, and what I would, are as secret as maidenhead: to your ears, divinity, to any other's profanation. Good madam, let me see your face."

(Note: this is one of the sexiest and most romantic passages in all of Shakespeare. Leo plays Olivia to the hilt. He's a grande dame, vain and resplendent. The tone shifts at Meg's speech "With adorations, with fertile tears," and from that point on, the tone is lushly romantic.)

LEO: "Have you any commission from your lord to negotiate with my face? You are now out of your text. But we will draw the curtain and show you the picture."

(She unveils and shows her face.)

"Look you, sir. Is't not well done?"

MEG: "Excellently done, if God did all."

LEO: "'Tis in grain, sir, 'twill endure wind and weather."

MEG: "O, if I did love you in my master's flame,
    With such a suff'ring, such a deadly life,
    In your denial I would find no sense,
    I would not understand it."

LEO: "Why, what would you?"

MEG: "Make me a willow cabin at your gate
    And call upon my soul within the house,
    Write loyal cantons of contemnèd love,
    And sing them loud even in the dead of night;
    Halloo your name to the reverberate hills,
    And make the babbling gossip of the air
    Cry out 'Olivia!'"

(Silence. Leo is so smitten he can barely speak.)

LEO: . . . We should get married.

MEG: What?

LEO: *You.* You should get married. Are you married?

MEG: No. I'm not.

LEO: Oh good! Isn't that splendid.

MEG: But I'm getting married next month.

(Leo turns white and he almost falls.)

LEO: What? You are? Next month?

MEG: That's right.

LEO: But-but-but you haven't met me yet!

MEG: I'm sorry?

LEO: Met-met-met-me. To met-me. It's an Old English expression. It means
    to live life to the fullest. From the French, metmoyer. And who exactly is
    the lucky man?

MEG: You met him just now. Duncan. Reverend Wooley.

LEO: *Him?* Reverend Woo — But-but my dear, you . . . you don't have an en-
    gagement ring.

MEG: Duncan says that rings are earthly symbols of material wealth.

LEO: You mean he's cheap. And where's the honeymoon?

MEG: He doesn't believe in honeymoons, either. But can I tell you a secret?
    Someday I want to go to Paris.

LEO: Well of course you do. And you *should* want to. But are you in love with Reverend Whosits?

MEG: *(Taken aback.)* Wooley. Yes, of course I am. You see, he was friends with my mother and father, here in York, and they passed away when I was young. And he was very kind when they died and helped me get through it. And so it means a lot to me. That we can talk about them.

LEO: Ah.

MEG: I think that's what love is, don't you? Having something you can share, then letting it grow.

LEO: No, no, no, no, *no*! My dear, love is lightning. It makes you ache and cry and laugh and scream. It lingers your desire and makes you count the minutes till your wedding night so that your heart stops beating with the anticipation of it.

MEG: *(In awe.)* . . . Have you ever been in love like that?

LEO: Oh, *yes* . . . But what am I saying? I'm interfering and I shouldn't. I wish you every happiness in the world with that man. Duncan. Reverend Woolsack.

MEG: Thank you. You will be here for the wedding, won't you? Oh please say yes! It's three weeks from Sunday.

LEO: Well, I'm afraid that all depends. I may have to . . . meet someone in New York. A very dear friend of mine. Leo Clark. One of the greatest actors in the English-speaking world. I'm sure you've heard of him.

MEG: Yes, I have!

LEO: You have?

MEG: I saw him about two years ago in Philadelphia doing "Scenes from Shakespeare." He was wonderful! I fell in love with him! Is he your boyfriend?

LEO: Hm? No. No! Not at all. We're just very close. Inseparable, you might say.

MEG: This is so amazing. I was supposed to go see him last night. In Shrewsbury. Which is only twenty miles from here. In fact, you could go visit him right now, unless . . . Maxine? . . . Hello?

(But Maxine is lost in thought.)

LEO: I wonder . . .

MEG: What?

LEO: *Shh!* Don't interrupt. *(Silence.)* . . . I am getting the most marvelous idea. Margaret, what if Leo Clark came here to meet you . . . and the two of you put on a performance of Shakespeare, together.

MEG: . . . You're teasing me.

LEO: I am not, now listen. You get married in just three and a half weeks. Right? So, in honor of your wedding, we plan a special event to make it truly unforgettable: a scene from Shakespeare — *no!* A *whole play* — *Twelfth Night* — starring you and Leo Clark.

MEG: You are teasing me!

LEO: No I am not! Look, Leo is close by. You are my cousin. And I would love the two of you to spend some time together . . .

MEG: Well first of all, he wouldn't do it.

LEO: Of course he would! He's devoted to me!

MEG: But he'll be too busy! He must work all the time!

LEO: Well, not *all* the time.

MEG: But he wouldn't do it with me! I'm not a real actress! I'm not good enough!

LEO: Nonsense.

MEG: I'm not!

LEO: Margaret, I just heard you! You were marvelous!

MEG: But I have no training.

LEO: *So he'll give you lessons! Private acting lessons!* And you'll spend a lot of time together! — which believe me, he wouldn't mind at all.

MEG: Oh he'd hate that.

LEO: He would kill for it.

MEG: But —

LEO: Margaret. Didn't you tell me not five minutes ago that you would love to be an actress? More than anything in the world? Well here's your chance — and believe me, it isn't every day that chances — any chances — come along. Do it now, before life gets cold.

MEG: . . . All right, I'll do it.

LEO: That's my girl!

MEG: *Eeeee!* Oh my God. I can't believe it. And listen! Aunt Florence is giving a party the night before the wedding. We could do the performance then.

LEO: Well that's perfection!

MEG: But it won't interfere with the wedding, will it? I mean, you don't think Duncan will mind, do you?

LEO: Noooooo. Of course not.

MEG: Eeeee! This is incredible! *Leo Clark!*

LEO: Yes? . . . Oh, yes! Leo Clark. *The* Leo Clark.

MEG: *The New York Times* called him "a living legend." It was on one of his flyers.

LEO: Yes, I remember that one . . .

MEG: So you'll call him?

LEO: Who?

MEG: Mr. Clark.

LEO: Oh, yes yes yes. No problem. Leave it all to me.

MEG: All right. *(Pause.)* Would you like to see your room now? You must be exhausted.

LEO: I think I'll wait here for Stephanie. If that's all right.

MEG: Oh yes.

LEO: You're sure?

MEG: Of course. Anything you want.

LEO: Anything?

MEG: You just have to name it and it's all yours.

> *(Leo groans.)*
>
> Well. I'll be upstairs. When it gets really warm like this, I . . . no, I can't tell you.

LEO: Oh tell me, please.

MEG: I can't.

LEO: Of course you can.

MEG: You won't tell anybody?

LEO: I promise. It'll be just between us girls.

MEG: Well . . . when it gets really warm, I like to take off all my clothes and sprinkle water on my chest and just lie down on the bed spread out like a flag!

> *(Leo gulps.)*
>
> Have you ever tried it?

LEO: I do it all the time.

MEG: I'll see you later.

> *(Meg runs up the stairs to the door on the balcony.)*

LEO: Oh, Margaret. By the way, which room is mine and Stephanie's?

MEG: This one. Mine. We're all sharing. The three of us. Isn't that great?!

LEO: . . . Great.

> *(Meg exits, closing the door. Leo buckles at the knees.)*

LEO: Oh God. Now we're in trouble. Jack! Jack! . . . *Stephanie!*

> *(Leo dashes out through the garden. The instant he's gone, Jack and Audrey enter through the doors to the hall.)*

AUDREY: COME WITH ME. I'LL SHOW YOU WHERE YOUR BED-ROOM IS.

(Audrey leads Jack up the stairs.)

AUDREY: Now this is your *bedroom. Sleep. Snore. ZZZZ.* Okay? I'll see ya later.

(Jack hugs her.)

Aw . . . Bye-bye. Now go ahead. Into your room.

(Jack goes into the room and closes the door.)

AUDREY: Gee, what a nice girl.

(She walks away.)

JACK: *(Off.) AHHHHHHHHH!!!*

MEG: *(Off.) AHHHHHHHHHH!!!*

(Jack reels out of the room and stumbles across the balcony. Meg hurries out of the room with a towel around her. Leo reenters from the garden at the same time.)

JACK: *Oh my God! Oh my God!*

MEG: Stephanie, it's all right!

JACK: *Oh my God!*

AUDREY: *Wait! Wait! Meg, listen! Holy cow! Stephanie is talking!*

(Meg gasps.)

MEG: Maxine! Did you hear that. She's *talking!*

(Leo drops to his knees and throws his arms up to heaven.)

LEO: *Oh thank God! It's a miracle!*

(Religious music. Trumpets and organ. Blackout.)

END OF ACT I

ACT II

SCENE ONE

The lights come up on the living room, late afternoon, three days later. Florence is hurrying out the door of her downstairs bedroom, pursued by Doc, who has a stethoscope around his neck.

DOC: *Florence!*

FLORENCE: *Shut up!*

DOC: *Will you please stay in bed!*

FLORENCE: *No!*

DOC: Florence, if you don't listen to me, you are going to die!

FLORENCE: How would *you* know?

DOC: Because I will strangle you to death.

FLORENCE: I want to see Stephanie! My baby is talking! Someone could have told me about it *three days ago*!

DOC: You were hardly breathing three days ago, you were on life support!

FLORENCE: *Well I still had ears, didn't I?!! I could have listened! I could have nodded my head!!*

(Florence makes a break for the front door.)

DOC: *Florence get back in that bed.*

(At which moment, Jack enters dressed as Stephanie, in a day dress.)

FLORENCE: *Stephanie! Stephanie, there* you are! I just heard the news. Let me hear you speak.

JACK: *(At a loss; then, wispy and flowerlike.)* . . . I need a drink.

FLORENCE: Oh, my heart! Did you hear that? The tone. The lightness. It's her mother's voice.

JACK: Dear Mama. So sweet. So gentle. When she entered the room it was like a summer breeze.

FLORENCE: She weighed three hundred pounds.

JACK: Yes. Of course. But so light on her feet . . .

FLORENCE: It's true, it's true! Now tell me, how does it feel, speaking aloud for the first time? Is it exciting?

JACK: Well, it is quite a surprise in some ways. In my head, I always sounded like Lucille Ball.

(Duncan enters.)

DUNCAN: Well, good morning. Florence. Stephanie. I was looking for Margaret.

JACK: I believe that she and Maxine went shopping for the day. In Philadelphia.

FLORENCE: Isn't it amazing, Duncan. Stephanie, talking after all these years.

DUNCAN: Amazing. Almost miraculous.

JACK: But as a man of the cloth, surely you believe in miracles, Reverend Wooly.

DUNCAN: Well, I believe that miracles happen to people who are deserving of miracles.

JACK: And you don't think that I'm deserving?

DUNCAN: Well, you might be, but I don't know you very well, now do I? You came onto the scene somewhat unexpectedly. At a rather unfortunate time.

JACK: *(Starting to whimper, trying to hide the tears.)* Oh, dear, I'm sorry if I'm a nuisance . . .

DUNCAN: I didn't say that —

JACK: Perhaps Maxine and I should just go home . . .

FLORENCE: Don't even think about it!

JACK: *(Weeping now.)* But he said that we're unfortunate!

DUNCAN: I didn't say that either!

FLORENCE: Duncan, be quiet!

JACK: But if he doesn't like us, then we *should* go.

FLORENCE: Oh, who cares what he thinks. I never liked him anyway.

DUNCAN: Florence!

FLORENCE: Stephanie, come to my room!

JACK: Actually, I thought I might take a walk . . .

FLORENCE: *To my room! Now!*

JACK: Yes, Aunt Florence.

DOC: Florence, I'll be back tomorrow.

FLORENCE: Don't do me any favors, Dr. Crippen. *Just stay away from me! Stephanie!*

JACK: Coming!

(Florence exits, followed by Jack.)

DOC: I don't understand it. She's getting stronger by the minute. It must have something to do with the rise of evil in the world, it's giving her strength.

DUNCAN: Doctor, don't you find it incredible that a woman who has been deaf and dumb all her life is suddenly talking like this?

DOC: Well, there have been cases like this before, medically speaking. Usually caused by some jolt to the system. Apparently in her case it was the shock of seeing Meg lying there on the bed, buck naked.

DUNCAN: Doctor —

DOC: Of course, that would do anybody a lot of good. If I'd been in her shoes I'd have done a lot more than start talking. Ha!

DUNCAN: Doctor, please!

DOC: Please what?! It's called living, Duncan. Sex. Living. Humor. Have you heard of these things?! I have to go. I have patients to see. I have a real job.

(When Doc is gone, Duncan looks around furtively, then he goes to the telephone and dials a number.)

DUNCAN: Hello? Inspector Ballard, please . . . Ah, good, it's Reverend Wooly. Now, have you made any progress concerning the two women? . . . Yes, I know it's only been two days, but . . . No, I don't have any evidence. That's what I want *you* to find . . . No, I don't *know* that they're frauds. I *suspect* they are . . . Because they're odd! . . . Well for one thing, they're very large women, and . . . Well yes, people do vary in size, but . . . well one of them was deaf and dumb since birth and now she's talking! . . . Well yes, I suppose I'm happy for her, but . . . Look, officer, I can't put my finger on it, but they're not being honest about something. They're sort of . . . shady . . . No, they haven't tried to get me in a card game! I don't play cards, I'm a minister! . . . Well . . . yes, bridge occasionally.

MEG: *(Off.)* Duncan?

DUNCAN: *(Quickly.)* Look, I have to go now, just keep working on it. I'll call you later. Good-bye.

(As Duncan hangs up, Meg hurries in carrying several purchases, including a dress box. She's wearing a pretty new hat and a duster over her dress. She's in high spirits.)

MEG: Oh, Duncan, wait till you hear! Maxine and I had a day out together and we had the most wonderful time! First we went shopping at Saks Fifth Avenue, and Maxine insisted I get this dress for the party. At first, in the dressing room, I couldn't even get it on. But then Maxine helped me into it. Poor thing. As she was pulling it over my hips, she got faint. Then we had lunch at the Bellevue and we ordered snails, then we had our nails done, then more shopping at this little boutique where they simply *worship* Maxine, then tea at the Ritz, at the corner table, and I had a *champagne cocktail*!

DUNCAN: Ah.

MEG: Is something wrong?

DUNCAN: No, no . . . I would have liked to have known you were going, that's all . . .

MEG: I'm sorry, Duncan. I forgot to tell you. But Maxine says it's so important to be spontaneous in life. Try new things, take chances. As they say in French, metmoyer!

(Meg removes her coat to reveal that she's wearing a stylish new dress.)

DUNCAN: Margaret!

MEG: Do you like it?

DUNCAN: It's a little snug isn't it?

MEG: Maybe a little . . . But listen, I have something to tell you. We went to a bridal shop and looked at wedding gowns.

DUNCAN: Margaret! We agreed on business attire!

MEG: I know. She just wanted me to look. But she says that a bride *should* have a gown. And an engagement ring. She says it means so much to a girl.

DUNCAN: Well, heh heh, not all girls would agree with her there. Mm? Right?

MEG: Well, I do think a ring would be nice, Duncan.

DUNCAN: You do?

MEG: Yes. I do.

DUNCAN: *(Nettled.)* Well why didn't you say so before?

MEG: I did but you weren't listening.

DUNCAN: No you didn't.

MEG: Yes I did.

DUNCAN: You did not!

MEG: Do we have to argue about it?

DUNCAN: We are not arguing! If you want a ring, you can have a ring. I just want to make you happy. You know that.

MEG: Maxine says that *you* have to pick it.

DUNCAN: Of course I'll pick it.

MEG: She says it should have a diamond in the middle.

DUNCAN: Fine, I'll get a diamond.

MEG: With a platinum setting.

DUNCAN: Who is this for?! You or Maxine?!

MEG: Duncan, you're yelling at me.

DUNCAN: *No I'm not!* It's just . . . I have been under a great deal of strain. Now if you'll excuse me, I have some charity work to do.

(Duncan leaves. Meg passes a mirror and notices herself. She poses, admiring herself in her new dress. Leo appears at the garden doors, dressed as a man, but she doesn't see him. He looks every inch the star actor.

Meg strikes another pose, more daring. She notices how the dress empha-
sizes her breasts — she has cleavage! — and she starts to shimmy in front of
the mirror, like a stripper, really going way out on a limb. As she gyrates in
front of the mirror, Leo walks further into the room and watches . . . and then
she sees him.)

MEG: *Yahhh!*

LEO: Excuse me. Sorry. Is this the home of a Miss Florence Snider?

(Meg recognizes him immediately as Leo Clark and gasps.)

MEG: . . . Yes, it is.

LEO: Oh, good. I'm looking for someone who's staying here —

MEG: Maxine.

LEO: That's right. How do you . . . ?

MEG: You're Leo Clark, aren't you?!

LEO: *(Puzzled.)* Yes.

MEG: *(Curtseying instinctively, overcome with awe.) Oh, how do you do! Please,*
come in. I'm Maxine's cousin. Meg. And I am just so thrilled to meet you!
Maxine has told me all about you. Which I knew already! Because of who
you are. I mean, Leo Clark . . . She'll be along in a minute. We just got
back from a little shopping spree. She had something to do at the station.
Well. She had to use the bathroom, but I suppose I shouldn't say that.
(She laughs nervously.) Would you like to sit down?

LEO: I'm fine.

MEG: I just want to say how . . . kind it is of you to come all this way. And I
am so thrilled about being in a play with you . . . and-and if you want to
back out of it, I understand. I mean, you're an actor. A real actor. You
have a body . . . I mean, your body is *trained.* It's an instrument. A treasure. And my treasure isn't trained at all. My instrument. My body! The
way yours is.

(She looks away and makes a face. She wants to kill herself.)

LEO: *(Quietly.)* You have the most beautiful eyes I have ever seen. I'll go find
Maxine.

(Leo exits through the garden. Meg is in a daze. Then Jack, still dressed as
Stephanie, enters from the hall.)

JACK: Margaret? . . . Did you have a nice outing? Are you all right?

MEG: Oh, Stephanie. I just met the most intriguing man.

(Without warning, Leo reenters.)

LEO: Sorry, just one more thing . . .

JACK: *AHH!*

MEG: Stephanie, this is Leo Clark. The famous actor!

JACK: You-you-you —

MEG: She's speechless. I know just how she feels. Stephanie is Maxine's sister. Have you two met before?

LEO: No, but she's even prettier than Maxine said she was. Anyway, I just wanted to say that rehearsal starts tomorrow at ten.

MEG: I wouldn't miss it for the world.

(To Jack.)

We're putting on a play at the wedding.

JACK: Oh, really? Well, that's news to me.

MEG: Maxine is directing and Mr. Clark and I are starring in it! Wait. Do you think that Stephanie could be in it?

LEO: Well, I suppose we could put her in the dance at the end. Like some enormous elf or sprite . . .

MEG: Oh, that's wonderful. Isn't he wonderful?

JACK: Mmmmm. . .

MEG: Wait! There are some lines I need to ask you about. For the play. I marked them in my copy and it's in my room someplace. I'll be right back. Don't go way. All right?

LEO: Of course.

(Meg backs away, trying to be sophisticated, and trips on her packages. Then she gathers them all up and runs off. But she's gone out through the wrong door — and she hurries right back into the room.)

MEG: The, uh, bedroom's upstairs . . .

(She fumbles her way up the stairs and into her bedroom, closing the door with a bang. Jack turns, furious.)

JACK: You crumb.

LEO: I can explain —

JACK: You traitor.

LEO: I did it for both of us.

JACK: You did not! You did it to get Meg! So you could just-just-just —

(He indicates sexual intercourse.)

LEO: Jack!

JACK: You have put my entire life in jeopardy so you could have a little snog in the grass!

LEO: That's not true!

JACK: You want to play the hero and wear *trousers* and *fool around*, while I have to wear this stinking *dress* and this *GODDAM BRASSIERE!*

LEO: Would you keep it down!

JACK: *NO! Hey! Where are you going?!*

LEO: *(Exiting.)* Any place until you keep your voice down.

JACK: Get back here, I'm not finished! . . . Leo! *Get back in here or you can go to* hello . . . !

(As Jack runs out, Duncan enters — so Jack has to immediately turn his galloping man walk into a mincing female walk.)

Ta-ta, good-bye.

(Jack exits, and Duncan strides into the room, simply ecstatic.)

DUNCAN: Meg! Meg?! Meg, get down here!

(Meg enters from above.)

MEG: Duncan, what is it? Where's Mr. Clark?

DUNCAN: Who?

MEG: Leo Clark, the actor. He was just here.

DUNCAN: Fine, fine, fine, now listen. I was walking past the house just now and one of those Western Union boys was coming to the door. I said can I help you, he said do you live here and I said yes —

MEG: But you don't live here.

DUNCAN: I know that. That's not the point! He brought this telegram addressed to you. I gave him a tip by the way, so you might want to re-im . . . no, forget it. But listen to this!

MEG: Duncan —

DUNCAN: Just listen! "Saw advertisement in *London Times*. Stop. Both of us thrilled. Stop. Embarking from Southampton tomorrow and will arrive your house morning of June 8. Stop. Love, Maxine and Stephanie!" Ha, ha! Ha, ha, ha, ha, ha, ha!

MEG: *(Taking the telegram.)* I don't understand.

DUNCAN: Understand what? It's obvious. These two are your real cousins! They arrive here the day before the wedding. And so the ones who came on Monday, those horrible, big, pushy creatures, are both frauds. Hee, hee, hee, hee, hee! I knew it! Oh, it'll be just like old times.

(With a Russian accent.) "Dahnce vit me, my dahlink."

(He dances her around the room.)

MEG: Duncan, stop it! This is ridiculous!

(He gives her a big kiss on the lips. The news has made him passionate. When the kiss breaks off, she keeps talking as though nothing has happened.)

MEG: Maxine is wonderful. And so is Stephanie. They can't be frauds.

DUNCAN: Margaret, they are not your cousins. They have come here to fool you and take your money.

MEG: I don't believe you.

DUNCAN: Well then how do you explain this telegram? Huh? *"Love, Maxine and Stephanie!"*

MEG: Well . . . I suppose that . . . wait. It's simple. *They* must be the frauds. That's it, I'm sure of it!

DUNCAN: Oh, Margaret —

MEG: They *have* to be, and I'll tell you why. I can prove it. Because Maxine — our Maxine, the real one — knows Leo Clark, the famous actor, and they're old friends! She even asked him here and he just arrived!

DUNCAN: So what? That doesn't prove anything!

MEG: Of course it does! He's an established actor, everyone knows him, and she's one of his *best friends*!

DUNCAN: Well maybe this best friend of his is a con artist.

MEG: Oh, stop it.

DUNCAN: And maybe *he's* in on it, too! Have you thought of that?! They could be splitting the boodle!

MEG: Oh, Duncan. He's Leo Clark. He's in the theater. Theater people wouldn't do that kind of thing!

DUNCAN: Wouldn't d — !! *Meg, they are actors, they lie for a living! That's their profession! They are all big liars!!* Look, look, look, we can decide this easily, right now, no problem. We will show your so-called friends this telegram, you will stand here and watch their reactions and that will settle it, *case closed.*

MEG: Duncan. You will not show them that telegram. *Ever.*

DUNCAN: What?

MEG: I will not have them offended in this house.

DUNCAN: But Marg —

MEG: They are the sweetest, kindest women that ever lived and I will not let you do it.

DUNCAN: But they are *not your cousins*!

MEG: *Yes they are!* And if you tell them a single word about that telegram — just one word — I'll-I'll-I'll *do something.* And that's final! Especially now that Leo Clark is here.

DUNCAN: "Leo Clark." What is he doing here anyway?

(*Beat. Meg takes a breath. Her heart is pounding, but she tries to look unfazed.*)

MEG: He's starring in a play . . . which we're putting on the night before the wedding . . . which I will be playing in as well . . . as an actress. So now you know.

DUNCAN: Margaret!

MEG: I'm sorry, Duncan, but that's how it is. Now please go. I have to study my lines. I'll see you later.

(Duncan tries to say something, but he's speechless. He turns and leaves with as much dignity as he can muster. Meg has never stood up for herself like this before, and it's been the ordeal of a lifetime. When Duncan is gone, she takes a deep breath to calm herself. Then she snatches up her copy of the play and bounds to the French doors.)

MEG: *(At the doors; romantically, as Viola in* Twelfth Night.*)*
O time, thou must untangle this, not I;
It is too hard a knot for me t'untie.

(With a look of determination, she hurries out of the room — as the scene changes to:)

SCENE TWO

The living room, ten days later, midmorning. Doc enters in his Elizabethan costume for the play, as Sir Toby Belch, including scarlet tights, a doublet, a sword, and an impressive codpiece.

DOC: Butch, come on!

BUTCH: *(Off.)* No!

DOC: Butch now stop it! The rehearsal starts in two minutes!

BUTCH: *(Off.)* No! I'm not coming out!

DOC: Butch, I'm telling you, it's a nice costume. You look terrific. Now get out here!

(Butch enters dressed as Sir Andrew Aguecheek. He wears baggy hose, a moth-eaten doublet, and a floppy hat from which emerges a wig of straight blond hair that looks like yellow straw sticking to his shoulders.)

BUTCH: I look like a broom with shoes on.

(Audrey enters in costume. She's dressed as Sebastian, an Elizabethan man.)

AUDREY: Good morning, everybody!

DOC/BUTCH: Morning!/Morning!

AUDREY: *(Striking a pose.)* "This is the air; that is the glorious sun;"

(Jack enters dressed as Stephanie — but not in costume for Twelfth Night.*)*

JACK: Good morning!

AUDREY: *"This pearl she gave me, I do feel't and see't . . . "*

BUTCH: *"En garde! Ha! Ha! Ha! . . . Ha! Ha!"*

DOC: *"What a plague means my niece to take the death of her brother thus."*

JACK: *"Item, two lips indifent red; item, two grey eyes with lids to them —"*

(Leo enters, as Leo, carrying his script.)

LEO: Good morning, everyone.

(Everyone responds with "morning.")

It's time for rehearsal. Let's get started. Sofa, please.

(Everyone pitches in to move the furniture out of the way.)

JACK: *(To Audrey.)* Oh, isn't this fun! I just love rehearsals. Here, give us a hug.

AUDREY: Aww . . .

JACK: Give us another.

AUDREY: Aww . . .

JACK: Give us a —

(Leo coughs pointedly.)

Oh, sorry.

LEO: Right. Sit down, sit down.

(Meg enters dressed as Viola/Caesario — and so her costume is identical to Audrey's. It's a glorious costume with mirrored patchwork and rakish hat with a feather.)

MEG: Hi everyone, I'm sorry I'm late.

(She and Audrey see each other — and realizing that they look identical, scream for joy, then strike a mirror-image pose.)

LEO: *One face, one voice, one habit and two persons;*

A natural perspective, that is, and is not.

Sit down, please.

(Everyone sits on the floor facing Leo.)

Now Maxine, our esteemed director, has asked me to give you a few notes while she's out looking for props.

JACK: I thought she did that yesterday.

LEO: She's doing it again.

JACK: Oh. She does that quite a lot, doesn't she?

LEO: Well, Stephanie, there are a lot of props in the play.

JACK: And therefore she just disappears.

LEO: Exactly.

JACK: Aha. That's very informative. Thank you, Leo, you good-looking hunk of man, you.

LEO: *Thank you,* Stephanie. Now Meg, I want to . . .
(Jack/Stephanie raises his hand.)
Yes, Stephanie?

JACK: May I be excused? I have to use the little ladies.

LEO: Please do.

JACK: Thank you. I'll be back in a moment.
(To Audrey.)
Give us a hug. Ta ta.
(Jack exits.)

LEO: Now Meg we'll start with you. A general note, remember to keep your head up so we can see your face.

MEG: Right.

LEO: And I want you to articulate every word. "My father had a daughter." Try it.
(Meg stands, takes a breath; then does the Viola speech from Act II, Scene Four — and does it beautifully.)

MEG: "My father had a daughter loved a man —
As it might be perhaps, were I a woman,
I should your lordship."

LEO: *(As Orsino.)* "And what's her history?"

MEG: "A blank, my lord. She never told her love,
But let concealment, like a worm in the bud,
Feed on her damask cheek. She pined in thought,
And with a green and yellow melancholy,
She sat like Patience on a monument,
Smiling at grief. Was not this love indeed?"

LEO: Much better. Just keep practicing. Tongue, tongue. "Was not this love indeed."

MEG: *(With her own meaning.)* "Was not this love indeed."
(She sits.)

LEO: Good. Doctor. Because you're doubling as the Sea Captain and Sir Toby, you might want to create a different physical presence for each one. Perhaps, as the Captain, you might stoop a little. The old sea-dog type. Then as Sir Toby, you might be more . . . rollicking.

DOC: Rollicking. Got it.

LEO: Butch.

BUTCH: Yes sir!

LEO: Don't rush your lines so much.

BUTCH: I can't help it. I get nervous.

LEO: Try it for me.

BUTCH: Now? In front of everybody?

LEO: Butch, in ten days, you'll be doing it in front of a hundred people. Stand up.

(Butch groans. He stands up and poses stiffly.)

LEO: Now just relax.

(Leo does a relaxing exercise, shaking his arms and humming. Butch imitates it. Butch then does each of the things that Leo now suggests:)

Bend your knees a little. Now let your arms hang at your sides. Look up. And relax your jaw.

(By this time, Butch looks like a gargoyle with rickets.)

We'll get there.

(At which moment, Jack enters through the garden, dressed as himself.)

JACK: Knock knock? Leo! It's me! Jack!

(Leo is shocked. How did Jack do that so fast? Perhaps he screams as Jack did when Leo first appeared as Leo in the previous scene.)

Your friend, Jack! I heard you were in these parts, so I thought I'd drop by.

AUDREY: Oh my gosh. Hey, remember me? We met on the train!

JACK: Audrey.

MEG: Hello, I'm Meg. I saw you in Philadelphia —

BUTCH: My name's Butch!

AUDREY: I was wondering if I'd see you again . . .

DOC: Hi, I'm Doctor Myers . . .

LEO: Excuse me. *Excuse me!* . . . We're having a rehearsal.

THE ACTORS: Sorry . . . sorry . . .

(They retreat to their seats on the floor.)

LEO: For those of you who don't know him this is Jack Gable, who used to be an old friend of mine.

(The following exchange is one of utterly false bonhomie.)

JACK: Are you surprised to see me? Huh? Just a little?

LEO: No, I've been expecting you for quite some time. I was simply waiting for you to think of it.

JACK: Well, when I heard that you had arrived here, I thought "Now why should he have all the fun?"

LEO: Because I thought of it first and I have a real reason for being here. Ha.

JACK: Ha, ha.

LEO: Ha, ha, ha.

JACK: Ha ha ha ha.

BOTH: Hahahahahahahahahaha.

(The cast joins in the fun.)

LEO: Now please sit down, we're rehearsing.

JACK: Right.

(Jack and Audrey sit next to each other, quite cozy together.)

LEO: All right. Butch. Your lines. And don't rush.

BUTCH: "Sir-Toby-Belch-how-now-Sir Toby! I'll-stay-a-month-longer-I-am-a-fellow-of-the-strangest-mind-in-the-world-I-delight-in-masques-and-revels-sometimes-altogether-and-I-excel-at-kikshaws-of-every-kind-and-I-think-I-have-the-back-trick —

LEO: *Stop, stop, STOP! THAT'S TOO FAST!*

(Butch turns away, hurt.)

No. I'm sorry. I-I shouldn't have yelled. I'm sorry.

JACK: You know, I think Maxine could help right now. She listens better than you do.

LEO: Surprisingly, that's a good idea. I'll go find her. Everybody, take five.

(Leo exits. The actors relax and start chatting. Butch is low.)

BUTCH: Gee, I'm tryin' to slow down. I really am.

JACK: You'll be fine, I promise. Look. Try this. After every, say, five words, take a breath and say to yourself the word . . . Mississippi.

BUTCH: I can do that!

DOC: Of course you can! You could be a star! It just takes practice.

BUTCH: Thanks, Dad. And you're doing great!

DOC: Aw. Come on. As they say in showbiz, let's "run your lines."

(They move away, leaving Audrey and Jack alone together.)

AUDREY: Hey. You're really nice, ya know that?

JACK: You know what? The feeling is mutual.

AUDREY: Aw, get outa here . . . So what brings you to York, PA?

JACK: The truth? I've been having dreams about roller skating and I thought of you.

AUDREY: Gee that's nice.

JACK: How's the play coming?

AUDREY: It's coming great. But the thing is, I'm playing somebody of the opposite sex. His name is Sebastian. He's supposed to be Meg's twin brother,
which is nuts. Me as a guy! But I've thought up an angle. See, I'm gonna
play him as a real tough guy. I do this great Marlon Brando imitation, but
I figure I won't tell Maxine till later. I'll just surprise her.

JACK: What a good idea.

AUDREY: So how do you know Maxine and Stephanie?

JACK: Me? Oh, they . . . didn't they tell you? Well, they-they practically
raised me.

AUDREY: No kiddin'.

JACK: I can still remember Stephanie singing me to sleep every night.

AUDREY: But I thought she was deaf and dumb till recently.

JACK: She used a tape recorder and moved her lips.

AUDREY: Are you puttin' me on? Get outa here.

JACK: Here, give us a hug . . . I mean, me a hug. Give me a hug.

*(Audrey hugs him, slightly confused. At this moment, Leo enters from the hall,
dressed as Maxine in a very chic pants outfit, having changed in a hurry. She's
in director mode now, flying everywhere, half business, half Bernhardt.)*

LEO: Darlings! Oh, my darlings, forgive me!

(Into the garden.)

Thank you, Leo! Take your time! I was scouting for props amid the roiling
sea of the York County merchants. Jack! Jack! My dear boy!

JACK: Maxine! How good to see you!

LEO: Oh let me look at you. Why, you've put on weight. You're getting enor-
mously fat.

JACK: Well you look marvelous. You've always had that big, raw-boned mannish
look.

LEO: Why thank you. Aren't you sweet.

*(Leo pinches Jack's cheek and has to restrain himself from doing Jack an in-
jury.)* Now Jack dear, do me a favor and go find Stephanie. I need her for
rehearsal. And tell her to get into costume.

JACK: Costume? Now?

LEO: Yes *now*, dear, before anyone gets hurt.

JACK: Oh all right.

(Jack exits.)

LEO: Now let's all take another minute while I settle down. Chat among yourselves. Whoo. Hot. I'm afraid I rushed too much . . .

(He blows down into his blouse and sits next to Meg.)

LEO: So. My dear. How is it coming along? Do you feel bright-eyed and bushy-tailed?

MEG: *(Troubled.)* Well, it's coming, I guess. But not the way I hoped it would.

LEO: Is something wrong?

MEG: Well, not really.

LEO: "Well, not really." That doesn't sound very promising at all. Can you tell me about it?

MEG: Well, it's just . . . I've never done any real acting before and there's so much to remember. Head up. Enunciate. Move left, move right. You and Leo are professionals. And you work with professionals. From the Royal Academy! And they're all sophisticated, and they know everything, and they've been everywhere . . . I just . . . I can't imagine what Leo must think of me.

(She's ready to cry by this time.)

LEO: Margaret.

(He takes her hand.)

Let me tell you something. I'll say it once, and I don't want to say it again. You are an extraordinary woman. You can do anything you set your mind to. And *everyone* has to start some place. Olivier was born in some dinky little town in southern England, and Katherine Hepburn was born in Cape Cod someplace with a knife in her teeth. You are not defined by where you start, but by where you end up. As for the play, there are two rules for every actor: remember your lines and don't bump into the furniture. That is *my* line. Noël Coward stole it from me. As for traveling or not traveling, you will get to Paris one of these days if I have to carry you on my back and swim. And when you get there, you will look around and say to yourself: I was just as sophisticated before I left only now I need a bath. All right?

MEG: . . . All right.

LEO: Good. And remember: Lines.

MEG: And furniture. Got it. Maxine . . . thank you for staying for the wedding.

LEO: My dear, I think of nothing else.

(At this moment, Jack reenters as Stephanie, only he's dressed for his role as Olivia in something wildly seductive and outrageous — Spanish perhaps — and he's not happy about it.)

JACK: Well. Are you happy now?

LEO: Stephanie. You look as ridi — as charming as I hoped you would. All right, everyone, line up, please. Line up. Let me see my cast all together. Let's go . . .

(The cast lines up, a truly motley crew of all shapes and sizes, variously terrified [Butch], overconfident [Doc], confused [Audrey], annoyed [Jack], and thrilled [Meg]. They should remind us of the mechanicals in A Midsummer Night's Dream *— a valiant band of well-meaning locals who haven't got a clue.)*

LEO: Now I want each of you to recite your favorite line from the play, in character, reaching way down deep, showing me the absolute finest performance of which you are capable. Sir Toby.

(Each character steps forward, does his or her speech, and steps back in line.)

SIR TOBY/DOC: *(Rollicking, hands on hips — truly awful.)*

What a plague means my niece to take the death of her brother thus?! *Ha! Ha!* I'm sure care's an enemy to life! *Ha ha! Ho ho! Ha ha!* Rollicking.

SIR ANDREW/BUTCH: *(Strikes his pose.)*

Methinks sometimes I have no more wit, Mississippi

Than a Christian or an ordinary man has, Mississippi!

Oh had I but followed the arts, Mississippi!

OLIVIA/JACK: *(The great diva.)*

By the roses of the spring,

By maidenhood, honor, truth and everything,

I love thee so, in spite of all thy pride,

Nor wit nor reason can my passion hide!

VIOLA/MEG: As I am man,

My state is desperate for my master's love.

As I am woman (now alas the day!),

What thriftless sighs shall poor Olivia breathe?

SEBASTIAN/AUDREY: *(Very Brando, both in voice and gesture.)*

Ah, me. My stars shine darkly over me.

I seek in this strange land my sister,

My twin, in hope she is not drowned.

LEO: And there you have it. Each one better than the next. Soon this room will be decorated like a fairyland and we, the actors of this comedy called life will be presenting a one-in-a-million performance of *Twelfth Night,* and all I can say is May God Be with Us!

(The lights change and the cast scatters.)

SCENE THREE

As the lights change, we hear a dance band in the garden playing "Just in Time" over the clinking of party glasses. In a blue half-light, our company of actors helps move the furniture back into place; simultaneously, stagehands dressed as caterers begin decorating the room with flowers, a screen, and a punch bowl and glasses. Small white fairy lights come on in the garden — and by the end of the transition, the room looks joyfully partylike.

It's ten days later and the party is in progress. Just as the caterers finish decorating the room, the lights come up on the balcony above the living room, and Duncan enters from down the hall. There's a telephone up there, outside Meg's bedroom, and he picks up the receiver and dials, furtively. He's extremely upset.

FLORENCE: *(Off.) Duncan, get down here!*
DUNCAN: *(Calling.)* I'll be down in a minute, Florence!
(To himself.)
You old bat!
(Into the phone.)
Ah, Inspector Ballard, it's Reverend Wooley again. Sorry to bother you at this . . . Yes, I know it's seven-thirty, but I've been trying to get you all . . . Well, you didn't answer any of the messages! Now listen, I'm at Florence's house right now, at the *party* . . . Well I'm sorry you weren't invited but I wasn't in charge of the guest list . . . Well, yes, I had *some* influence, but . . . Yes, the food *is* excellent, I'm very sorry you weren't invited, but please just listen! Do you remember I told you about the telegram from the real Maxine and Stephanie — well, it said they'd arrive this morning and they aren't here yet! Of course it has me worried! I told you about this whole thing weeks ago! You were supposed to help me! Yes I am, *very* upset, and I'll tell you why. Because Maxine, the *big* one, told me this morning that she overheard Florence changing her will. She's leaving everything to Stephanie, the *smaller* one . . . Yes, they're both large, but one is bigger than the other! The point is, Stephanie doesn't deserve it! . . . Well, yes, I hope Florence lasts forever, *but it isn't very likely now is it*!?
FLORENCE: *(Off.)* Duncan!
DUNCAN: *Shut up! (Into the phone.)* All right, I'll tell you what I think you should do. I think you should arrest them both. Right now. Send a squad

car . . . Of course you need evidence, but you were supposed to find it! That's your job! . . . *I'm not criticizing you! I'm stating a fact!*

FLORENCE: *(Off.) Duncan! Where the hell are you?!*

DUNCAN: *I'M COMING!*

(Into the phone, desperate.) Look, just do something, but do it now! . . . *Thank* you! *(He hangs up.)* God!

(He realizes what he just said — at which moment, the lights change and a tango starts to play. Florence appears, dressed to the nines, and starts tangoing. She has taken years of lessons and has great flair. Duncan enters and joins her. He's miserable. They complete the first section of the dance and dance out — as Audrey and Butch dance into the room. Audrey is terrific, Butch is trying hard to keep up. They perform the second section and then go — as Stephanie and Doc enter tangoing up a storm. Shades of Some Like It Hot. *When they complete the third section, the other couples come back on, and all three couples dance the coda in unison and end with a flourish. Note: this should be choreographed as a real dance number. When the dance is over, everyone filters off into the garden, except Florence and Audrey, who linger for a moment.)*

AUDREY: Ooh, this is such a good party, I can tell already. And just wait'll you see the play tonight. You'll go insane.

FLORENCE: Well, that's something to look forward to.

AUDREY: You know, I've just gotta say, it's really nice of you to do this for Meg. Next time somebody says to me you're nothin' but a nasty old bat, I'm gonna say, "Oh yeah? You only know the *half* of it."

FLORENCE: Thank you.

(As they exit, Leo and Jack enter simultaneously, Jack from the garden. Leo is Leo, dressed in a dinner jacket, and Jack is Stephanie, in a party dress, just having danced.)

LEO: Jack — !

JACK: If I have to dance one more minute in high heels, I'll kill myself. You should see them out there, hip, sway, hip, sway. I'm telling you it's a whole other sex.

LEO: Jack listen! We have to stop the wedding.

JACK: Stop the . . . Why? What are you talking about?!

LEO: So that I can marry Meg.

JACK: *Marry* her? I thought you just wanted to . . .

(He indicates sexual intercourse.)

LEO: Jack, I'm in love with her!

JACK: Oh, really? So you've been stringing me along the whole time under false pretenses! And what about *Julius Caesar*?! Huh?! And-and-and *King Lear*, and *Hamlet*! That's what you live for!

LEO: Yes. I did. And I want all that. If it's possible. But Jack, I'm in *love*. Deeply in love. I want a house, and neighbors and a front door.

JACK: That was my idea!

LEO: And you were right! You were exactly right! And we're almost there. It could be *us*.

JACK: "Us"? What have I got to do with this?

LEO: Well you and Audrey.

JACK: What do you mean?! We're . . . friends.

LEO: Jack, whenever she walks into the room, you start drooling. And last night she told me she's in love with you. She wants to marry you.

JACK: . . . She said that?

(*Leo nods. Jack is speechless, then he explodes with joy.*)
Hoo-hooooo! Ha-haaaaaaaa! Yes!!! Yyyyyyyyyyyes!!! I knew it! Ha-haaaaaaaa!
Did she really say that?

LEO: No, but you can see the effect it has on you.

JACK: *Leo* — !

LEO: Now listen. Jack. You've got to help me. I have spent three weeks trying to convince Meg to leave Duncan and marry me and I've gotten nowhere. She feels obligated to him. So, I have a plan. The final gambit. I want *you* to seduce *Duncan*. Offer him your body. As Stephanie, of course.

JACK: What?

LEO: You see, this morning I told Duncan that I overheard Florence talking to her lawyer, cutting Margaret and Maxine out of her will and leaving everything to Stephanie. Well Duncan is beside himself! He wants the money for some foundation or something. So if you give him even the slightest encouragement he'll go after you. Now here's the trick: Meg and I will be hiding behind this screen watching everything. We'll jump out and catch him the second he starts to undress you.

JACK: Un-un-undress —

LEO: It's the old screen gambit, like in *Twelfth Night* and *School for Scandal*.

JACK: Are you crazy? *ARE YOU NUTS?!!!*

LEO: Jack! You have to do this. When Meg sees him for what he is, she'll give him up! Then I can marry her!

JACK: No.

LEO: Please.

JACK: No!

LEO: Jack, you're my best friend! If I ever needed you in my whole life, I need you now!

JACK: I have spent the last four weeks of my life dressed as a woman, I can't take a bath without you guarding the door, and I have nightmares, really horrible nightmares, about *talking brassieres*!

LEO: Is that a yes?

JACK: *(Whimpering.)* Yes.

LEO: Good. Here's the letter.

JACK: What letter?

LEO: From you to Duncan. *(Points to the envelope.)* See? "Duncan." It says that you'll meet him here at eight o'clock and that you find him sexually attractive.

JACK: Oh, God!

(Audrey enters from the garden.)

AUDREY: Has anyone seen Jack?

JACK: Yes? *(Catches himself.)* No! No Jack. Not here. All gone.

LEO: Stephanie, you can ask her now.

JACK: Huh?

LEO: She's so shy. She wants you to deliver this letter.

AUDREY: Sure, no problem.

(She takes the envelope — as Meg enters at the top of the stairs dressed for the party and looking gorgeous. We hear the song "Fascination" wafting in from the garden.)

MEG: Hi everybody. Sorry to interrupt. Has anyone seen Duncan?

LEO: Duncan, Duncan, never heard of him. Their playing our song. Shall we dance?

MEG: Well . . . all right.

(They dance around the room like Fred Astaire and Ginger Rogers — then sweep out into the garden, leaving Audrey and Jack alone. Audrey sighs.)

AUDREY: Isn't love great. Some day I'm gonna find just the right guy. And believe you me, on that wedding night, in some big soft comfy bed, I'm gonna make him *really happy*. Hey, come here, you're drooling.

(She pulls out a hankie and mops around his mouth.)

Aw. Here. Give us a hug. *Ooh!* Stephanie, watch your fingers!

JACK: Sorry, sorry . . . I-I-I-I think I should go now. Bye-bye.

(He reels up the stairs and through the door.)

AUDREY: Gee she's a nice girl.

(Audrey turns and accidentally drops the envelope in the punch bowl. She fishes it out and wipes it with her sleeve.)

AUDREY: *Ahh!* Oh, darn! Would you look at this envelope? I'm supposed to deliver it and now I can't read it. Let's see . . . D. It starts with a D. D-U. Or is that an O? Who do I know that starts with a D . . . ?

(Doc enters.)

Hi, Doc . . . Wait! Doc. "D." Doctor. Doc, this letter is for you. It's from Stephanie.

DOC: For me?

AUDREY: She asked me to give it to you. See you later.

(And Audrey exits. Doc is alone.)

DOC: From Stephanie? That's odd.

(He opens the letter and reads.)

"My dear friend, You are a healer of souls. You are a man of compassion to those in your care. You are my sunshine, my only sunshine, You make me happy when skies are gray . . . As the song says, I adore you." . . . *What?* "As you know, I am now an heiress, but please don't let my millions stand in your way. I never felt religious until I met you, but now I want to sit on your pulpit. May you enter my house and dwell there forever." The woman is an animal! A very large animal! "Take me. Ravish me. Meet me tonight in the living room at eight o'clock." That's in ten minutes! "Your loving and devoted Stephanie. P.S. Don't take no for an answer." God in heaven. She's just been playing hard to get! I should have known from that first time we met. She just looked at me and never said a word. Of course, she was deaf and dumb at the time. But still. She had those bedroom eyes. Droopy. Sensuous. Astigmatic. I shall return.

(He hurries out, as Meg and Leo dance in.)

MEG: Well. I can't believe it's finally happening. The wedding, I mean. I've actually been remarkably calm about it. Up to now. I don't know why, I guess it seemed so far away. But then suddenly, last night, as I was lying there in bed, my stomach got very tight, and my heart started

(He stops her mouth with a kiss. A really great kiss.)

MEG: No!

LEO: Meg. I love you.

MEG: Leo, stop.

LEO: I can't. I love you more than anything in the world.

MEG: I'm getting married tomorrow!

LEO: Then don't. Not to him. Marry me instead.

MEG: Leo, I can't do that! I promised Duncan!

LEO: But he's not right for you! Meg, you deserve a life! You have to see Paris, and do some acting and travel the world! Now I have a plan, so just listen. You and I are going to stand right here, behind this screen and watch Duncan try to make lo —

MEG: I've got to go.

LEO: Not yet.

MEG: I need Maxine! I have to talk to her!

LEO: Maxine?!

MEG: I have to find her right now!

LEO: Oh no. No no. No no. No no. *Wait!*

(Too late. Meg is gone. As Leo runs after her, Duncan enters jovially, carrying a telegram.)

DUNCAN: Why hello there, Leo.

LEO: You're early. Go away and come back.

(Leo runs out to the garden, following Meg, leaving Duncan alone in the room. Duncan is in high spirits.)

DUNCAN: "Go away and come back." Ha! I knew I was right. Why look at this. It's another telegram — and it just arrived. *(He kisses the telegram with a big smack. "Mwa!")* "Apologize for delay. Stop. General strike at fault. Stop. Will arrive at eight-fifteen tonight. Stop. Maxine and Stephanie." *Ha! Ha! Ha!* Oh, Justice is sweet, sayeth the Lord, *hallelujah!*

(Jack now enters from the bedroom at the top of the stairs, still in his party gown, looking as sexy as all get out. He sees Duncan, kicks the door shut, and drapes himself along the door frame.)

JACK: . . . Hello, big boy.

DUNCAN: I beg your pardon.

JACK: Is that a chopstick in your pocket or are you just glad to see me?

DUNCAN: Are you speaking to me?

JACK: Oh, *yes.*

DUNCAN: Well don't bother.

JACK: Fine, fine. No words, just action, is that your game? Well go ahead, mister! I'm ready for you!

(He poses with his dress hiked up above his knee. When Duncan isn't looking, he gives a high sign to the screen, believing that Leo is behind it. Duncan turns and just stares at him.)

What's the matter?

DUNCAN: The matter? Nothing's the matter for me. No-o-o. But it is for you. I have a surprise.

JACK: Here it comes.

DUNCAN: A *big* surprise.

JACK: Now you're just bragging.

DUNCAN: In fact, I have two surprises.

JACK: You have two of them?

DUNCAN: That's right. And they have long flowing hair.

JACK: Have you thought about surgery?

DUNCAN: Don't change the subject!

(Jack covers his eyes with his hand and keeps them covered throughout the following.)

JACK: All right. Go ahead.

DUNCAN: You want to see it, eh? *(Duncan goes through his pockets, looking for the telegram.)* Wait a second . . . I'll get it out . . . Oh, damn, now I can't find it . . .

JACK: You can't find it?

DUNCAN: Just give me a second . . .

JACK: And you call this a *big* surprise?

DUNCAN: Here it is. I found it. *(He pulls out the telegram and holds it up. But Jack is still hiding his eyes.)* There. Do you see it?

JACK: No.

DUNCAN: You're not looking.

JACK: I can't.

DUNCAN: At least look at the signature.

JACK: It's *signed*?

DUNCAN: *Of course it's signed! How else would you know where it came from?!* *(Bing bong! The front doorbell rings.)*

DUNCAN: It's them. I know it is. Ha! Here! Keep it as a souvenir!

JACK: A souvenir . . . ?

(Duncan stuffs the telegram into Jack's hand and exits. Jack hurries over to the screen to talk to Leo — who isn't there, of course — when Doc enters. Jack puts the telegram into his sleeve and forgets about it.)

DOC: Hello, gorgeous.

JACK: *Ah!* Oh, Doctor, thank God it's you. I just had the most awful experience!

DOC: Oh, you poor thing. You poor baby. You're upset, I can tell. Now you just sit down. Just tell your doctor aaaaall about it.

(Doc starts making love to Jack, stroking his hair and cheek.)

JACK: . . . What are you doing?

DOC: Am I doing something?

JACK: Yes, now stop it.

DOC: Stop it, she says. Stop it. Ha! Can I have a kiss?

JACK: No!

DOC: Ouch! Give me that hand! Oh, you have such interesting hands. For the record, I do electrolysis.

(Doc really goes after Jack, who wriggles away and starts crawling across the floor.)

JACK: Hey! Would you stop that! *Stop it! Just-just-just —That's personal property!*

DOC: Who said "Don't take no for an answer"?

JACK: I have no idea.

DOC: "You are my sunshine, my only sunshine."

JACK: I think you've had too much punch.

DOC: "I want to sit on your pulpit!"

JACK: You do?

DOC: You can't deny it. You feel just as I do! It was all there, in your letter.

JACK: My letter?

DOC: "Take me. Ravish me. Enter my house!"

JACK: *Leo! Come out already! It's time to come out! . . .* Oh, no. *The screen! There's nobody behind the screen!*

DOC: Good idea. We can do it back there.

(He drags Jack behind the screen.)

JACK: No!

DOC: Please! Darling. Stephanie. I'm on my knees.

(He realizes he's not, so he drops to his knees and takes Jack's hand.)

Marry me.

(At this moment, Butch and Audrey burst into the room having a fight.)

BUTCH: I can't believe you want to break up!

AUDREY: Butch I'm really sorry!

BUTCH: It's that Jack guy, isn't it? Oh, I'm gonna punch him —

AUDREY: Leave him alone!

BUTCH: I could have other girls, you know. Father wants me to marry Stephanie. And look at her! She's beautiful! Maybe I *should* marry her!

JACK: No, I really don't think —

(Butch kisses Jack.)

YAAAH!

DOC: Butch, listen to me. I know this may hurt you a little, but Stephanie and I are in love.

JACK: We are?

BUTCH: Father! You can't have her! She's mine now!

DOC: She wants *me*, Butch. Not you!

(And Doc kisses Jack.)

JACK: *YAAAH!... Would you two stop it!*

(Jack runs around the room pursued by Doc, Butch, and Audrey.)

DOC: Stephanie, darling, come back!

BUTCH: Hey, leave her alone! She's mine!

AUDREY: Butch, wait!... *Butch!*

(They all run out of the room. As soon as they're gone, Leo enters as Maxine — just as Meg enters from the other direction. She's extremely upset.)

MEG: Oh, Maxine! Where have you been?! I need to talk to you!

LEO: My dear, what's the matter?

MEG: I need your advice! I don't know what to do!

LEO: Now, now, just calm down and start at the beginning. And whatever it is: Follow your heart. It's always the way.

MEG: All right. It's about Leo. You know how well I've gotten to know him over the past few weeks and oh, I just think the world of him. He's gentle, and thoughtful, and . . .

LEO: Kind and handsome. Go on, go on.

MEG: Well, tonight, while I was dancing with him, he . . . kissed me. And when he did, something totally unexpected happened. Inside me. And I realized, while I was kissing him . . . oh, I don't know how to say this.

LEO: Try, try.

MEG: I'm sure it's wrong.

LEO: Tell me.

MEG: Oh, I can't do it!

LEO: Margaret, tell me *right now*.

MEG: . . . All right.

(They sit together on the sofa.)

While I was kissing him, I was . . . thinking about you.

(She leans amorously into Maxine.)

Maxine, I think I'm in love with you.

(Pause.)

LEO: . . . No. You're not.

MEG: I think I am.

LEO: You are not! Oh, darling, you're just confused. I mean, of course Leo and I are similar in some ways . . .

MEG: Like two halves of the same apple! I mean, do I love him at all? Yes of course I do. He's funny and kind and . . .

LEO: Sexy?

MEG: Well I guess a little bit. But the thing is, I love you more! I guess it's wrong, but it just feels, when you're not around me, that something is missing. I wouldn't have dared say anything, but I know you feel the same way. I *know* it. I can see it sometimes when you look at me. Sort of cross-eyed with your mouth hanging open.

LEO: No, that's just me.

MEG: Maxine, I'm being very brave and you aren't helping me!

LEO: I will help you, just listen! Life can be complicated. Right now it's extremely complicated. For reasons that have nothing to do with you.

MEG: You don't love me, do you?

LEO: Of course I love you —

MEG: But not the same way.

LEO: Well not exactly —

MEG: Oh, Maxine, I shouldn't have told you. I should just marry Duncan.

LEO: No, you shouldn't!

MEG: I'll never mention it again.

LEO: Mention it, please —

MEG: I am *so sorry!*

(*She kisses Leo on the cheek and then runs up the stairs and into her room.*)

LEO: No. Meg, wait — ! Wait!

(*She's gone. At which point, Jack enters still dressed as Stephanie, but completely disheveled.*)

JACK: *Where the hell were you!* You weren't there! Behind the screen! And I was attacked!

LEO: By Duncan?

JACK: No! By Doctor Lust, Monster of Medicine. He thought the letter was for him.

LEO: Why?

JACK: *How should I know!* Duncan must have thought I was insane.

LEO: Did he try anything?

JACK: No, he stuffed a telegram in my hand. Maybe, for a minister, that's foreplay.

LEO: What telegram? What did it say?

JACK: I don't know! I didn't read it!

LEO: Do you still have it?

JACK: I guess . . . Yes, here it is. So what?

LEO: "Apologize for delay. Stop."

JACK: "General strike at fault. Stop."

LEO: "Will arrive at eight-fifteen tonight. Stop."

JACK: "Maxine and Stephanie."

LEO/JACK: . . . *YAHHHHH!*

LEO: *Eight-fifteen! That's in five minutes! What do we do?!*

JACK: *Get the hell out of here!*

LEO: But I can't leave Meg.

JACK: Forget about Meg! We're about to get arrested as women! They'd put us
in a woman's prison. With *female truck drivers with tight T-shirts and tat-
toos!* . . . Well, maybe that's not so bad . . .

LEO: Wait a second. If we're men, we're in the clear.

JACK: What do you mean?

LEO: When the girls arrive, everybody will be looking for the first Maxine and
Stephanie. So we have to change and become Leo and Jack again!

JACK: Good idea.

DUNCAN: *(Off.)* Florence, just don't ask questions!

LEO/JACK: . . . Duncan!

> *(They hide under the stairs, as Duncan enters at a run from the garden,
> pulling Florence along with him.)*

DUNCAN: Oh, damn, I thought I saw them in here.

FLORENCE: Duncan, what are you *doing*?!

DUNCAN: All right, listen. The women you know as Maxine and Stephanie are
frauds. The real ones are arriving tonight.

FLORENCE: How do you know?

DUNCAN: A telegram just arrived. And there was one before that.

FLORENCE: Let me see them.

DUNCAN: I don't have them right now.

FLORENCE: Oh, please —

DUNCAN: It's the truth!

> *(Bing bong! The front doorbell rings.)*

DUNCAN: It's them. It has to be. Come on!

FLORENCE: *Ah!*

> *(Duncan pulls Florence off at breakneck speed. As soon as Duncan and Flo-
> rence are gone, Leo and Jack come out of hiding. Simultaneously, Meg enters*

from her bedroom at the top of the stairs. She sees the men from above, but they don't see her.)

JACK: Oh, God in heaven. It's incredible! Just look at us! Two grown men dressed as women!

(Both men pull off their wigs. Meg reels backward against the wall, then clings onto the banister, peering down through the rails.)

JACK: I'm wearing a dress, for God's sake. And a petticoat! And lace knickers! With little flowers on them! I think they're peonies!

(Audrey now enters from down the hall. She starts to say something to Meg, but Meg silences her and points over the balcony to the men below.)

JACK: If my mother ever saw me like this, I'd kill myself!

(Audrey takes it in — and swoons into Meg's arms. Meg pushes her back to her feet.)

JACK: Oh, how did I ever let you talk me into this?

LEO: You weren't complaining for the last four weeks, while you were slobbering over Audrey.

JACK: Well what about you? If I hadn't gone along with all this, you wouldn't have met Meg.

LEO: Well that's true. Except now she says she's attracted to Maxine.

JACK: Attracted?

LEO: *Attracted.*

(Audrey turns and looks at Meg — then inches away from her.)

JACK: But you're not even pretty as a girl.

LEO: Look who's talking!

JACK: Well, I can't be too bad, because two men just kissed me on the lips!

(The women react.)

LEO: Look, that's not the point! The point is, I'm in love with Meg. She is the greatest woman that ever walked this earth. I don't care if she's slow, I don't care if she's gullible, I don't even mind that squint she has in the one eye. I'm in love with her.

JACK: Gee, that's really nice, it's a lovely thought, I know just how you feel. *BUT I NEED MY CLOTHES!*

LEO: All right, all right! Come on. We'll both change, then find the girls and tell them everything. But we have to do it just right, because this whole thing makes them look really, *really stupid.*

(The men exit and the women head down the stairs.)

MEG: *(Beyond furious — ready to eat nails.)* I'll kill him. *I'm going to kill him!*

AUDREY: I think we should kill all *four* of them! . . . Oh. I get it, I get it.

MEG: Unh!

AUDREY: But, you know, when I think about all they've been going through just to spend a little time with us, I'm incredulous. That means —

MEG: *Shut up!*

AUDREY: Yeah! I'm gonna shut up now!

MEG: I can't believe I shared a bedroom with him for four weeks!*(A horrible thought suddenly strikes her.)* Oh my God. He saw me in my . . . curlers! *(She's seething now.)* Revenge. *I want revenge!*
(Meg exits in a fury into the garden.)

AUDREY: *(Calling.)* Yeah! Me, too!
(At which moment, Jack hurries in from the kitchen, dressed as himself.)

JACK: Audrey!

AUDREY: Jack!

JACK: Listen. There's something I have to tell you.

AUDREY: Well, I have something to — !

JACK: Please don't interrupt. *(He takes a breath and it all pours out.)* I did something terrible. It all started a month ago. Leo and I were on a train.
(Audrey reacts as if to say "no kidding.")
Well you know that. And we read about Florence dying and leaving her money to Max and Steve. And by this time I had met you and all I wanted to do was take you in my arms. But then you told us her nephews were Maxine and Stephanie, and you see we're *actors* and we had these *costumes* and so . . . well the fact is, we dressed up as women!

AUDREY: No!

JACK: Yes! *I* was that beautiful creature. Stephanie. It was me.

AUDREY: Wow!

JACK: I know, but I didn't mean to make you look stupid. I–I did it because of your thighs. I mean your eyes. I wanted to be with every inch of you. Your lips. Your forehead. And I wanted your bust. I mean your trust. And I want a home so badly. A real home with a picket fence, and a gate, and little Audreys skating to school every morning. And so I lay my soul at your feet and I ask — nay, I beg — your forgiveness.
(He kneels before her.)
Audrey, will you marry me?

AUDREY: You are the most obstreperous, abominable, loathsome, odious, deplorable, despicable, obnoxious, vile, detestable man I have ever met! And of course I'll marry you! You just had to ask! *Now give us a hug!*
(She grabs him; they hug and run off. The moment they're gone, Leo and Meg

enter from opposite directions. Leo is now in his suit, as Leo. Meg plays it cool, enjoying her revenge to the hilt.)

LEO: Meg!

MEG: Leo, listen to me, I have to talk to you!

LEO: Well I have something to tell you too.

MEG: Let me go first, it's important. After I left you on the dance floor, I went to see Maxine. I was confused, and oh, I said some silly things, but while I was with her, she gave me some very good advice. She told me that I should follow my heart. And now that I've had a chance to think, I know exactly what she meant. So I'm marrying Duncan tomorrow morning.

LEO: Huh?

MEG: "Follow your heart." I made a commitment to him. That's what she meant. She *wants* me to marry him.

LEO: No, she doesn't.

MEG: That was her way of reminding me that honor and trust are so important!

LEO: *No they're not!* That's not what she meant!

MEG: Leo. Thank you for everything. Good-bye.
   (She kisses him sadly on the cheek and starts to go. She has to do this, but now it's breaking her heart.)

LEO: No! Wait! Look, look, look! Wait, wait! Look! Wait! Look! I'll go find Maxine and she'll tell you exactly what she thinks.

MEG: I know what she thinks.

LEO: *No you don't!* I mean, you-you-you think you know . . .

MEG: I'm sorry, Leo.

LEO: Please. *Please!* Just one more chance! Let her talk to you! *Please!*

MEG: . . . All right. I'll give her *one minute* to come in here and tell me what she thinks. And if she isn't here by then I'm marrying Duncan. Oh, and I want you to be here too. You and Maxine together. Then we'll get it all straightened out.

LEO: Together?

MEG: That's right.

LEO: Together! Right! One minute! Me and Leo. Me and Maxine! I'll find her. And mail her. Bring her. We'll be here! *(He dashes off through the garden. Off.) Shit!*
   (At that moment, Duncan and Florence enter from the hall.)

DUNCAN: Margaret! We've been looking all over for you. I'm afraid I have some rather distressing news.

FLORENCE: Don't listen to him! He's an idiot.

DUNCAN: Florence, please. Margaret, I now have conclusive proof that the two women who have been here for the past four weeks posing as Maxine and Stephanie are *not* your cousins.

MEG: *(Sadly.)* I know that, Duncan.

DUNCAN: You do? How?

MEG: It doesn't matter.

DUNCAN: Oh. Well, I do have some good news. Your real cousins have just arrived. They're in the garden.

FLORENCE: And I don't particularly like them!

DUNCAN: That's not the point! And Meg, listen, I've spoken to them and they're willing to take only $100,000 each and go back to England. We'll have the rest for the foundation! Now as soon as the police arrive, this will all be over.

MEG: *(Alarmed.)* The police? What for?

DUNCAN: To arrest Maxine and Stephanie. That is, the supposed ones.

FLORENCE: I told him not to do it!

DUNCAN: Florence, they have deceived you.

FLORENCE: But I *like* them, Duncan!

DUNCAN: Well I'm sorry, but they have broken the law! They have made a mockery of your entire household and they should not be rewarded for their . . . theatrical behavior. So typical of actors, it's always me, me, me, look at me!

(At this moment, we hear the whine of a siren as a police car screeches to a halt in the driveway.)

DUNCAN: Oh, good! Now all I have to do is find them and hand them over.

MEG: Duncan! Wait! I saw one of them in the front yard! Just now!

DUNCAN: Which one?!

MEG: Stephanie. And Maxine. They were both there.

DUNCAN: I'll be right back!

(He runs off. The moment he's gone, Leo hurries in dressed as Maxine, but slightly askew, since everything has been pulled on in such a hurry.)

LEO: Darling girl, there you are! Now listen, you misunderstood me. I want you to marry Leo, that divine young man — and he's right outside.
(Calling.) Come in, darling! . . . What?! What's that you said?!
(To Meg.) Oh no! He's hurt his leg! I'll send him in. You stay right here.

MEG: Leo —

(He runs off and now plays both parts, putting his head around the door as necessary.)

LEO: *(Off — as Leo.)* Meg, I'm right out here! I've hurt my leg and I can't come in! *(Off — as Maxine.)* Of course you can, just put a little weight on it. *(Off — as Leo.)* Ow, that really hurts!

(He pops his head around the door, without the wig and with his jacket on, as Leo. The more he can pop in and out as the two characters and make this a tour de force, as in The Mystery of Irma Vep *and other similar plays, the better. It should build to a fever pitch.)*

LEO: *(As Leo.)* Here I am, Meg! Now Maxine says you should marry me — but I've hurt my leg so I'll let her do all the talking. Bye!

MEG: Leo —

LEO: *(Off — as Maxine.)* Oh you brave young man! Of course she should marry you and not Duncan! *(Off — as Leo.)* Then go inside and tell her! *(Off — as Maxine.)* I'll do it right now!

MEG: Leo — !

(He runs back on as Maxine.)

LEO: I'm right here! Here I am! Now Meg, you really must marry Leo. He's such a lovely boy, and so handsome and —

MEG: Leo, stop it!

LEO: Leo? *(Beat; then he calls through the door.)* Leo, she's talking to you so listen carefully!

MEG: *Would you please just stop it!* I know it's you! I know you're Leo! And that Stephanie is Jack! I know everything!

LEO: You do?

MEG: Yes! Now get out of here, fast. The police are here!

LEO: But I can't leave you.

MEG: You have to! You'll be arrested!

LEO: Meg, I love you.

MEG: I know that! And I love you!

LEO: You do?

MEG: *Yes.*

LEO: Will you marry me?

MEG: *Yes!*

(He's about to kiss her, but stops abruptly.)

LEO: Wait! I came here to take your money.

MEG: *I know that!*

(They kiss. Another really great kiss.)

FLORENCE: If I were you, I'd get the hell out of here.

LEO: *(To Florence.)* Aren't you even a *little* surprised?

FLORENCE: Why? Because I'm old? Now listen carefully. Old: smart. Young: nitwits. *Now go!*

LEO: Right.

(Leo pulls his wig on and rushes to the garden doors — and runs straight into Duncan.)

DUNCAN: *Aha!* Gotcha!

MEG: Oh, no.

(Beat — then Leo transforms himself right back into Maxine.)

LEO: Duncan. My dear old friend. How delightful to see you again. *"Ah, the friends thou hast, grapple them to thy soul with hoops of steel."*

DUNCAN: How very apt. Because you're under arrest.

(Jack enters.)

JACK: Hey. What's going on?

MEG: Duncan, let her go!

DUNCAN: I will not! She's a fraud!

MEG: But wait a second! What if she's the real one and the ones outside aren't genuine?

DUNCAN: Margaret, please. You admitted she was a fraud, not five minutes ago. You may like this creature, but your real cousins are in the garden waiting for you!

(From the garden, we hear voices and gunshots.)

A WOMAN'S VOICE: *(Off.) AHHHHHHHHH!*

(They all look up.)

Leave me alone! Get your hands off me! Stop it!

(Bang!)

A SECOND WOMAN'S VOICE: *(Off.) Get away from me! Do you hear me?!*

(Bang! Bang!)

MEN'S AND WOMEN'S VOICES: *(Off.) Grab 'em! Hold 'em! Ahhhh! I got 'em! Ahhhhh!*

(Bang! Bang!)

A MAN'S VOICE: *(Off.) Quiet down! You're under arrest!*

(Audrey rushes in from the garden, with Butch and Doc trailing behind. They're crazed with excitement.)

AUDREY: Oh my gosh! The most incredible thing just happened! I'm out there talking to these two women, and they tell me their names are *Maxine and Stephanie*. And my jaw, it hits the floor, ya know?! Then out of the blue two policemen show up and then *whamo!* They take one look at these women and go *"Aha! Trixie McCall! Bubbles Schaeffer! Hands up!"* Then the girls make a run for it, and the policemen knock 'em down! It turns out the girls are well-known crooks! They sent a telegram and *pretended* to be your nieces just to get your money! Can you *imagine*?!

LEO: Oh, this wicked, wicked world.

DUNCAN: Oh, no.

MEG: Duncan. I believe you owe "Maxine" an apology.

LEO: No, no, please. Don't. We all make mistakes. It is forgiveness that makes the world a better place. Reverend Wooley got a little confused, and don't we all sometimes?

MEG: Yes, we do.

AUDREY: Yeah. Tell me about it. Hey Jack.

(She kisses Jack on the lips. A great kiss.)

DUNCAN: Audrey!

LEO: Now it's our turn.

(Leo/Maxine kisses Meg.)

DUNCAN: *Margaret!!!*

MEG: Oh, stop it. We should tell him the truth.

DUNCAN: Tell me what?!

LEO: *(As Maxine.)* Margaret and I are getting married.

DUNCAN: *AHHHHHHHHHHHHHHHHH!*

DOC: Don't you get any ideas, Florence. You're too old for me.

(There's no answer. They all look at Florence. She's slumped over in her chair.) Florence . . . ? *Florence!*

(Everyone freezes. Doc tries to get a pulse at her neck, but there is none. He feels her hands. They're stone cold. Doc goes white.) She's gone.

MEG: Oh, no . . .

AUDREY: Florence . . .

(Everyone is in shock. Meg takes Leo's hand. Doc shakes his head sadly.)

FLORENCE: . . . You are the worst doctor that ever lived.

(Shock, then cries of relief, as everyone clusters around her, jubilant.)

MEG/AUDREY/BUTCH/JACK: Aunt Florence! / You're alive! / You really had us scared that time / Oh, Lord . . .

(A bell sounds.)

AUDREY: Oh my gosh. It's time for the show!

LEO: Places, everyone! Act one places! Let's go!

(Everyone scurries around to prepare for the play, moving furniture and pulling a costume basket in from the kitchen. During the following, the actors pull costume pieces from the basket and put them on.)

EVERYONE: The chair! Put it here! / We need the hats! / I've got mine. / What about the wig? / Where's my sword! I need my sword! / My line! I can't remember my first line!

(Meanwhile, Leo and Meg have a moment alone together, and we hear them over the words above.)

LEO: What did you mean that "*maybe*" I was a little sexy?

MEG: I was just teasing. Because I knew it was you all along.

LEO: You did not!

MEG: I did so! From the moment you walked through the door, I knew there was something funny going on because

(He stops her mouth with a kiss.)

JACK: *Would you two stop it! We have a show to put on!*

LEO: I'm ready!

MEG: Me too!

DOC: Ready!

BUTCH: Ready!

JACK: Ready!

FLORENCE: Ready!

DUNCAN: Ready.

AUDREY: All set!

LEO: *Ladies and gentlemen, the curtain is going up,*

EVERYONE: *AND THE PLAY BEGINS!*

> *(Blackout.)*
> *(Curtain.)*

END OF PLAY

SHAKESPEARE
IN HOLLYWOOD

Pictured: Emily Donahoe (Puck), Casey Biggs (Oberon)

ORIGINAL PRODUCTION

Shakespeare in Hollywood premiered on September 5, 2004, at Arena Stage, Washington, D.C.: Molly Smith, artistic director; Stephen Richard, executive director; Guy Bergquist, producer. The set designer was Thomas Lynch, the costume designer was Jess Goldstein, the lighting designer was Nancy Schertler, and the sound designer was Susan R. White. The company manager was Jill A. Mauritz, the casting director was Eli Dawson, and the technical director was Jim Glendinning. The stage manager was Brady Ellen Poole, the assistant stage manager was Amy K. Bennett, the choreographer was Karma Camp, the fight choreographer was Brad Waller, the dramaturg was Michael Kinghorn, and the speech and vocal consultant was Lynn Watson. The production was graciously sponsored by Esthy and Jim Adler. It was directed by Kyle Donnelly. The cast, in order of appearance, was as follows:

LOUELLA PARSONS	Ellen Karas
MAX REINHARDT	Robert Prosky
DICK POWELL	David Fendig
JACK WARNER	Rick Foucheux
DARYL	Michael Skinner
LYDIA LANSING	Alice Ripley
OBERON	Casey Biggs
PUCK	Emily Donahoe
OLIVIA DARNELL	Maggie Lacey
WILL HAYES	Everett Quinton
JOE E. BROWN	Hugh Nees
JIMMY CAGNEY	Adam Richman
ENSEMBLE	Bethany Caputo, Scott Graham Eric Jorgensen, Robert McClure

AUTHOR'S PREFACE

Shakespeare in Hollywood came about as a commission from the Royal Shakespeare Company. (At the end of this preface is an essay by Simon Reade that describes some of the background.) However, what I remember best about the genesis of *Shakespeare in Hollywood* is the story of a different play — the one that almost got written in its stead but died quietly on the banks of the River Avon in England.

Originally my idea for a play for the RSC was based on the events surrounding David Garrick's Shakespeare Jubilee of 1769. In that year, the small market town of Stratford-upon-Avon decided to put itself on the map by exploiting the fact that it was Shakespeare's birthplace. To this end, the burghers of Stratford invited the most famous actor of his day, David Garrick, to hold a three-day festival in the town, at which time Garrick and his friends would eulogize Shakespeare with odes, ballads and a parade of characters. Garrick came through on the bargain, and in early September 1769, distinguished guests from all over England streamed into the town of Stratford for the Shakespeare Jubilee. Despite heavy rains that week, the festival succeeded in its goal, putting Stratford on the map forever as a tourist destination of the Shakespeare industry. It seemed to me that this premise was a natural for a theater devoted to the works of Shakespeare; and I realized from the beginning that I needed to get the distinguished director Adrian Noble, then artistic director of the RSC, on board with me.

Cut to two months later, in Stratford, England, on a bright sunny day in spring as Adrian and I sat on the balcony of a restaurant on the banks of the Avon, just across the river from the RSC's Memorial Theatre. I was feeling quite confident (always a bad sign), certain that Adrian would love this wonderful idea, which would not only keep his patrons rolling in the aisles, but give them a valuable insight into the origins of the whole Shakespeare industry.

We lunched, we drank, we laughed, and then I got down to it.

"Okay, Adrian, brace yourself. The play is a comedy set during the Shakespeare Jubilee of 1769 — "

"Stop."

"What?"

"Stop talking."

"Me?"

"You."

"Why?"

"Because we just commissioned a play from Peter Barnes on that subject, and if you say anything about your ideas for the plot or characters and they then pop up in his play, or vice versa, you or he or both of you could sue me and/or the RSC for plagiarism or something, so for God's sake don't say anything!"

What happened next I recall only as a blur. It involved dragging myself back to my hotel room, locking the door, pacing, thinking, and scribbling on a pad of paper until about five in the morning. I remember thinking: the RSC wants a comedy from an American playwright. Hmm. American. The movie industry. 1930s. On-and-off craze at the time for Shakespeare movies. Several filmed with big stars. Movie studios innately funny. Movie stars playing Shakespeare innately funny. Hmm. I then slept briefly, felt invigorated by the new idea, and went back outside to meet the RSC.

· · ·

In doing research for *Shakespeare in Hollywood,* I had the pleasure of immersing myself in the history of the Hollywood studio system in the 1930s as well as in the history of Shakespeare on film, particularly the version of *A Midsummer Night's Dream* directed by Max Reinhardt. The first thing I learned was that in the 1930s, the talkies discovered Shakespeare in a big way. Four significant movies based on Shakespeare plays were made within a span of four years: *The Taming of the Shrew* starring Douglas Fairbanks and Mary Pickford; *As You Like It* starring Laurence Olivier and Elizabeth Bergner; *Romeo and Juliet* starring Leslie Howard and Norma Shearer; and, the subject of this play, *A Midsummer Night's Dream* directed by Max Reinhardt.

The film studios in the 1930s recognized quickly that movies based on Shakespeare plays were "box office poison." However, as I continued to do research for this play, it became clear to me that the Shakespeare films of that time were often made (despite bad box office) so that the mistresses or wives of the studio heads could star in "prestigious" movies to enhance their reputations. Elizabeth Bergner, who starred in *As You Like It,* was married to Robert Czinner, the director of the film. Irving Thalberg, production chief of MGM, put Norma Shearer into *Romeo and Juliet* despite her age. And for Fairbanks and Pickford, who were married, *The Taming of the Shrew* was a family affair as well. (This is the movie that caused great hilarity in its opening minute by announcing that the play was "by William Shakespeare with additional dialogue by Sam Taylor.")

In writing *Shakespeare in Hollywood*, I stuck to the historical record as much as possible. Thus, Max Reinhardt, the most famous stage director of his generation, did — in life as in the play — come to Hollywood from Austria as a refugee from the Nazis and directed his first (and only) motion picture: *A Midsummer Night's Dream* for Warner Brothers Pictures in 1934. Jack Warner did have three brothers, Harry, Albert, and Sam, who ran the studio with him. Their father did start out as a shoemaker. And Louella Parsons, the most famous gossip columnist of her day, was born Louella Oettinger in Dixon, Illinois.

Dick Powell, who played Lysander in the movie, was indeed — in life as in the play — a heartthrob of the 1930s, and he starred in a string of successful musicals, including *42nd Street*. James Cagney, the biggest star of the movie, did play Bottom, though he was best known at the time for gangster pictures. The emerging child star Mickey Rooney ultimately played Puck in the movie; however, his filming was indeed delayed by the accident he had while skiing with his mother. Also, as Olivia mentions in the course of the play, for the two hundred fifty years prior to 1900, Puck was often played by a woman.

The terms of the Production Code that Hays outlines in the play are virtually verbatim from the actual Production Code that caused untold misery for every studio in Hollywood. Moreover, the objections that Hays raises in the play are the ones that the Hays Office actually raised at the time of filming. (Jack Warner himself wanted Reinhardt to cut the "love scene" in "Pyramus and Thisbe" because both characters were played by men, and he was afraid that the Hays Office was going to object.) The biggest objection of the Hays Office was to the black fairy overcoming the white fairy toward the end of the movie. Reinhardt said that he created the black fairy to represent the evils of Nazism. Ultimately, this and the other objections were withdrawn. No one knows exactly why.

To me, one of the most surprising aspects of Shakespeare in the movies is that dozens of silent pictures were made from Shakespeare's plays before the advent of sound. Obviously, the producers in those days thought that Shakespeare's stories alone were strong enough to carry the films. Many of these silent movies can be seen on a DVD entitled *Silent Shakespeare*, released by Milestone Film & Video (2000).

• • •

I enjoyed writing *Shakespeare in Hollywood* tremendously. To me, Hollywood in the 1930s is the bee's knees, and as a lifelong student of Shakespeare, I loved living for a few months in the land of Oberon and Puck. So my thanks to Simon Reade and Adrian Noble for the commission, and equal thanks to Molly Smith, Arena Stage, and my clever director Kyle Donnelly for the first production.

P.S.: I am still working on that play about the Shakespeare Jubilee.

SHAKESPEARE IN HOLLYWOOD
by Simon Reade
for the Arena Stage Production Journal

The name rang a bell. "He's called Ken Ludwig, Simon," said Adrian Noble, then artistic director of the Royal Shakespeare Company. "He's in Stratford. Big supporter of the RSC in the States. He's got some ideas he wants to run past us." Ken Ludwig? Surely not Lend-Me-A-Tenor-Crazy-For-You Ken Ludwig? What on earth would that master of American screwball comedy want with a classical Shakespeare ensemble? As literary manager at the RSC at the time, I was a champion of poetic theater, pursuing commissions that tended toward political epics. The imp in me surmised that the RSC could well do with upsetting its own applecart; but it is a state-subsidized theater. This Ken Ludwig is the darling of commercial theater.

Curious, I met the guy.

Well, never judge a writer entirely by his output. Just as Dostoevsky probably wasn't all doom and gloom, wisecracking Ken Ludwig's got his serious points too. Sure, he's fun, full of beans. But he's also exceptionally well read, bright as a button, with an enthusiasm for comedy and music theater across the centuries. He's an expert who kept — who keeps — putting me to shame in my lack of appreciation of the popular stage, of the movies. And I don't just mean the cheesy matinees we'd snigger and sneer at today. He can extemporize on the clown in European Renaissance drama, on the wit of the eighteenth-century playwrights, on the interwar stars of the silver screen . . . On our first meeting, in the sunshine of Stratford-upon-Avon, he charmed me, he delighted me. And, canny fellow he is, he'd pitch several ideas at me before I'd even realized he'd started.

Some had been long in gestation: a rewrite of a Regency Tony Lumpkin sequel to *She Stoops to Conquer*. We read the original and realized why it necessitated a rewrite. It was trash. We decided not to go there. Some ideas had been dreamt up on the hoof — inspired by walking backstage, along the narrow passage where the huge 1930s Royal Shakespeare Theatre collides with the Elizbethan-style Swan Theatre. Ken had seen the actors from contrasting shows comingle, midperformance. What if, in this collision, the modern-dress performers get confused with the doublet-and-hosed ones, take a wrong turning, and end up on the wrong stage in the wrong play, mused Ken. We laughed and laughed as he improvised and then had the good grace to admit Michael

Frayn had written *Noises Off,* Alan Ayckbourn *House and Garden.* Ken's is still an even wilder idea, but we didn't pursue this either.

We also talked about the whole Shakespeare industry and how the recent movies — from Ken Branagh, via Baz Luhrman, to *Shakespeare in Love* — had introduced the plays and the man to a whole new generation who'd rejected the works in the classroom or in the lyric theater. *Shakespeare in Love* in particular inspired us. Marc Norman and Tom Stoppard's marvelous screenplay had illustrated how the Elizabethan theatre of ruthless producers and jobbing script writers wasn't a million miles away from the Hollywood studio system.

It was then that Ken mentioned something in passing and we both had that "ping" lightbulb moment. A film I should have known about, but didn't — Max Reinhardt's 1936 movie of *A Midsummer Night's Dream* — was even more amazing in its making than the finished product itself. It was a story that got right to the heart of the commercialization of art, the opportunism of Hollywood, the use and abuse of the most venerated writer of all time, Shakespeare. It charted the creative quirks of a meister of mittel Europische Kinema, Max Reinhadt. And it had a cast of stars, including Mickey Rooney and Jimmy Cagney. And the more he talked, the more animated he became. Ken explained to me about Will Hays, the daffy self-appointed censor, whose application of the Hays Code to the sexiness and magical realism of Shakespeare's dream play was an outrage — very funny, but an outrage nonetheless. And there it was, the embryo of a play that embraced the Shakespeare industry, Hollywood exploitation, U.S. cultural imperialism, the clash of ideologies (liberal and philistine, European and American), and dreams versus nightmares, with fascism in Germany a distant but significant rumble. I saw a serious play in the making. I guess Ken had the genius to see that its seriousness could be conveyed through an accumulation of farcical mayhem.

Key to that, and what I learnt from Ken, is this brilliant genre, which I believe is peculiar to the American psyche: high-jinx screwball comedy. British people would never be that zany. We're too knowingly cynical. Funny, yes. But don't we just know it. It is a genre specific to the American stage and screen of the mid-twentieth century. And Ken is the modern master of it, his passion for its vaudevillian high-octane antics fueling his messianic zeal to recapture its essence for contemporary audiences.

Ken's passion for Shakespeare (his family, even his personal e-mail address all seem to be named after one Shakespeare character or another) is also evident in his new play. *Shakespeare in Hollywood* is thus a deeply personal play as much as a popular play. And in the spirit with which I used to commission plays at the RSC, it's also poetic and political and, let's not be afraid to say it, something of a miniepic. Yet it's also got a screw loose, the playwright's having a ball. Screwball. Good comedy. Good drama. Good fun.

SIMON READE is associate producer for Theatre Royal Bath Productions for whom he adapted Jane Austen's *Pride and Prejudice*. He was literary manager and dramaturg for the Royal Shakespeare Company and artistic director of Bristol Old Vic. His plays include: Salman Rushdie's *Midnight's Children*, Ted Hughes' *Tales from Ovid*, Philip Pullman's *The Scarecrow and His Servant*, and Michael Morpurgo's *Private Peaceful*. Simon is also a director and has worked in television drama for the BBC. His books include *Dear Mr. Shakespeare* (published by Oberon Books).

CHARACTERS
> OBERON
> PUCK
> JACK WARNER
> MAX REINHARDT
> WILL HAYS
> DARYL
> OLIVIA DARNELL
> LYDIA LANSING
> LOUELLA PARSONS
> DICK POWELL
> JIMMY CAGNEY
> JOE E. BROWN
> ALBERT WARNER
> HARRY WARNER
> SAM WARNER
> GROUCHO MARX
> COWBOY
> JOHNNY WEISSMULLER/TARZAN

The play is written for twelve actors: four women and eight men. The actors playing Hays, Brown, Cagney, Powell, and Daryl double as Albert, Harry, Sam, Groucho, Tarzan, and the Cowboy. If extra actors are available, they can play movie stars at the opening of the play, cameramen, seamstresses, and so on.

PLACE AND TIME
Hollywood, 1934.

SHAKESPEARE IN HOLLYWOOD

> What is love? 'Tis not hereafter,
> Present mirth hath present laughter;
> What's to come is still unsure:
>
> In delay there lies no plenty;
> Then come kiss me, sweet and twenty;
> Youth's a stuff will not endure.

> *Twelfth Night*
> Act II, Scene Three

ACT I

Hollywood, 1934. An orchestra is playing "Hooray for Hollywood," and lights are criss-crossing the sky like enormous, reckless fireflies. We feel the excitement and glamour of movieland at its height.

We're at the world premiere of a new movie in front of Grauman's Chinese Theater. Louella Parsons, the iconic gossip columnist for the Hearst newspapers and well-known radio personality, is at a microphone, broadcasting live, and a rope barrier separates her from hundreds of screaming fans who have shown up to see their favorite movie stars. Some of these stars, glamorous and trendy, wave to the crowd as they parade into the theater past Louella.

LOUELLA: Good evening, good evening to all of you out there in radioland, this is Louella Parsons, your eyes and ears in Hollywood, at the sensational premiere of the new motion picture *A Midsummer Night's Dream* by the Warner Brothers. That's right, we have a night of culture ahead of us, a movie by the Swan of Avon himself, Mr. William Shakespeare, and if he could only see the excitement here tonight, he would be swimming down that river just as proud as a peacock. And don't let that word "culture" frighten you, my darlings, because the word on this movie is sock-o entertainment from start to finish. And what else would you expect from a talking picture starring Mr. Dick Powell!
(Screams from the crowd.)

Miss Anita Louise!

(More screams.)

And Mr. James Cagney!!

(Even bigger screams — as Cagney goes by and waves to the crowd.)

Wait a moment. A limousine is pulling up. Someone is getting out . . . Oh my darlings, how exciting, it's the director of the movie himself, Mr. Max Reinhardt!

(A disappointed "Ohhhh . . . " from the crowd as Max Reinhardt enters. He's a pixieish man in his sixties and he has a pronounced German accent.)

LOUELLA: Max! Over here! . . . He's coming this way . . . Ah, Professor Reinhardt, it's Louella Parsons. Welcome to the opening of your new cinematic sensation.

REINHARDT: Thank you, Louella, I'm —

LOUELLA: *(To the radio audience.)* I'm sure you all know that Professor Reinhardt is considered the most distinguished director working today in the live theater. Now tell us, Max, did it scare you a little, directing your first motion picture ever?

REINHARDT: No, not really. But I —

LOUELLA: "No, not really." *(Laughing.)* Oh, Max, you're priceless. Now do I hear an accent in your speech? Are you from abroad?

REINHARDT: Ja, I am from Austria. And I have —

LOUELLA: "From Austria." How adorable. And what brings you to the United States?

REINHARDT: Heh heh, this is going to make you laugh, is funny story. There is man in my country named Hitler who is killing people.

LOUELLA: Oh yes of course. And we're just *thrilled* that you got away. Wait! A limousine has just pulled up . . . Oh, it is! It's Dick Powell!

(Screams — and Dick Powell enters. He's a good-looking, boyish actor in his late twenties. He waves to the crowd and sings:)

POWELL: "I'm young and healthy, and you've got chaaaaarm!"

(Bigger screams.)

LOUELLA: Dick! Dick! It's Louella!

(Louella chases after Powell, leaving Reinhardt stranded. He turns and speaks to the audience.)

REINHARDT: And for this I have left my homeland. True, alternative is the Nazis, but is very close race. So: vhy am I here, you ask? It all began one year ago when I found myself for very first time in this legendary place called *Hollyvood:* land of glamour and gluttony, palm trees and poodles, sequins and sin. At this time, I have just put on big stage production of Shakespeare's masterpiece *A Midsummer Night's Dream*, and I get raves and kudos you vould not believe. So, I ask myself, vhy not make a film of this production using big hotshot Hollyvood stars. It vould be a great contribution to world culture, a real treat for lovers of Shakespeare, and, between you and me, I could make a few bucks in the process. With this in mind, exactly one year ago today, I go to see Jack Warner of Warner Brothers Pictures. *(The scene shifts to Jack Warner's office at the Warner Brothers Studio. Jack Warner is behind his desk. He's a natty dresser and tough as nails. Sitting nearby is Daryl, who's known in the trade as a "yes-man." He's twenty-five to thirty and wears glasses. As the set is changing, Reinhardt continues:)*

REINHARDT: Mr. Warner, I say to him, you are great producer and famous man. But you have not yet achieved the respect you deserve as man of innovation and artistic vision. So what do you say about making movie of Shakespeare's play *A Midsummer Night's Dream*.

WARNER: *You're an idiot!*

REINHARDT: Okay, but what do you say?

WARNER: Listen, Mel — can I call you Mel?

REINHARDT: Sure, but my name is Max.

WARNER: Right, Max, now I've been asking around about you, and people tell me that you're really smart.

REINHARDT: Is true, I am genius.

WARNER: Good. Then you'll understand this perfectly. *It's a dumb idea.* Am I right, Daryl?

DARYL: Yes sir!

WARNER: Now why do you think we make movies, Max? Take a wild guess.

REINHARDT: To make artistic contribution to world culture?

WARNER: Wrong. We make movies to make money. They even have the same first letter. Movies. Money.

REINHARDT: Ah, but what if you use that money to make *Midsummer Night's Dream*. Is another M.

WARNER: And so is moron! It ain't gonna happen!

REINHARDT: But you could make it happen!

WARNER: *You're an idiot!*

REINHARDT: *Okay, fine!* I take project back to Adolph Zukor at Paramount, he is *begging* me for this picture!

WARNER: You're a liar!

REINHARDT: *(To the audience.)* And he's right, of course, I am lying through my head. But at this moment, a miracle occurs. A fairy princess, like in Shakespeare play, comes through that door and changes everything.

LYDIA: *(Striding into the room.)* I'm a slut!

(Lydia Lansing is a beautiful blond starlet with a whiny, showgirl voice. She sleeps with Jack Warner, not just to get ahead, but also because she likes him. She's just come off the set of a historical action picture, and she's wearing a cheap, bright-red costume, torn and shredded along the skirt to show she's been in a battle and across the chest to show that she has a lot of cleavage. Somewhere deep inside that cleavage is a nice kid. She carries a fan magazine, and she's fuming.)

WARNER: Lydia!

LYDIA: That's what they call me, Jack! A slut! Look at this! *Photoplay Magazine.* "The Ten Biggest Sluts in Hollywood." And who do ya think is number one? The Queen of the Sluts? Take a guess.

WARNER: You?

LYDIA: Bingo! You got it, Jack. And do you know why it's me? Huh? *Do ya?! 'Cause I do all the stinkin' pictures you give me!*

WARNER: But darling —

LYDIA: *Gun Moll Mama.* Remember that one? And *Hold My Pistol.*

WARNER: But they made you a star!

LYDIA: A star? You call this a *star*?! *(Her costume.)* Look at me! I'm in a fucking French Foreign Legion picture! "Oh Major Waverly, I feel so frightened by those nasty heathens surrounding Fort Chutney." *(She wiggles — her trademark wiggle.)* "How will I ever get back to my ancestral home in Dundee, Scotland?"

WARNER: But sweetie pie —

LYDIA: Don't touch me! Now I want somethin' decent for a change. Somethin' with *prestige.* You're makin' biography pictures, give me one of those. I'd be great in a biopic. I could play Madame Curie. Listen to this, I wrote it myself: "Oh, Dr. Mendel, just look at them squiggly things under the microscope. I think they could cure somethin'! Somethin' bad, like disease! Wait! We'll call it . . . penicillin!"

WARNER: But we just did a doctor picture about Louis Pasteur.

LYDIA: *Well they ain't the same person are they?!*

REINHARDT: She has a point.

LYDIA: Who's he?

REINHARDT: *(Kissing her hand.)* How do you do, I am Max Reinhardt, and I am famous director.

LYDIA: Gee.

REINHARDT: Good-bye.

LYDIA: Hey, where ya goin'?

REINHARDT: Alas, there is nothing here for me to do. I have just offered to make classic *prestige picture* for your boyfriend here. *Shakespeare* picture. Only he tells me he does not have leading lady who could perform in such a picture.

WARNER: That's a lie!

LYDIA: *Shut up! (To Reinhardt.)* What's it about?

REINHARDT: It is about a fairyland forest that is ruled by a handsome king named Oberon.

LYDIA: Wow.

REINHARDT: He and his helper, named Puck, devise a plan to use a magic flower that makes you fall in love with the very first person you see.

LYDIA: This is really good!

REINHARDT: So Oberon uses the flower on a group of lovers who have fled to the forest — one of whom could be you, Lydia Lansing, in the part of Helena, a ravishing maiden who speaks only in poetry.

LYDIA: Holy cow.

WARNER: Don't listen to him!

LYDIA: Why not? Cause you want me to appear in nothin' but *dreck*?

WARNER: But honey pie —

LYDIA: I want this picture.

WARNER: Well you can't have it! Because I ain't makin' it! Right, Daryl?!

DARYL: Yes sir!

LYDIA: Shut up, Daryl!

DARYL: Yes ma'am!

LYDIA: Jack, listen to me, I'm gonna tell ya somethin', and I'll say it slow and calm so it's really clear. You get me this picture and you make it fast, *or ya never touch these hips again! Comprendo?!*

(All sweetness to Reinhardt.) So very nice to have made your acquaint-tinyance.

WARNER: *(To Reinhardt.)* You son of a bitch.

REINHARDT: *(To the audience.)* And so it happened in a flash of magic that I was soon making film of *Midsummer Night's Dream*, and I assure you that all four Warner brothers could not have been happier.

(The lights change, and we see the Warner Brothers on a telephone conference call with each other, each in his own pool of light. They include Harry, the

elder statesman; Albert, the smart one; Sam, the dumb one; and Jack, who we just met. Their dialogue crackles along quickly.)

HARRY: *Jack, you're a schmuck!*

JACK: Harry, that ain't fair!

SAM: I agree with Harry.

JACK: Sam, stay out of this.

ALBERT: You did it for some toostie, right?

JACK: Al, that's a lie!

SAM: He wanted to get in her pants.

ALBERT: I'll bet it was that girl that wiggles.

SAM: He's got a Hawaiian girl?

ALBERT: Not that kinda wiggle.

JACK: Would you guys just shut up and listen!

HARRY: The big shot is telling *me* to shut up.

JACK: Harry, please I'm telling you straight. This picture'll be good for the studio.

ALBERT: Like the plagues were good for Egypt.

SAM: Papa always said to us, "Stick to your last." That's what he said, you know, "Stick to your last."

JACK: *He was a shoemaker!*

HARRY: And what's so wrong with a shoemaker? Are you saying Papa didn't work hard?

ALBERT: He's criticizing Papa now.

JACK: *Boys would you just listen to me!* This Shakespeare stuff ain't all bad. I read some this morning and there are parts in English.

SAM: It's poison, Jackie.

HARRY: We'll lose a fortune.

SAM: Ya know the title ain't so bad. "Shakespeare." Sounds like a biopic.

JACK: It ain't called "Shakespeare"!

ALBERT: Sam, it's called *A Midsummer Night's Dream.*

SAM: Well that'll put us right in the crapper.

ALBERT: Maybe we should get a rewrite man.

HARRY: Mankiewitz is good.

ALBERT: Or Morrison.

SAM: Or pay this Shakespeare guy to do it.

ALBERT: He's dead, you idiot.

SAM: Then he'll cost us peanuts.

HARRY: I say we axe the project and we do it fast before he makes any more commitments to this dame of his —

ALBERT: He's got a girl that wiggles, let her wiggle in somebody else's picture. I need this whole thing like I need a goiter —

SAM: So how come I'm the one who needs my head examined when he's the one who gets us in trouble? Tell me that —?

JACK: Boys . . . *Boys, would you listen to me!!* I happen to be head of production for this company, and we are making this film whether you like it or not. *End of discussion!*

(They all hang up.)

(The lights come up, and it's midmorning on the back lot of the Warner Brothers Studios. We're on the sound stage where A Midsummer Night's Dream *is being shot. We see a tree and some foliage as well as lights and cameras. After a beat, there's a crack of thunder and a flash of lightning, the stage goes dim in a magical way — and Oberon, King of the Fairies from* A Midsummer Night's Dream *appears from nowhere. The stage effect by which he appears should be as magical as possible, so that we realize instantly that this is not a human but a being from another world. As for the creature himself, he has all the characteristics of the Oberon we know from Shakespeare. He's imperious, impatient, and commanding. He has a childlike temper, and there's a sense of whimsy about him. He's also extremely attractive.)*

OBERON: Home,

Home at last to the Magic Wood near Athens,

Aweary from a night of escapades

And frolic, where lovers meet, embrace and dream of

Immortality.

(Calling.)

Puck! Robin Goodfellow! Come hither!

(Another crash of thunder, and Puck magically appears. This is the real Puck from the same play, that "shrewd and knavish sprite" called Robin Goodfellow, the mischief maker of the fairy world. Though Puck is a boy/man, he's played in this case by an actress.)

PUCK: I am here, my Oberon, swift as a shadow

And brief as the lightning in the collied night!

OBERON: Wither wander you, spirit?

PUCK: Over hill, over dale,

Through bush, through briar,

Over park, over pale,

Through flood, through fire —

I do wander everywhere,

Swifter than the moon's sphere,

And I serve —

(At this moment, Groucho Marx crosses the lot with his characteristic stride and walks right up to Oberon and Puck.)

GROUCHO: *(To Oberon.)* Why hello. Do you always wear your pajamas on the set, or is it just because I'm good-lookin'?

(Johnny Weissmuller enters dressed as Tarzan and gives his famous yell.)

TARZAN: *Aiiiieeeieiiiieieiiieeeeieieee!!*

(A Cowboy enters.)

COWBOY: Hey, Johnny, wait up! *(He playfully pulls his six guns and pretends to shoot Oberon and Puck.)* Blam, blam, blam, blam, blam! Ha ha!

(Groucho, Tarzan, and the Cowboy all exit. Beat. Oberon looks at Puck.)

OBERON: . . . Where in Depths of Hell are we?!

PUCK: I have no idea.

(Hollywood, we come to realize, is our modern equivalent of a Wood near Athens. It's a land of enchantment where anything can happen. It's a place of liberation and reassessment, where the illusory is part of the total experience of reality.)

OBERON: *(Angry.)* I gave thee but one instruction, lead us

Home from Athens to the magic wood,

But no, he has to flub it up!

PUCK: "Flub it up"? That doesn't sound like you. Could we be dreaming?

OBERON: We are such stuff as dreams are made on.

PUCK: Now that sounds more like your old self.

OBERON: Oh shut up!

I have just had one of the longest nights of my life!

First I have an argument with my Queen.

Then I try to sort out four Athenians

Who are so excited by the sex

Of one another they can barely keep their

Pants on. Then I drop the liquor of the

Magic flower on Titania's eyes

And she awakes and makes an ass of herself,

Or rather *he* does, Bottom, so she couples with him,

Good joke, ha, ha, then it's

Back to the lovers, we watch the play, we get them to
Bed, we give them our blessing, and by this time
I'm so tired I could drop,
And all I ask is a good day's sleep
And you *can't even find the way home!*

PUCK: But I know I used all the usual spells.

I bayed at the moon like a wolf and rolled my eyes,

Then spun around three times to the left and . . . uh-oh.

OBERON: To the left?

PUCK: Well —

OBERON: You normally spin to the right.

PUCK: Ay, there's the rub.

OBERON: I have a blockhead for a henchman.

A coddle-pated, lack-brained, thick-eyed, three-suited, rabbit-sucking
Ignoramus-is-too-good-for-him having
No more brain than a Christian!
Do you have anything to say?!

PUCK: I think we came to the wrong Wood Near Athens.

WARNER: *(Off.)* Now listen to me and listen good.

OBERON: But who comes here? We are invisible

And we will overhear their conference.

(Zzzzing! And just as in the "Dream," Oberon makes a gesture with his hand and renders himself and Puck invisible. That is, they remain onstage, and we can see them, but no one on the stage can see them. [Note: whenever they magically disappear or reappear throughout the play, we hear the distinctive sound you get when you run your fingernail across the strings of a harp. This sound will be indicated in the script by the word "zzzzing!"] Warner and Daryl enter. The following Warner lines — up to "Daryl, my boy . . . " — are meant to cover moving a director's desk and chair onto the set.)

WARNER: Daryl, my boy, I need your help. I want you out of my office.

DARYL: *(Getting teary eyed.)* Well may I say, sir, what a pleasure it's been working
for you all these years —

WARNER: No, you idiot, I'm not firing you. I'm assigning you to this Shakespeare project. I want you to be Reinhardt's assistant.

DARYL: Me?

WARNER: The son of a bitch will try to spend me into the grave, I know it. I want you to watch him every minute. If the bastard goes over budget by *one penny* I want to know about it.

DARYL: Yes sir.

WARNER: And most of all, keep an eye on Lydia.

DARYL: Lydia.

WARNER: She's one in a million.

DARYL: A million.

WARNER: I'm insane about her.

DARYL: You're insane.

WARNER: The poor little thing. She doesn't know Shakespeare from sheep dip. And if she so much as looks at another actor without her legs crossed, I want her . . .

(Lydia walks in wearing her costume.)

walking onto the set like a vision from classical drama! What a costume!

(She's happy as a clam and bursting with excitement about her new role. She's carrying her script.)

LYDIA: Thanks, Jack. Pretty classy, huh? It kinda itches around the crotch but that's okay because you gotta make sacrifices for art.

WARNER: Maybe it's just the underwear that's itchy.

LYDIA: It can't be. I ain't wearin' any. Now listen — I got the script and it's fabulous! Real class. I don't understand a single word of it.

WARNER: I'll send it to rewrite.

LYDIA: Good. 'Cause there's a word in here with like fifteen syllables. Oh, and guess what! I hired a vocal coach. This guy's really cute. He's Irish, I think. His name is Larry O'Liver.

WARNER: Laurence Olivier?

LYDIA: Yeah, that's it.

WARNER: He's big stuff. He just starred in a movie. How much are you paying him?

LYDIA: Don't worry. I know how to pay him.

(She pats his cheek and walks off. Warner reacts.)

WARNER: *(Running after her.)* Lydia! Lydia, *I'll* pay him! Daryl, stop her!

DARYL: Yes sir!

WARNER: Lydia, come back here! Listen to me . . . !

(And they're gone.)

(Oberon gestures with his hand so that he and Puck reappear. Zzzzing!)

OBERON: Well at least it won't be boring.

(The telephone on the director's table rings. Ring!)

OBERON/PUCK: *Ahh!*

OBERON: What was that?!

PUCK: It's that black thing. There.

   (Ring!)

   Is it alive?

OBERON: I have no idea. But if that's its mating call, where's the other one?

   (Ring!)

   No, wait.

   (Oberon has figured it out. He picks up the receiver.)

VOICE THROUGH THE PHONE (WARNER): Hi, is Reinhardt there? We've got a problem.

OBERON/PUCK: *Yahh!*

   (Oberon and Puck jump backward in fear, dropping the receiver.)

VOICE THROUGH THE PHONE (WARNER): What was that?! . . . Hello? Are you there, because if you are, you're fired!! . . . Hello?!

   (Oberon hangs it up with a bang.)

OBERON: . . . O brave new world that hath such creatures in it.

A WOMAN'S VOICE: *(Off.)* Oh, now what do I do!

DARYL: *(Off.)* Miss Darnell!

OBERON: Someone's coming. Go quickly. Find us a way out of here.

PUCK: I go, I go, look how I go,

   Swifter than arrow from the T —

OBERON: *Just go!*

   (As Puck runs off, a young woman hurries in from the other direction. Her name is Olivia Darnell. She has the sass, beauty, and natural charm of a heroine from the screwball comedies of the 1930s. She's wearing an attractive day dress.)

OLIVIA: Hide me!

OBERON: What?

OLIVIA: Hide me! Please! Quick!

OBERON: Where?

OLIVIA: Anyplace!

OBERON: Here!

DARYL: *(Off.)* Miss Darnell!

OLIVIA: *(Popping up.)* And tell him you haven't seen me!

OBERON: Get down!

   (He hides her behind his cloak — and Daryl runs on.)

DARYL: Have you seen a young woman run past here?

OBERON: Black hair, red dress, this high?

DARYL: Right!

OBERON: I haven't seen her.

DARYL: Hey, come on! Mr. Reinhardt's looking for her!

OBERON: Sorry. I couldn't help it. She went in that direction.

DARYL: Thanks!

(He runs off.)

OBERON: The coast is clear.

(Olivia emerges.)

OLIVIA: Thank you for hiding me. I guess I panicked.

OBERON: Are you in trouble?

OLIVIA: No. I mean yes. A little. See, I'm in this movie. I play Hermia. And I
fought so hard to get the role, you have no idea! I did screen test after
screen test, and I memorized the entire part. Only a different part. I
wanted to play Puck.

OBERON: Puck?

OLIVIA: I know, you think a *boy* should play him, but until this century, Puck
was always a girl.

OBERON: *(Horrified.)* He was? I had no idea.

OLIVIA: Anyway, I got the part of Hermia, which is tremendous, it's the biggest
break I ever had, and of course to play opposite Dick Powell, the biggest
heartthrob in Hollywood, he's such a sweetheart, God in heaven, but I
was going to really memorize the lines last night, at least get a start and
learn the ones for today, but then my brother got a cable from his base
that he was being sent to flight school in the morning! So anyway, we
stayed up the entire night so we could spend a few more hours together,
and we tried to make a party of it, and I guess I got a little drunk and then
I woke up this morning and I hadn't learned the lines, at least the way I
want to, and I just can't bear to face the great Max Reinhardt without
being well prepared, so I'm hiding out to get some time alone so I can
memorize it better since I'd look like such a fool if I didn't know it really
well, do you see?

OBERON: It's perfectly clear.

OLIVIA: I'm Olivia.

OBERON: Oberon. King of the Fairies.

OLIVIA: Oberon? Oh, dear. I hope your heart's not set on it.

OBERON: Set on what?

OLIVIA: *Oberon.* The part's been cast. Haven't you heard? It's Victor Jory.

OBERON: What's a Victor Jory?

OLIVIA: Are you serious? He's a movie star. Where are you from, outer space?

OBERON: No, but it's another world.

OLIVIA: I knew you were foreign. I could tell from the way you speak. It reminds me of a bell, tolling in the countryside.

OBERON: When the sweet wind did gently kiss the trees
And they did make no noise.

OLIVIA: That's from *The Merchant of Venice*.

OBERON: Is it? I thought I made it up.

(She laughs.)

REINHARDT: *(Off.)* Miss Darnell!

OLIVIA: Oh no, that's Mr. Reinhardt. I've got to run.

OBERON: No, stay. You'll be all right.

OLIVIA: But I told you, I don't know all the lines yet!

OBERON: You will. Just speak the speech, I pray you.

OLIVIA: Hamlet.

OBERON: I thought you said it was Reinhardt!

OLIVIA: *It is!*

OBERON: Then just do as I tell you! Look over there. He comes.

OLIVIA: Where?

(Oberon has deliberately made her look away. When she does, he gestures with his hand and makes himself invisible again. Zzzzing! Reinhardt enters.)

REINHARDT: Ah, there you are. I have been looking for you everywhere.

OLIVIA: I was taking a walk, that's all, and I've just been talking to . . .
(She looks around; he's gone.) Where did he go? He was right here . . .

REINHARDT: Okay, fine, now listen to me. I want to take a few minutes right now to rehearse your big speech in Act One.

OLIVIA: Now? I mean, does it have to be now? Could we do it later?

REINHARDT: No. Is first shot of filming, so I want it to be extra good. Let's hear what you've got. Start with scream.

OLIVIA: Scream?

REINHARDT: Big scream. Of frustration. You are angry because your father says you cannot marry boy you love. Go. Big scream.
(Olivia takes a breath. She prepares herself. Then:)

OLIVIA: Ahhh!

REINHARDT: Dat vas terrible. It stunk. *Big.* I want *big* scream. Go.

OLIVIA: . . . *Ahh!*

REINHARDT: Oy vey iss mir. *Big! You know what is big scream? Is opposite of little pathetic scream!*
(Olivia closes her eyes to get her courage up. Oberon has by this time picked

up a pair of scissors from the director's table — and he sticks them into her
rear end.)

OLIVIA: *AHHHHHHHHHHHHHHHH!!!*

(Oberon happily tosses the scissors in his hand and puts them back.)

REINHARDT: Okay. Not bad. We continue. Now remember, you are speaking
to the Duke of Athens, and he says that you must do exactly as your father
tells you and marry a man you do not love. So what do you say?

(Pause. Olivia takes a breath. And now Oberon starts to prompt her. He whispers in her ear, and the effect of their two voices echoing and mingling with each other is very sexy.)

OBERON: "I do entreat your grace"

OLIVIA: "I do entreat your grace to pardon me."

OBERON: "I know not by"

OLIVIA: "I know not by what power I am made bold."

OBERON: "Nor how it may"

OLIVIA: "Nor how it may concern my modesty
    In such a presence here to plead my thoughts.
    But I beseech your grace that I may know
    The worst that may befall me in this case
    If I refuse to wed Demetrius."

OBERON: "Either to die the death"

OLIVIA: "Either to die the death? or to abjure
    Forever the society of men?
    Oh, so will I grow, so live, so die, my lord,
    Ere I will yield my virgin patent up."

REINHARDT: *(Framing the shot.)* And you turn slowly and look into the face of
man you love . . .

(She turns and faces Oberon — but of course she doesn't know it.)

OBERON: "My good Lysander"

OLIVIA: "My good Lysander,"

OBERON: "I swear to thee"

OLIVIA: "I swear to thee by Cupid's strongest bow,
    By his best arrow with the golden head,
    By the simplicity of Venus' doves,
    By that which knitteth souls and prospers loves,"

OBERON: "And by that fire"

OLIVIA: "And by that fire which burned the Carthage queen
    When the false Trojan under sail was seen,

By all the vows that ever men have broke —
In number more than ever women spoke —
In that same place thou hast appointed me
Tomorrow truly will I meet with thee.
(Pause. It's finished. The magic of it sinks in.)

REINHARDT: Magnificent. I am genius for choosing you. Come now, we shoot the scene.

OLIVIA: I'll be right there. Please. Just a moment.

REINHARDT: I give you one minute, and I'm counting!

(He exits. Zzzzing! Oberon reappears, and Olivia turns and sees him.)

OLIVIA: There you are! Where have you been? Oh, how can I ever thank you enough? You were right, I remembered every word. Every syllable. And I was really good!

OBERON: Bravo.

OLIVIA: It was astonishing. It just took hold of me.

OBERON: Upon your words
Sit laurel victory, and smooth success
Be strewed before your feet.

OLIVIA: Anthony and Cleopatra.

OBERON: *(Looking around.)* Where?

OLIVIA: *(Laughing.)* Oh you're so silly. You make me laugh.

OBERON: Do I? I don't think I've ever made anyone
Laugh before. I've made them frightened.

OLIVIA: I don't believe that.

REINHARDT: *(Off — perhaps over a speaker.)* Miss Darnell! Now!

OLIVIA: I've got to run. Oh God, I hope I don't forget the lines.

OBERON: You won't, I promise.

OLIVIA: Thanks again. *(She kisses him on the cheek.)* I hope you get a part in the movie!

(Puzzled, Oberon touches his cheek. Something has happened, and he's not sure what it is. He exits, and Olivia is now alone. She turns front and is lit as though in another place.)

OLIVIA: Mrs. Joan Darnell
46 Mountain Lane
Sioux City, Iowa
Dear Mother,
Well, the filming has started and I'm playing opposite Dick Powell, and he's being so nice to me. Anyway, this morning I met the most interesting

man. He's an actor who wants to be in the film and he's somehow . . . strangely inspiring. I like him very much. No, don't call Aunt Ethel and start planning the wedding. We're just friends. I may never even see him again.

Write soon.

Love,

Olivia

(As she goes, the lights change, and Will Hays enters. He's in his fifties, full of bluster and vanity. He wears a suit. He wields immense power in Hollywood, and he knows it.)

HAYS: Hello?! . . . Anybody here?! . . . Typical.

(He looks impatiently at his watch. Oberon enters.)

Ah, good. Will Hays. Hays Office. I'm looking for a Max Reinhardt.

OBERON: I know not where he is.

HAYS: You "know not"?

OBERON: No, but I do wager he'll return without delay.

HAYS: Oh, really?

OBERON: Yea. Have patience and endure, I urge thee.

HAYS: Oh, I see. Well, let me suggest to "thee" that you "cutteth" the crap and go find Reinhardt for me! *Right now.* And don't be such a smart-ass!

OBERON: Do you insult me? Call me villain? Break my pate across?

HAYS: Oh, brother. Look, I'm asking for some cooperation around here! Is that so hard to follow?!

OBERON: Sir, if you but *ask* you'll get a fair reply. If you demand, I'll have to take revenge.

HAYS: Revenge?! I'm Will Hays! Do you know what I'm capable of?!!

OBERON: A lot of wind, apparently.

HAYS: All right, what's your name?! Now! I want your name right now. Let's go. Name!

OBERON: Oberon. King of the Fairies.

HAYS: Don't you try to be funny with me. I could have you out on the street by tomorrow morning *selling apples*!!

OBERON: Oh, I don't think so.

HAYS: *Do you want to bet?!*

OBERON: *Done!* It's a bet! A fair wager! Before I leave this place, you will *beg* me for forgiveness!

HAYS: *(Astounded.)* . . . Beg you?

OBERON: Plead with me, on your knees, with tears

In your eyes, like Niobe, turned to stone
And weeping for eternity!
Puck! Ho! Robin Goodfellow!
(Oberon exits in a rage.)

HAYS: The man's a crackpot. He's insane.
(Reinhardt enters in a foul mood. He's followed by Daryl.)

REINHARDT: *Hello? Do I hear yelling on my set?!*

HAYS: Are you Max Reinhardt?

REINHARDT: Ja!

HAYS: Well thank God. At last. Will Hays. Hays Office.
(Hearing the name Hays, Daryl runs off.)
Now listen, I'm afraid I've got some problems with your script.

REINHARDT: Oh really? How vonderful. He's got problem with my script. I just found out that my Oberon — Victor Jory? — he just quit, my Puck, Mickey Rooney, broke his leg while skiing with his mother, so I am now missing my two big stars, *AND YOU GOT PROBLEMS VITH MY SCRIPT?!* And you are who again?

HAYS: Will Hays. Production Code Administration.

REINHARDT: Never heard of it.

HAYS: Oh of course not. You're a foreigner, from *Eastern* Europe? Let me fill you in. The Production Code is a set of rules to protect the American public so that movies do not contain anything vulgar, salacious, profane or obscene. We look askance at scenes of sex, adultery, lust, passion, seduction, nudity, venereal disease, sexual hygiene, and childbirth.

REINHARDT: You have good memory.

HAYS: I wrote the Code. At the request of the Legion of Decency — which is composed of millions of Americans who have pledged to boycott any movie that does not receive my seal of approval. No seal, no movie. Are we clear now?

REINHARDT: Ja, very clear. Is censorship.

HAYS: No, it's the will of the people. Now let's discuss your film, shall we? Here is a list of things I'd like to see cut from your script as soon as possible. It includes, of course, the scene on page, let's see, here we are, page 58, where someone named Titania sleeps with a man who has been changed into a donkey.

REINHARDT: So?

HAYS: It is disgusting! It smacks of bestiality. If this Bottom fellow has to be transformed, turn him into something human. It could still be funny.

Perhaps he could have a club foot or something. Next item, it's in the stage directions, aha, right here, page 108, it says "the *black* fairy overpowers the *white* fairy and carries her off." A black man carries off a white woman, and you expect to have no problems? And who *is* this black fairy anyway? It doesn't even say!

REINHARDT: He is spirit of evil.

HAYS: "Evil"? What "evil"? What are you talking about? That's irrelevant.

REINHARDT: It is? With what is happening in my country, it is irrelevant? People being dragged screaming from their homes. Families separated. Children murdered. This is irrelevant?

HAYS: I meant irrelevant to the picture. It isn't set in Germany.

REINHARDT: And because it's not *set* in Germany, it cannot be *about* Germany? It cannot remind us who we are. Are you blind?

HAYS: I beg your pardon?

REINHARDT: You must be blind or stupid.

HAYS: *(Enraged.)* How dare you?! Are you *insane*?! Mr. Reinhardt, here is a list of all of the offending passages in your script. *I suggest you clean it up!*

REINHARDT: *(Equally enraged.)* Mr. Hays. Here is confetti! *I suggest you clean it up!*

(He tears up the list and tosses the bits of paper in the air.)

HAYS: *(Nose to nose.)* I'll be back! You *foreigner!*

REINHARDT: *And I'll be waiting! You native!*

(They exit in opposite directions. As they go, Oberon enters.)

OBERON: Puck! Puck! Robin Goodfellow!

(Puck runs in.)

PUCK: I'm here, your grace! Right here! I was looking for you!

OBERON: *(With the urgency and excitement of a great discovery.)* Listen to me. I think I've figured out what's going on around here. We're in the future, and this place is a kind of theater. They put on plays here.

PUCK: That's what I heard! Only they're called "movies."

OBERON: Right. And they record them on something called flim, using a coma.

PUCK: Film and camera.

OBERON: That's it. And when you sit and watch this "movie," you're not seeing the actors themselves, just flickering shadows. Which is very profound, because it implies that nothing lasts forever. That we are all just flickering shadows. Mere images on the spleen.

PUCK: Screen.

OBERON: Right. Moreover, *everybody* wants to be a movie actor. It's the great thing to be! They get paid enormous sums of money, they're treated like gods, they do nothing to deserve it, and everyone calls them moons!

PUCK: Stars.

OBERON: That's it. And here's the big surprise — guess who their current movie is about? Hmm? *Us!*

PUCK: It is?

OBERON: Yes! Apparently at some point in the past we became famous. People *love* us. They *read* about us. Our exploits have been chronicled by some cowardly Indian named Shaking Spear. People adore us!

PUCK: Everybody?

OBERON: Yes! No. That reminds me. There is a human here who pollutes this place — his name is Hays, he insulted me! — and I intend to make him *suffer* for his crimes.

PUCK: *(A guttural whisper.)* Hays . . .

OBERON: Now listen, I have a plan.

My gentle Puck, come hither.

(During the following, as Oberon gives Puck instructions, Reinhardt enters and listens. Oberon and Puck don't see him. Oberon speaks with urgency.)

OBERON: Thou rememb'rest

Since once I sat upon a promontory

And heard a mermaid on a dolphin's back

Uttering such dulcet and harmonious breath

That the rude sea grew civil at her song

And certain stars shot madly from their spheres

To hear the sea-maid's music?

PUCK: I remember.

OBERON: That very time I saw, but thou couldst not,

Flying between the cold moon and the earth,

Cupid, all armed. A certain aim he took

At a fair vestal thronèd by the West,

And loosed his love-shaft smartly from his bow

As it should pierce a hundred thousand hearts.

Yet marked I where the bolt of Cupid fell,

It fell upon a little western flower —

Before milk-white, now purple with love's wound —

And maidens call it love-in-idleness.

Fetch me that flower, the herb I showed thee once.

The juice of it on sleeping eyelids laid

Will make or man or woman madly dote

Upon the next live creature that it sees.

Fetch me that herb and be thou here again

Ere the Leviathan can swim a league.

PUCK: I'll put a girdle round about the earth

In forty minutes!

REINHARDT: *(Applauding.)* Excellent! That vas vonderful. You boys are good! How did Mr. Varner get you here so fast?

PUCK: Mr. "Varner"?

REINHARDT: That was terrific audition.

OBERON: Thank you, but what exactly is an "audition"?

REINHARDT: Ah! That is exactly how I feel. Bravo. There is no such thing as audition, we must be truthful every second. You just scored big point with me. So, let's continue. Your names please.

PUCK: Puck.

OBERON: Oberon. King of the Fairies.

REINHARDT: Ja, but that remains to be seen. I want your real names.

OBERON: Oh, our *real* names.

PUCK: Ralph.

OBERON: Hector.

(They look at each other and shrug as if to say "why not.")

REINHARDT: Now tell me about yourselves. Where did you last appear?

OBERON: Just outside Athens. We were playing at the palace.

REINHARDT: You played the Palace? Ooh, that is very good venue. Now have you ever played Oberon and Puck before?

OBERON: Well, yes.

PUCK: Quite a lot, actually.

REINHARDT: Good. Now what about your film experience. What have you shot?

OBERON: Well, once I shot a unicorn. But I was very young.

REINHARDT: "A Unicorn." That was the title?

OBERON: He didn't have a title. He was just a common unicorn. I also did some shooting for the Amazons. I had to, it was the birth of their nation.

REINHARDT: *The Birth of a Nation.* Hoo. That was very big hit. Gentlemen, I have good news. You are hired. Congratulations.

OBERON: "Hired"?

REINHARDT: I want you to play Oberon and Puck in my new movie.

PUCK: In this movie?

REINHARDT: Ja.

OBERON: You mean as . . . actors?

REINHARDT: Ja.

OBERON/PUCK: *Ha haaa! Yahoo! We're movie actors!*

OBERON: *(Very showbiz.) I'm gonna be a moon!*

PUCK: Star.

OBERON: Right!

(*Olivia enters.*)

OLIVIA: Excuse me, Mr. Reinhardt, but there's a rumor that Mr. Jory has left!

REINHARDT: Ja, is true, he quit, who needs the bum. I have found someone ten times better. Miss Darnell, meet your new Oberon.

OLIVIA: . . . You? Is it really you?

OBERON: Apparently.

(*She almost jumps for joy.*)

OLIVIA: Oh, my God. I'm so happy for you! You did it! You actually did it! (*She runs to him and hugs him with affection.*) Wait! I think we should celebrate. Have you been to the commissary yet? It's like a fairyland. You see one big star after another and they sit right next to you! And don't worry, we'll go dutch.

OBERON: All right, but I don't think I can do the accent.

OLIVIA: Oh, Mr. Reinhardt, could we have our lunch break, please, I mean the cameramen are still setting up the shot and we'll be back before they're done, I promise!

REINHARDT: Ja, go, but don't be long.

OLIVIA: Thanks! Come on! It's my treat!

(*And as she drags Oberon away, Puck throws his hat in the air and lets out a cry of happiness.*)

PUCK: *We're going to be in the movies. Yipeeeee!*

[If the play was in three acts (as it is structurally), this would be the end of Act I.]

(*As Puck dances out happily, Lydia enters, dressed to the nines in her costume, with Louella following her, getting an interview.*)

LOUELLA: Lydia! My dear! You must be so excited arriving for your very first day on such a prestigious picture! May I ask you some questions for my column?

LYDIA: Why of course, Louella, I would be utterly enchanted.

(*Lydia is really putting on the dog now that she's such a classy actress; alas, she is betrayed by her chorus-girl accent.*)

LOUELLA: First of all, tell me: who do you play in the picture?

LYDIA: I play a beautiful and delightful young woman named Helena. She is the star. But alas, her boyfriend loves another, and so she flees into a forest.

LOUELLA: How thrilling.

LYDIA: Only this ain't no ordinary forest. It's full of magic, including a magic flower! Of which the *juice* of it is so powerful that if you get it in your eye, you fall deeply in love with the very next person you look at, *whammo!* Which, as you can well imagine, makes for some very funny complications. Ho ho.

LOUELLA: How exciting. Now tell me, what does all this mean for Lydia Lansing? Can we expect to see you in other prestigious movies in the future?

LYDIA: Yes, Louella, I think you can. And I would like to add that I personally find it thrilling to be doin' a movie written by the immortal Shakespeare, because he is truly one of our great Americans. And I do hope this is just the beginning, because there are so many other classic roles I hope to play in the future. Like Madame Curie and Moby Dick. Thank you.

(*At this moment, Powell, Reinhardt, and Daryl enter.*)

DARYL: Okay, let's go! Shot 128. The Wood Near Athens. Lights, check. Set, check, We've got a moon, we've got a tree. Lysander over here, Helena enter here. Quiet, please ladies and gentlemen! *Quiet!*

REINHARDT: Roll them. And action!

(*Lysander, as portrayed by Dick Powell, is asleep on the ground. After a beat, Lydia, playing Helena, enters. She is a truly terrible actress. She makes Snout and Tinker look like Laurence Olivier. But she tries her best and gives it all she's got.*)

LYDIA AS HELENA: (*Her Brooklyn accent as strong as ever.*)

"O, I am out of breath in this fond chase.

The more my prayer, the lesser is my grace.

Happy is Hermia, wheresoe'er she lies,

For she hath blessèd and attractive eyes."

(*She smiles broadly and sighs. That part's out of the way!*)

"But who is here? Lysander on the ground?

Dead — or asleep? I see no blood, no wound. [She pronounces it to rhyme with "ground."]

Lysander, if you live, good sir, awake!"

POWELL AS LYSANDER: "And run through fire I will for thy sweet sake!
   Not Hermia, but Helena I love.
   Who would not change a raven for a dove?"
LYDIA AS HELENA: "Good sooth, you do me wrong — good sooth, you do!
   In such disdainful manner me to woo! To woo! To woo!"
REINHARDT: Cut! Cut! Cut! What is this "to woo to woo"?! You sound like bird!
   There is only one "to woo"! "In such disdainful manner me to woo!"
LYDIA: I thought it kinda helped my character. It makes her seem really sad. Ya
   know? "To woo, to woo."
REINHARDT: Ja, is sad all right.
LYDIA: Gee, thanks! If ya want, I could do some cryin'.
REINHARDT: I will do that for both of us. *Now do it again! And do it right
   this time!*
   *(The scene shifts to the Warner Brothers Commissary. Oberon and Olivia sit
   together at a table. The effect is very romantic.)*
OBERON: Thank you for . . . "lunch."
OLIVIA: Isn't the commissary a dream?! It reminds me of . . . Omigosh. Don't
   look behind you. Don't! *Don't!* It's Bing Crosby!
OBERON: And he does what again?
OLIVIA: He's a singer. And he smokes a pipe. He's very famous.
OBERON: Well no wonder. It must be hard to sing and smoke at the same time.
   Can I have some more of that brown liquid with the bubbles?
OLIVIA: Coca Cola.
OBERON: And I love those little square things with the layers.
OLIVIA: Sandwiches. I would have thought that every place in the world had
   sandwiches.
OBERON: Not where I come from.
OLIVIA: Outside Athens.
OBERON: Right. I mean, in a way.
OLIVIA: What way? And don't change the subject this time.
OBERON: *(Hissing.)* Look! I mean don't look! The man behind you! He must
   be important, he's all in white and he has a weapon!
   (She peeks over her shoulder.)
OLIVIA: He's the waiter. That's a ladle.
OBERON: Oh. He's not a star?
OLIVIA: No. Well he might be someday, if he's in lots of movies.
OBERON: And then, if he becomes a star, he gets treated like royalty.
OLIVIA: That's right.

OBERON: Doesn't your king get upset at this?

OLIVIA: We don't have a king. Or a queen.

OBERON: Then who runs the place?

OLIVIA: The people do. It's a democracy.

OBERON: Well that'll never work, believe me. They tried it once in Athens, it
was chaos.

(She laughs.)

OLIVIA: Come on, tell me the truth. Where are you from?

OBERON: And if I said: a land of magic?

OLIVIA: I'd say how interesting and tell me more.

OBERON: *(Gently.)* Think of a world that's full of groves and green,
With fountains clear and spangled starlight sheen.
Where argument between the jealous queen and king
Makes riot of the middle summer's spring.
A land of pavèd fountain and of rushy brook
Where in the beachèd margent of the sea
We dance our ringlets to the whistling wind.
Would you come to such a place with me?

(Their faces are an inch apart. They could kiss at any moment.)

OLIVIA: Oh my gosh, look at the time. We have to go. Reinhardt'll be furious.

(She leaves money on the table and drags him off.)

Quick! Come on! We can't be late!

*(As they run off, the action shifts to the Warner Brothers costume shop where
Joe E. Brown is being fitted by a seamstress with pins in her mouth. Brown is
a good-natured fellow with a wide grin who always looks bemused and slightly
baffled by life. He's holding a copy of the movie script and calling to someone
offstage.)*

BROWN: I can't get over it. Why would they put me in a Shakespeare movie? I
can hardly speak regular English.

CAGNEY: *(Off.)* Aw it ain't so bad.

BROWN: That's easy for you to say. You're the great Jimmy Cagney. I'm in baseball movies.

(Jimmy Cagney walks in wearing a large ass head.)

Yaaah! . . . What's that?!

CAGNEY: *(With the head still on.)* It's my costume. For the movie.

BROWN: You're kidding me.

CAGNEY: Nope.

(Brown walks around Cagney in amazement.)

BROWN: But I don't get it. I thought you were playing a guy named Bottom.

CAGNEY: I am. But during the movie, I turn into a donkey. Then everybody gets scared and runs away. Except a fairy princess who falls in love with me.

BROWN: And this is by Shakespeare?

CAGNEY: Uh-huh.

BROWN: Frankly, I expected more out of him.

(Cagney pulls off the ass head — and we see the real James Cagney, the famous movie star. Despite his image playing tough guys, he's very likeable. As he pulls the head off, Oberon enters in an urgent mood.)

OBERON: *Puck!* . . . Oh where is he? I need that flower. *Robin Goodfellow!* *(He sees Cagney in the ass head.)* Bottom! What are you doing here?

CAGNEY: *(From inside the head.)* Making an ass of myself.

BROWN: That's a good one.

(Cagney takes off the head.)

OBERON: *Ah!* How did you do that? I thought I was the only one who could take your head off.

CAGNEY: Then you haven't met Mrs. Cagney.

OBERON: Oh, you must be a . . . star.

BROWN: He's the great Jimmy Cagney. Joe Brown, how are ya.

OBERON: Hector.

CAGNEY: Oh, you're the new guy playing Oberon. You look the part. Nice costume.

OBERON: Have you seen Ralph?

CAGNEY: Who?

OBERON: *Puck!*

(Puck appears magically from a hamper or box.)

PUCK: Right here, my liege.

(Cagney and Brown are startled. Puck is dressed like a star now: sunglasses, bright yellow blazer, designer slacks, the works. And he's carrying packages with logos of expensive stores. He's gone Hollywood.)

OBERON: What in the name of Venus are you wearing?!

PUCK: They're called sunglasses. It's what the *stars* wear! I bought you a pair. Try 'em on.

(He hands the glasses to Oberon, who puts them on.)

OBERON: Well?

PUCK: *(Brooklyn chorus girl.)* Honey, they were made for you.

(To Cagney and Brown.) You like 'em?

CAGNEY/BROWN: Uh, yeah./Sure do.

(Puck snaps his fingers and two more pair jump out of the basket and into his hand.)

PUCK: Here. One for you and one for you. Now we can all be stars together!

CAGNEY: Uh, excuse us . . .

BROWN: We gotta go now . . .

(Cagney and Brown exit, spooked and uncertain about these new guys.)

PUCK: Sire, I'm telling you, this being a star is even better than we thought! Cash advance, great clothes, hot chicks . . .

OBERON: "Hot chicks"? As in little braised poultry?

PUCK: As in *women. Babes.* When they realize you're a star, they're all over you! And here's the capper: you know they're giving that party tonight.

OBERON: Party? No.

PUCK: The studio gives a party after the first day of filming. It's a tradition. So: guess what? I got us two girls for the party! One each! Mine's called Heather, yours is named Delores. I got you a blond. I thought she'd look good with your coloring.

OBERON: No, I can't.

PUCK: You can't?

OBERON: No.

PUCK: But these are quality women. They talk and everything!

(At this moment, Olivia rushes in.)

OLIVIA: Excuse me. I'm sorry to interrupt, but can you believe it, we left our scripts on the table at the commissary. I ran back and got them and this is yours, it's fine but has a little ketchup in the corner so I wiped it off so you can hardly see it, but now I've got to run.

(Beat; he just stares at her, so in love that he's tongue-tied.)

Thanks for lunch. I had a wonderful time. *(She kisses him on the cheek and heads off.)*

OBERON: Olivia. My friend here tells me there are revels planned this evening. May I have the pleasure of your company?

OLIVIA: To answer by the method, you may indeed, sir. With all my heart.

OBERON: We shall go coupled and inseparable, like Juno's swans.

OLIVIA: *As You Like It.*

OBERON: How very kind. If there be dancing, shall we rock the ground?

OLIVIA: Absolutely. But I warn you, I'm a *really* good dancer.

OBERON: And so am I.

OLIVIA: *(Demonstrating each dance.)* Do you do the jitterbug?

OBERON: Yes, I do.

OLIVIA: Big Apple?

OBERON: Indeed.

OLIVIA: The Lindy?

OBERON: Why not?!

OLIVIA: Then pick me up at seven. My place.

OBERON: I'll be the one with the eye shadow.

PUCK: Sunglasses.

OBERON: Sunglasses.

(She exits.)

O Robin. Did you see her?

I would live in her heart, die in her lap,

And be buried in her eyes.

PUCK: Well, I guess Heather is out. Does she know how you feel?

OBERON: I think so.

PUCK: Does the difference in your ages give her any pause?

(Oberon takes this in and gets angry. We hear the rumble of thunder. Puck realizes what he's said and starts backpedaling madly.)

I-I mean, of course, there isn't really much difference at all, when you think about it. What's a few thousand years, here or there . . . I think I'll go look for the flower again.

OBERON: You haven't found it yet?!

PUCK: No, my Lord.

OBERON: Well keep looking, it's important! I have a score to settle with that creature Hays.

PUCK: The one who insulted you?

OBERON: *Yes!*

PUCK: All right, all right! I was just asking.

I go, I go, look how I go,

Swifter than arr —

OBERON: *Just go!*

(Puck disappears down the hamper. Oberon is alone.)

OBERON: Difference in our ages . . . We're spirits. We grow to maturity, reach the age of our greatest perfection and stay there. Which is as it should be. No wonder mortals are so depressed all the time. They reach their pinnacle and then decline. Then they limp, limp on to the end, sans teeth, sans eyes, sans taste, sans everything. And for what? Because intimations of mortality make them write better books? Compose better operas? Well it isn't worth it. If I thought for a minute that *I* was going to leave the planet, I'd —

(He looks at his hands and stops abruptly. He sees something strange about them.) That's odd. I can see light . . . through my skin . . . Maybe that's part of being a star. People can see right through you.

(At this moment, Dick Powell enters.)

POWELL: Knock knock? Hi. I don't think we've met. I'm Dick Powell. I play Lysander.

OBERON: How do you do.

POWELL: Listen. I'm sorry to bother you, but I have a sort of favor to ask. Well. It concerns Miss Darnell. Olivia? See, I've just been talking to her and it's clear to me that, well, she thinks the world of you. She looks on you as a sort of . . . father figure.

(Oberon reacts. We hear thunder. Perhaps Powell looks up.)

Okay, now here's the thing. It's hard to put into words, but . . . well . . . *I am just so in love with her!* See, I met her a few weeks ago. And then I asked her out, and she couldn't go, and, well, the fact of the matter is, she barely knows that I'm alive! And I don't know what to do! And then I thought . . . oh, it's stupid.

OBERON: Go on.

POWELL: Well, I thought that maybe *you* could say something to her. About me. Sort of get in my corner. I bet she'd listen to you. I know she would! And, well, that's it.

OBERON: . . . I don't know what to say.

POWELL: I guess it's pretty stupid, huh? Thanks for listening.

(He walks away.)

OBERON: Wait. Mr. Powell. I have an idea. I think I can help.

POWELL: Really? Gee, that's great! You mean you'll talk to her?

OBERON: I'll do something appropriate.

POWELL: No kidding! Gee thanks! I mean just . . . thanks! *(He wrings Oberon's hand.)* What a guy. It's like she said. You're the tops! Thanks . . . pal.

(He exits.)

OBERON: I don't think anyone has ever called me "pal" before.

(Puck reenters in some wonderful way. Perhaps he's driving one of those go-carts they use at movie studios.)

OBERON: Welcome wanderer. Hast thou the flower there?

PUCK: Here it is.

OBERON: I pray thee give it me.

> *(It glows from within with an aura of mystery. We're in the world of magic now, and Oberon intones his instructions with an air of danger.)*

OBERON: Mark me, Robin.

> Take this herb and seek through this place
> Find a youth with handsome face.
> Be not deceived, his design is foul,
> He'll answer to the name of Powell.
> Lull him to sleep, then streak his eyes
> So that the next thing he espies
> Is a ravishing woman.

PUCK: What woman?

OBERON: Any woman that you find provided it is *not* Olivia. Offer him some sacrificial virgin or something.

PUCK: It's hard to find a virgin. We're in Hollywood.

OBERON: Look. Just find *some woman* and let him fall in love! But he cannot have Olivia. She's *mine!*

PUCK: Yes, Master. But I thought the flower was for Hays.

OBERON: It was. It may be. But now it's for Powell. Go to thy errand!

PUCK: *(Leaving.)* I go, I go, look how I go,

> Swifter than arrow from the Tartar's bow!
> Thank you for letting me finish it, O King!

> *(As Puck disappears, Oberon exits in the opposite direction. The lights change with a snap. Olivia appears in her own light.)*

OLIVIA: Dear Mother,

> Do you remember that actor I told you about? Well I hope you're sitting down for this because he just asked me to the party tonight. *No, don't call Aunt Ethel!* You know her, she'll be sending out wedding invitations by sundown. It's just a date and I may never even see him again.
> Love, Olivia

> *(The lights restore and we're now on Sound Stage Number Two, where Reinhardt is about to film a scene from Act II, Scene One of the play with Olivia as Hermia and Powell as Lysander. Daryl is assisting Reinhardt.)*

DARYL: Okay, let's go. Shot 041. The Palace at Athens. Lights, check. Set, check. Rug, check. Lysander over here. Hermia over here. Quiet please, ladies and gentlemen.

REINHARDT: Wait. Where is Miss Lansing. *Miss Lansing!*

> *(Lydia hurries in, excited and happy.)*

LYDIA: I'm comin'! I'm right here! Now listen, I made this incredible discovery! You know how you keep tellin' us to "examine the text" and look at the words and discover new stuff and all?!

REINHARDT: Ja.

LYDIA: And you know how I'm always sayin' it doesn't make any sense to me —

REINHARDT: *(Impatiently.)* Ja, ja.

LYDIA: Well I just discovered that a lot of his speeches make just as much sense if you say 'em backwards as they do forwards! Listen to this. It's one of my speeches, the way it's written:

"You draw me, you hard-hearted adamant!

But yet you draw not iron: for my heart

Is true as steel. Leave you your power to draw,

And I shall have no power to follow you."

Okay? Now here it is backwards:

(She does it with great feeling as if it makes perfect sense.)

"You follow to power! No?!

Shall have I draw to power your leave?!

Steel as true is heart, not iron.

Draw you yet but adamant?! Hard-hearted you!!"

(Beat. She smiles and shrugs.)

You can't tell the difference.

REINHARDT: Miss Lansing, you have just made incredible stride in the history of Shakespeare scholarship. I can see whole book being written about Shakespeare backvards.

LYDIA: Gee . . .

REINHARDT: But I vant to film picture forwards and on time, *so into position get!*

(The actors scurry into position.)

Are you ready?!

LYDIA: *Yes sir! (She whispers to whoever is closest.)* I think he's jealous cause he didn't think of it first.

REINHARDT: Okay, roll 'em. Aaaaaaand action!

(The lights change and the scene begins. During this, Oberon enters and watches. No one sees him, because he's invisible.)

POWELL AS LYSANDER: "My Hermia, if thou lovest me, then

Steal forth thy father's house tomorrow night,

And in the wood, a league without the town,

Where I did meet thee once with Helena,

There will I stay for thee."

OLIVIA AS HERMIA: "I swear to thee by Cupid's strongest bow,

By his best arrow with the golden head,

In that same place thou hast appointed me

Tomorrow truly will I meet with thee."

POWELL AS LYSANDER: "Keep promise, love."

(He kisses Hermia passionately — in other words, Powell kisses Olivia passionately — and when they break it off, he's so weak in the knees he almost crumples to the ground. During the kiss, we see Oberon's jealous reaction — and perhaps we hear the thunder again.)

"Look — here comes Helena!"

(Lydia enters, playing Helena.)

OLIVIA AS HERMIA: "God speed, fair Helena!"

LYDIA AS HELENA: "Call you me fair? That fair again unsay!" Or, backwards . . .

"Unsay again! Fair that fair me you call?!"

REINHARDT: *Cut! Cut! Cut! Miss Lansing! JUST SAY THE LINES!!*

LYDIA: *I'm tryin', but they don't make any sense!*

REINHARDT: *Vell try harder!! . . .* We resume in ten minutes, when my blood pressure goes down!

DARYL: Okay, ten minutes everybody!

(Everyone leaves except Lydia. She starts to cry. She's trying so hard, and it just isn't working out. After a beat, Puck enters, holding the flower, talking to himself.)

PUCK: Powell, Powell. "Find a man named Powell . . . " Hello.

LYDIA: Hi. Gee, what a pretty flower. What kind is it?

PUCK: Oh, you wouldn't know it, it's quite rare.

LYDIA: Let me smell it.

PUCK: No! No! Give it back!

LYDIA: Ooh, it smells so nice.

PUCK: *No!*

LYDIA: Ow! *(The flower has attacked her eye. It does that.)* I think I got some pollen in my eye.

(As she dabs at her eye, Daryl enters.)

DARYL: Excuse, me, Miss Lansing — Mr. Warner asked me to tell you that he'll meet you at the party tonight at eight.

(She looks up and sees him — ping! — and falls instantly in love with him.

[Note: whenever anyone falls in love because of the flower, we hear the distinctive sound made when you pluck the string of a harp. This will be indicated in the text by the word "ping!"])

LYDIA: *(Her eyes glowing with adoration.)*

O I'll be there, I promise thee, my dove,

My precious boy, my everything, my love!

DARYL: . . . Right. I'll see you there.

(He exits.)

LYDIA: *Daryl! Please! Come back! I love you!*

(She drops the flower and dashes off.)

PUCK: Oh, no. Miss! Miss! Come back here! Stop!

(Puck snatches up the flower and runs to stop her. As he goes, he bumps into Powell, who is just entering.)

POWELL: Oh sorry.

PUCK: Sorry.

POWELL: Hey, you must be the new guy who's playing Puck.

PUCK: 'Tis I. Sorry, but I have to —

POWELL: Dick Powell. I play Lysander.

PUCK: . . . Powell? The actor? Excellent. I've been looking for you.

POWELL: You have?

PUCK: You must be getting very sleepy after all that filming. Very sleepy.

POWELL: No, not really.

(Puck snaps his fingers and Powell drops off instantly and snores.)

ZZZZZZZZZZ!

(Puck tosses the magic flower onto the ground, forgetting about it.)

PUCK: Nicely done, Mad Spirit.

Now upon thy eyes I throw

All the power this charm doth owe.

What thou seest when thou dost wake,

Do it for thy true love take,

Love and languish for her sake.

(Puck covers Powell up in the rug used for the film scene, hiding him from view.)

Now I go and find the girl

To tug the heart of snoring churl.

A buxom wench to join the chorus,

Heather, or perhaps Delores.

Till I bring her stay right here.

Do not arise till I appear.

I'll wake you when the coast is clear.

I am invisible.

(Zzzzing! He hurries off. A moment later, Olivia enters.)

OLIVIA: Mr. Reinhardt, I was wondering if . . . where is everybody? Hello?! . . . *Hello?!* . . . Well, I guess this gives me time to look at some lines. What's this? *(She sees the blossom of the Magic Flower that Puck accidentally left on the ground, and she picks it up.)* It's a flower. Oh, it's beautiful! And it smells so ow! *(The flower attacks her eye.)* Ooh, it's in my eye . . . There, that's better. *(She yawns.)* Oh, I'm so sleepy. I guess I'd better work on those lines. Let's see . . . *(She sits and looks at her script. She recites her lines with increasing weariness.)*

"Never so weary, never so in woe,

Bedabbled with the dew, and torn with briars —

I can no further crawl, no further go.

My legs can keep no pace with my desires."

(She gets no further.)

ZZZZZZZZZZ!

(She rolls over, pulling the other half of the rug over — hiding her from view. A moment later, Jimmy Cagney enters dressed as Pyramus.)

CAGNEY: *(Calling to Brown, who's offstage.)* Hey, Joe! Would you come on!

BROWN: *(Off.)* No!

CAGNEY: *(Calling.)* Would you stop it. You look great. It's what the part calls for.

(Joe E. Brown enters. He's dressed in drag as Thisbe, the young maiden in "Pyramus and Thisbe," which he and Cagney will perform in the movie. He wears a long blond wig and a dress with a Grecian pattern on the skirt and criss-crossed leather straps across the chest to emphasize his generous female figure — the same costume that Joe E. Brown actually wears in the movie.)

BROWN: I have to say, I don't know why this is necessary.

CAGNEY: Because you're playing Thisbe, who's a girl.

BROWN: I thought I was playing Francis Flute!

CAGNEY: You *are.* And in the play that Francis Flute is in, he's playing Thisbe. Which means you wear a dress. You talk "like this." And you walk like this.

(He demonstrates.)

BROWN: I don't know what girls you've been seeing.

CAGNEY: Then your big moment is when you kill yourself.

BROWN: I do?

CAGNEY: Yeah. See, you're in love with Pyramus. That's me. And I know there's a lion around. So I walk into the forest and I see your handkerchief covered with blood. *"She's dead!"* I cry. But you're not dead. I only think you're dead. So I kill myself. In grief. Then you come along and see *me* dead, and you kill *yourself.* In grief.

BROWN: That's a lot of grief.

CAGNEY: Okay, let's rehearse. You stand over here. Start when you're ready.

(*Puck enters. He's invisible, so the men don't hear or see him.*)

PUCK: A virgin. A virgin. Where am I supposed to find a virgin?!

BROWN AS THISBE: (*In a woman's voice.*)

"O wall, full often hast thou heard my moans,

My cherry lips have often kissed thy stones.

PUCK: O wingèd Mercury, I'm getting an idea.

CAGNEY AS BOTTOM: "I see a voice. Thisbe?! Thisbe?!"

PUCK: (*His voice magically coming through the public address system.*)

Attention please. Will James Cagney please report to the director's office. James Cagney to the director's office.

CAGNEY: I wonder what that's about. I'll be right back.

BROWN: I'll go with you.

PUCK: (*Still through the speaker.*) No, you stay right where you are.

(*Brown looks up, amazed. How do they do that? Cagney exits. Then Puck scampers up to Brown and spins him around and around, as though he's caught in a high wind.*)

PUCK: Up and down, up and down,

I will lead him up and down!

I am feared in field and town,

Goblin lead them up and down!

BROWN: Whoa . . . whoa! . . . Hey! What's happening?!

(*Brown spins across the stage and lands on Powell.*)

BROWN: Holy cow! I'm so sorry! I lost my balance!

(*Ping! Powell awakes and instantly falls in love with Brown.*)

POWELL: Tide life, tide death! What is this vision that I

See before me!

(*Note: as we saw with Lydia, the flower not only makes you fall instantly in love with the next creature you see, it also makes you speak in Shakespearean verse.*)

BROWN: I'm sorry?

POWELL: Goddess, nymph, divine creature!

O Cupid is a knavish lad
Thus to make poor fellows mad.

BROWN: Oh, I get it. That must be from the play. That's very good.

POWELL: Thou art my moon, my star, my sun,
More rare to me than Irene Dunne.

BROWN: No, you can't *do* that! Because with Shakespeare you can't ad lib.
It's a big no-no. Ooh.
(*Brown rubs his backside.*)

POWELL: What's the matter?

BROWN: I think I hurt myself when I fell.

POWELL: Oh, no! You poor darling! How you must
Suffer! What can I fetch you to make it feel better?

BROWN: It's fine.

POWELL: No. Please! Send me to the Antipodes,
To the furthest inch of Asia so that I can
Ease the pain.

BROWN: It's really not that —

POWELL: *Please!*

BROWN: Honestly, it's —

POWELL: *Anything!!!*

BROWN: . . . Well I guess I could use some aspirin.

POWELL: It shall be done at once! Now rest and stay.
And if perchance I see along the way
A little present? A little ring,
Or diadem or jewel or anything?
Is that of interest? Hm? Ha!
Ha ha! Ha ha ha ha ha ha!
And then when I return I'll kiss it where it
Hurts and make it aaaaall better.
(*Powell exits. Brown watches him go.*)

BROWN: He's a nice kid, but I think he's got a problem.

PUCK: This turns out even better than I hoped. I must tell Oberon.
(*Exiting, Puck squeezes Brown's chest:*)
Honk, honk!
(*And Puck is gone.*)

BROWN: It might be just me, but I think there's something funny going on
around here. Maybe if I sing, it'll go away.
(*Singing.*)

Take me out to the ballgame,

Take me out to the crowd,

Buy me some peanuts and Cracker Jack

I don't care if I never get back —

OLIVIA: What angel wakes me from —

(Ping!)

I pray thee, gentle actor, sing again!

Your voice transports me to another world!

BROWN: *(Beat; then sings:)* So it's root, root, root for the home team,

If they don't win it's a shame . . .

OLIVIA: And yet your voice is nothing to your face,

Your eyes, your lips that must be caressed and kissed!

BROWN: *(Fending her off.)* Hey, hey! Hold it! Get back! Now cut that out! You're teasing me and it isn't nice. I'll bet it's because I'm wearing this dress. Well it's not my fault. I've got to make a living, you know.

OLIVIA: "Love looks not with the eye but with the mind,

And therefore is winged Cupid painted blind."

BROWN: I wish you'd cut that out. It's really not nice.

OLIVIA: If only, like Titania, I had

A train of fairies here to make you happy.

(The fairies appear.)

"Moth! Peaseblossom! Mustardseed!

Be kind to this gentleman and gambol in his eyes;

I'll have my love to *bed* and to *arise.*"

(On the word "bed" she puts her arm around his neck. And on the word "arise" she puts her hand on his crotch. He looks down at her hand. He starts to object, but she stops his mouth with a long, passionate kiss.)

OLIVIA: Come with me now. We'll go to the party

Where we two shall dance the night away.

And every maiden there will stare at me

With longing in her eyes because you're mine.

BROWN: . . . *(Sings:)* "She'll be comin' round the mountain when she comes . . ."

OLIVIA: No more singing. Come. To bed.

And never change a hair on that sweet head.

(Music plays. With great ceremony, she leads him away.)

END OF ACT I

ACT II

SCENE ONE

We're at an outdoor party at Jack Warner's Beverly Hills mansion. Hollywood types walk by chatting and dancing, and we hear a big band playing hits of the great Swing era by Glenn Miller and Count Basie. After a moment, Reinhardt enters, dressed for the party, and addresses the audience.

REINHARDT: Hollywood! City of dreams! Like the Wood Near Athens, it is a place of magic. Anything can happen here. Especially at a fancy-schmancy party like this one on Jack Warner's estate. Do you see that leading man over there, big heartthrob? In January he was a chauffeur driving other people's cars. Now he has his own Mercedes Benz, the sporty, fun car made by Nazis. And that movie starlet over there? She couldn't pay her rent until six months ago when she was spotted in some drugstore sipping a cherry Coke. Now she has a swimming pool in the shape of her uterus. Lives change overnight. Love affairs appear like lightning and fade as quickly. Dreams are part of life, and after you dream, you bring back to the ordinary world what you learned in the world of imagination. And how bad can Hollywood be if they give parties like this one? The guests at this party alone confirm that yes, this planet has been visited by extra-terrestrial life.

(Louella Parsons enters. She's dressed extravagantly, as only Louella can dress.)

LOUELLA: *(Singing his name.)* Professor Rein-hardt . . . !

REINHARDT: *(To the audience.)* And it stayed.

(She bustles over to him clutching her notebook and pencil.)

LOUELLA: Oh, I have so many questions to ask you about your picture!

REINHARDT: I answer all your questions on one condition.

(Dramatically.) Dance with me!

LOUELLA: I thought you'd never ask!

(She flings her notebook over her shoulder, and they tango off. As they go, Oberon and Puck enter. They're both looking ultra-cool for the party. Puck is in high spirits.)

PUCK: Parties, parties, parties. I'm getting bored with them already. *NOT RE-ALLY!* Haaaa! By all that's sacred, this is fun!

OBERON: I wonder where Olivia is?

PUCK: I thought you were bringing her.

OBERON: I thought so too, but then I couldn't find her.

PUCK: Oh she'll be along. Now guess what? I found someone for that Powell creature to mate with. Ha! Oh, this really is my best work ever. Wait. Look. Here she comes. In full sail.

(Joe E. Brown enters, still in drag, dressed extravagantly for the party.)

PUCK: The barge she sat in, like a burnished throne,

Burned on the water!

BROWN: I still think this is wrong.

(Olivia sails in, dressed stunningly for the party. She has the magic flower behind one of her ears for decoration.)

OLIVIA: Then love is wrong, and Fate and Destiny

Are wrong. Oh, my darling love.

(She kisses him passionately. Oberon and Puck look at each other, then back at the couple.)

BROWN: Why can't I wear my normal clothes?

OLIVIA: Because this is how I fell in love with you!

BROWN: But I don't get it. Why pick me? I'm just a character actor.

OLIVIA: Love and reason keep little company nowadays.

BROWN: I guess I was okay in some of those baseball movies.

OLIVIA: Oh how I loved to see you in those pictures!

The way you sidled to the plate,

And held your *big strong bat* in front of you.

BROWN: Then fast ball down the middle of the plate and wham!, it's a home run!

OLIVIA: *(Approaching orgasm.)* O spirit of love, how quick and fresh art thou!

BROWN: And then another and another! Wham, wham!

(Olivia lets out an orgasmic scream on each wham.)

Then it's out with the glove!

OLIVIA: O that I were a glove upon that hand

That I might touch that cheek.

(The music changes to "Cheek-to-Cheek.")

Dance with me now, you mad fool.

(She takes him in her arms and they dance off. Oberon turns threateningly to Puck. Thunder is heard.)

PUCK: Wait. Wait wait. Wait. Just wait. Okay? I admit it. Something went wrong.

OBERON: "Something went wrong"?

PUCK: I don't know what happened! I mean, she must have gotten some of the flower in her eye!

OBERON: Oh, really? *DO YOU THINK SO?!*
You spongy, fawning, parasitical oaf! You lump of
Wind, you witless, unwiped, panderly puke-stocking!

PUCK: All right, all right! I made a mistake. I must have dropped it some place. She must have picked it up —

OBERON: And now it's behind her ear!

PUCK: Right.

OBERON: You useless, flap-eared measle, *get it back!*
We can't have a thing like that floating around
Hollywood. That's all they need out here,
Another excuse to copulate.

PUCK: Yes, my Lord.

OBERON: But more important, find the antidote.

PUCK: The antidote?

OBERON: To release her from the spell.

PUCK: I know what it is. I just don't know where to find it.

OBERON: Well then perhaps you should start looking *RIGHT AWAY!*

HAYS: *(Off.)* Where the hell is Warner!!

OBERON: Go.

PUCK: Yes sir, right away!
(As Oberon and Puck exit, Hays enters, slightly disheveled. He's wiping his jacket, mopping up a spill.)

HAYS: Lord I hate these parties! Look at this! That little tramp Claudette Colbert spilled her drink on me . . .
(He looks around to make sure that no one's watching, and he pulls a mirror out of his pocket. He looks into it and straightens his hair and eyebrows. He's even more vain than we realized.)
And they say that *I'm* unreasonable. Everything is *my* fault. They don't know anything about me!
(Puck reenters, carrying the flower.)
I'm not against art. I happen to love beautiful things. Real beauty. Like little furry animals.
(He gestures toward Puck, who is outraged.)
Or flowers. Like that one, there. Look at that. So delicate. So fragrant.
(Introducing himself.)
Will Hays. Hays Office.

PUCK: Did you say Hays? Here.

(Puck hands the flower to Hays. Hays smells it — and it attacks his eye.)

HAYS: Oooh! It's in my eye! *(He throws it down petulantly.)* Stupid flower! Ooh, it stings. Maybe I can get it out . . .

(He pulls out his mirror and looks into it, and — ping! — his jaw drops. He's enraptured by the image in the mirror.)

But soft! What light through yonder window breaks! It is the East, and I am the sun! Ooooh! My God! Tis beauty truly blent! Ha ha!

(He swaggers around in front of his image.)

Is this a swagger that I see before me?!

(He kisses his image in the mirror.)

My person beggars all description. I could hop forty paces through the street and make defect perfection! I could make me a willow cabin at my gate And let the babbling gossip of the air cry out "Will Hays! Will Hays!" God in Heaven, just look at that face. So strong, and yet so vulnerable. So harsh, yet so playful. Demanding, yet kindly. Noble, but with a common touch. It's no wonder people frown at me all the time. They're jealous. They all want to be me!! Ha! *To be or not to be me, That is the question!* Well I'll fix them. I'll fix them good. I'll listen to all their little complaints, and I'll smile and smile and be a villain and I'll say *NO!* You may *not* fill your films with smut in the name of art. I will not have it! You may not wheedle another concession out of me! You may not bribe me with fame or women or money! Unless it's a lot of money! There shall be *no more compromises! Ha ha ha ha ha ha ha ha!* Lead on, MacDuff! *Ha ha ha ha ha ha ha ha!*

(He holds the mirror out in front of him and follows it — so it seems to pull him off. [At some point above, he tossed the magic flower onto the floor — to be found presently.] The moment Hays is gone, Warner enters. He looks around impatiently.)

WARNER: Lydia? . . . Lydia?! . . . Where the hell is she? *(He nods graciously to some passing dancers.)* Hello. Hello.

(He looks around and shakes his head in amazement, not at all unhappily.) Just look at all this opulence. Two tennis courts. Four squash courts. I've got a boathouse — and there isn't a drop of water within fifteen miles. The American Dream. And it's meaningless without Lydia. Lydia. A chorus girl. I'm a fifty-year-old mogul and I fell in love with a chorus girl. I'm a walking cliché. On our very first date, she turned to me and said she wanted a starring part in my next movie. I said "Are you crazy?" She

looked at me with those liquid eyes and said "What's the use of sleeping with an old man unless he makes me a star?"

(He chuckles happily, then looks off dreamily.) If that wonderful girl ever knew how much I love her, she'd make my life a living hell.

(He sees Daryl passing.) Daryl.

DARYL: Yes sir! Yes sir! Right here, sir!

WARNER: Where's Lydia?! Have you been keeping an eye on her?

DARYL: Oh yes sir.

WARNER: And there's been no funny stuff?

DARYL: Funny stuff?

WARNER: Men. Has she been . . . entertaining anyone in her dressing room? Offering them a little chips and dip. Putting on a spread, as it were.

DARYL: No sir. I didn't know she cooked.

WARNER: That's a metaphor, you idiot. Has she been fooling around?

DARYL: Oh no sir.

WARNER: Good, good. I'm asking you because tonight could be special. I'm thinking of popping the question. Look at this ring.

DARYL: That's quite a pop.

WARNER: I want her to be happy. That's all that matters. As long as it's not with anyone else.

DARYL: Remember what she told me, sir. She wants to give you a "really big thank you."

WARNER: The vixen. Daryl, boy, I only hope that someday you find a girl even half as wonderful.

(Lydia enters. She's wearing a stunning, sexy dress. She looks toward Warner and Daryl, who are standing together.)

LYDIA: My darling, my darling, my darling . . . !

(Warner puts his arms out, but she sails right past him and goes straight for Daryl and kisses him passionately on the lips.)

Oh, *Daryl!*

DARYL: I-I-I-I

WARNER: What's going on here?!

LYDIA: Jack, come here.

(He does. She pushes him away.)

Go away! What's past is past.

I've found my beacon in the night at last.

DARYL: No you haven't! Sir, I never — ever — would have — sir, is this a joke?

WARNER: *A joke*?!

LYDIA: *(To Daryl.)* Daryl, how can you say that! Is *this* a joke? Or *this*? Or *this*?

(She puts his hands on her breasts and he screams.)

Oh, I've always dreamed of sleeping with a yes-man!

WARNER: *(Rolling up his sleeves.)* Lydia, stand aside.

(They circle the stage. It turns into a chase.)

DARYL: Sir! Please! It's not my fault!

WARNER: Traitor.

LYDIA: Don't touch him!

DARYL: Please. I bruise easily. *Heeeelp!*

(They dash off. We can hear them offstage as the chase continues: "Help!" "Don't touch him!" As they go, Louella Parsons enters, worn out by the party.)

LOUELLA: Parties, parties, every night. If I see one more scallop on a toothpick wrapped in bacon, I'll throw up. Still, who would have thought I'd end up in Hollywood, hobnobbing with the rich and the reckless, the base and the brazen, the vile and the vicious. It's like a dream come true. [Just look where I started. I was Louella Oettinger, from Dixon, Illinois. I had braces, bad skin, and my eyes were crossed. Now look at me. I'm gorgeous!] Ha! *(Beat.)* Oh look at that flower. It's beautiful. And the smell, it's oh, ooh! It's in my eye.

(Daryl runs in. He stops and leans against a statue. He's out of breath and panting hard. He doesn't see Louella.)

DARYL: I can't do this. I need a place to hide.

(Louella turns and sees him — ping!)

LOUELLA: And hide you shall forever by my side.

DARYL: Oh no.

LOUELLA: Kiss me, you fool.

(As she's kissing Daryl, Puck enters carrying the yellow antidote flower. Puck sees them kissing and screams.)

PUCK: Ahhhhh! I can't believe it. I did it again.

(Puck picks up the flower, as Hays reenters, gazing into his mirror.)

HAYS: He walks in beauty like the night,

Of cloudless climes and starry skies,

(Reinhardt enters.)

His eyes are Heaven, his smile is Gold,

He has those hips you love to hold.

REINHARDT: What's going on?

PUCK: *(Handing the red flower to Reinhardt.)* Nothing, nothing! Here, hold this.

REINHARDT: Thank you. Is beautiful. And the smell is *ooh!* It's in my eye.

(He rubs his eye and looks up. Ping! He's looking right at Hays.)

Vill Hays, Vill Hays, you have cheeks of bliss,
Und all I ask is a single kiss!

HAYS: Get away from me! Just stop it! If there's anybody I'm caressing around here, it's me!

(And now Lydia and Warner hurry in.)

LYDIA: There you are!

DARYL: Oh no.

WARNER: You low-life swine. Don't move or I'll call my guards and have you beaten to a pulp.

LOUELLA: Don't you threaten him, you bully! Can't you
See the boy is frightened? Look at that face!
That face those eyes those lips oh kiss me please my darling boy.

LYDIA: Leave him alone, he's mine!

LOUELLA: No, he's not, he's *mine*!

WARNER: I've got to admit, this kid must have something.

DARYL: *(Crying.)* Aw, please, would you cut it out! I know why you're doing this. Because I'm a yes-man with ambitions! But I want to *be* something when I grow up! I want to surprise the world! Once, just once in my life, I want to say *no*!

LOUELLA: *(To Lydia.)* You take one step in his direction and I'll scratch your eyes out, you slut!

LYDIA: Slut?! You're calling *me* a slut?

REINHARDT: Ja. Slut.

LYDIA: *Ahhhhhhh!*

(Lydia makes a running leap at Louella — and as she flies by, Warner and Daryl catch her under the arms and hold her dangling in the air. Hubbub. At this moment, Powell and Olivia enter fighting over Brown, who keeps trying to get a word in edgewise.)

OLIVIA: *I'm* being too forward? You had your hands all over him!

BROWN: No, he really didn —

POWELL: I cut in and we were dancing! You didn't have to make a scene!

(Now it's back to the other fight, as Lydia bites Warner's hand.)

LYDIA: Let go of me!

WARNER: *Ow!*

LYDIA: Look at you. You're old enough to be his mother!

LOUELLA: "Age cannot wither me, nor custom stale
My infinite variety."

WARNER: *(To Daryl.)* There's only one way to stop her but she'd never forgive me.

DARYL: I think you've got to, sir.

LOUELLA: Strumpet! Wench! Harlot!

LYDIA: Witch! Crone!

WARNER: Lydia?

(Warner taps Lydia on the shoulder, and — whap! — he gives her a right to the jaw and knocks her out.)

LYDIA: *(Crumpling to the floor.)* Geez . . .

WARNER: *(Reacting to what he's just done.)* LYDIA!

(Everyone goes mad:)

LOUELLA: *Ahhhhhh! Ahhhhhh! Ahhhhhh!*

POWELL: You want to settle this outside?

OLIVIA: That's exactly what I want to do. Let's go!

REINHARDT: Come, I show you my etchings.

DARYL: *No! I'm saying no! Ha ha! No no no no no no!!*

(Suddenly Oberon appears — perhaps from above.)

OBERON: *STOP!*

(Everyone magically freezes and there is instant silence. Oberon swings down, using a rope, Errol Flynn fashion. Then, to Puck:)

Give me the flower. The *yellow* one, you numbskull!

Take thou some of it and lead them awry,

Then crush this herb in Louella's eye.

To Lydia and Reinhardt do the same,

And put an end to this foul game.

I'll take these two about to fight

And remove the error also from their sight

And so restore some peace unto this night.

(Oberon leads off Olivia and Powell. Brown runs off in the other direction. Puck is left with Reinhardt, Lydia, Louella, Daryl, Hays, and Warner. He intones the following, making everyone onstage react in rhythm:)

PUCK: Up and down, up and down,

I will lead them up and down.

I am feared in field and town,

Goblin lead them up and down.

(Puck causes a mist to arise, so that everyone gets confused by the voices that Puck now imitates. In Lydia's voice:)

PUCK: Hey, Jack, Daryl, Will. It's me, Lydia! Come here, I need your help!

WARNER: Right away!

DARYL: Yes, ma'am!

HAYS: I'm coming!

PUCK: *(In Daryl's voice.)* "Louella! Lydia! 'Tis I, your darling Daryl!"

LOUELLA: You divine creature!

LYDIA: *(Orgasmically.)* I come, I come, see how I come . . .

(And so, they all leave the stage. As the last one exits, Oberon reenters, carrying Olivia over his shoulder in a fireman's carry. She's still under the spell of the flower and is kicking and screaming.)

OLIVIA: Let go of me! I need to see Joey! He'll miss me! Would you put me down!

(Oberon lowers Olivia so that she's standing in front of him. Then he puts his hand on her forehead, and she falls asleep. Oberon lowers her to the ground and presses the petals of the yellow flower on Olivia's eyes.)

OBERON: Be as thou wast wont to be;

See as thou wast wont to see.

Dian's bud o'er Cupid's flower

Hath such force and blessèd power.

Awake, my love.

(During the following, Joe E. Brown enters and is about to speak — then he overhears Olivia and listens . . .)

OLIVIA: . . . What's going on? Where am I? . . . Oh my gosh, I had the most incredible dream! I thought I was in love with Joe E. Brown! And I think he was in drag!

(She laughs. Brown pulls off his Thisbe wig and leaves downhearted.)

What a dream. I don't remember much about the party, though.

OBERON: Oh, it was one of those . . . unforgettable nights.

"In such a night,

When the sweet wind did gently kiss the trees

And they did make no noise, in such a night,

Troilus, methinks, mounted the Trojan walls

And sighed his soul toward the Grecian tents

Where Cressid lay that night."

OLIVIA: "In such a night

Stood Dido with a willow in her hand

Upon the wild sea banks, and waft her love

To come again to Carthage."

OBERON: In such a night

Did Oberon fall in love with a mortal
Named Olivia and vow to be
With her forever.
(He picks her up and holds her in his arms, kissing her passionately. She looks out.)
OLIVIA: Dear Mother,
Call Aunt Ethel.
(He carries her off.)

[If the play was in three acts (as it is structurally), this would be the end of Act II.]

(The next morning, the Warner Brothers are on another conference call.)
HARRY: *Jack, you're a schmuck!*
JACK: What'd I do?!
HARRY: We just got a call from your friend Will Hays. He's launching an investigation of the whole studio!
JACK: But why?
ALBERT: You didn't see the paper this morning? It says you had an orgy last night at your place. With the cast and crew of your big shot picture.
HARRY: It says that everybody in the place was drunk. That fights broke out. Screaming was heard. There was sex on the grass. It says there was even some *transvestism*!
SAM: What's transvestism?
ALBERT: When a guy dresses up as a girl.
SAM: Jack! I'm your brother, you didn't *invite* me?!
JACK: It wasn't that bad, I swear to God.
ALBERT: Tell that to Hays. He's issuing a press release denouncing guess which studio.
HARRY: And he says he's going to close your picture unless he gets compliance with his script demands and an apology from Reinhardt.
JACK: So I'll get him to apologize.
HARRY: You better or we're up the creek! We've got a lot invested in this film already.
SAM: Over half a million, I checked this morning.
ALBERT: *Half a million?!*
SAM: Something like that. It was higher than I can count.

HARRY: You had no business starting this film in the first place! You said the word "art" and I knew we had trouble!

ALBERT: I could have told you this would happen when he got the girl involved. Sex and business don't mix!

SAM: You want to drop that kind of money on a gangster picture, I say go ahead. But on some artsy-fartsy nonsense — ?!

JACK: All right, all right! Would you give me a break?!

HARRY/ALBERT/SAM: *(Together.) NO!*

(The lights change and we're at the sound stage that morning, as a number of actors straggle by. First we see Lydia, in her work clothes, holding a hot-water bottle to her head and weaving. Then Reinhardt, Daryl, Cagney, and Warner.)

WARNER: *(Going by, muttering.)* I don't know what happened. It started out real nice. Maybe the rum punch was too strong . . .

CAGNEY: *(Practicing his lines as Bottom:)* "I have had a dream past the wit of man to say what dream it was. Man is but an ass if he go about to expound this dream . . ."

(Oberon and Olivia now enter together. They're still wearing their clothes from the party — having spent the night together at her apartment.)

OLIVIA: I guess I'd better get to wardrobe. I had a wonderful time last night. Don't forget we're having lunch together.

OBERON: And dinner.

OLIVIA: And breakfast.

OBERON: I want to try one of those round crispy things with the indentations.

OLIVIA: *(Running into his arms and holding him tightly.)* . . . Waffles!

(Puck hurries in. He's very upset.)

PUCK: *Majesty, I need to speak to you right away!*

OLIVIA: "Majesty"?

OBERON: That's just his little joke . . .

OLIVIA: I've got to run. I'll see you later.

(She exits.)

PUCK: I'm sorry, sir, but I have dire news.

OBERON: So important that you have to interrupt?!

PUCK: *Yes! Look at this! (He puts out his hand.)* We're fading.

(Beat. Oberon turns gray. He looks at his hand.)

OBERON: *(To himself.)* That was it.

PUCK: I don't know why. Or how. I think it started in the middle of the night. I felt a sort of tingling. Then, since dawn, I've been seeing visions of the Wood near Athens. Ours. The real one. I think we're going home.

OBERON: We can't! Not now.

PUCK: I agree! It isn't fair! I'm a star! I gave an autograph this morning! And all those women. They want to mother me. They think I'm adorable. Can't you reverse it?

OBERON: I don't know how. *(He gives a cry of pain.) God in Heaven!*

PUCK: I wonder how much time is left.

OBERON: Time . . . Of course. It was about this time we arrived here yesterday.

PUCK: That's it.

OBERON: From sun to sun. Twenty-four hours. How much time does that leave us?

> *(Puck looks at his watch — and bursts into tears.)*

What's the matter?

PUCK: *(Pointing to his wrist.)* It's a *Rolex*! A few more days, I could have bought a *Studebaker*!

OBERON: *How much time do we have left!*

PUCK: It looks like twenty minutes.

OBERON: I've got to find Olivia.

PUCK: I've got to find a girl who's willing to have sex at nine-thirty in the morning.

> *(They exit. As they go, Warner, Reinhardt, and Daryl enter together.)*

WARNER: Hays will be here any second, now what did you say to him?!

REINHARDT: I vas reasonable. I listened to vhat he had to say. And then I told him he vas Nazi pig.

WARNER: Look. The fact is, if you don't do as he says, there will be no movie. He can pull the plug.

REINHARDT: So pull the plug.

WARNER: But we have five hundred thousand dollars invested!

REINHARDT: *(Shrugs.)* It's not *my* money.

> *(Warner staggers.)*

DARYL: Sir, it's all right. Keep breathing.

> *(Hays swaggers in.)*

HAYS: Well, well, well. That was quite a party you gave last night.

WARNER: Did you have a good time?

HAYS: No. I despised it. At least I had *me* for company.

WARNER: I believe you two know each other.

> *(Reinhardt and Hays look at each other and shudder, remembering last night.)*

REINHARDT: Vhatever he says, I take the Fifth Amendment.

HAYS: Don't even speak to me, you hypocrite! You tried to get on my good side last night, didn't you.

REINHARDT: You have a good side?

WARNER: He's kidding, that's a joke.

HAYS: Then here's a joke for you. I have decided that there will be no more compromises. Whatsoever. *None!* And you have *fifteen minutes* to agree to my alterations or I withhold the League certificate! In which case, you might as well stop filming because you won't get distribution. It'll be *all over*!

WARNER: *(To Reinhardt.)* So what do you say?

REINHARDT: What *can* I say? I cannot give in to censorship and bullying! That is just what happened in my country and look what happened!

HAYS: *Then your movie won't get made!*

REINHARDT: *Fine!*

WARNER: *Now wait a second!* You said you'd give us fifteen minutes.

REINHARDT: And I keep shooting film till final minute! Final second!

DARYL: I agree!

WARNER: Would you be quiet!

(To Hays.)

You'll hear from us.

REINHARDT: You'll hear bupkis.

WARNER: *(To Reinhardt.)* You! In my office now!

(Warner pulls Daryl and Reinhardt off, leaving Hays alone.)

HAYS: How dare he yell at me like that!

(Oberon enters, preoccupied.)

OBERON: Olivia . . . Where did she go . . .

HAYS: Oh, it's you again. Have you "losteth" your way? Or are you waiting to "appeareth" in the movie?

OBERON: I have to warn you that I'm in no mood for this.

HAYS: You're in "no mood for this"? You two-bit, piddling actor. Are you insane?! I can finish you! A single word from me and you'll be —

(Wham!! Oberon has pointed his finger at Hays — and with a crack of lightning, Hays is frozen solid. He's in the middle of a gesture, but he can't budge. Only his eyes can move, and they're open wide, darting in all directions.)

OBERON: Foolish mortal. *Do you know what I could do to you?! What I could turn you into?!* A meddling monkey or busy ape. A lion, cat or bear —

BROWN: Good morning. *(Joe E. Brown has entered. He looks at Hays.)* Is he all right?

OBERON: No. He has a rare medical condition. He makes other people sick.

BROWN: Oh. *I hope you feel better!* I've got to run. We're filming my big scene this morning.

(He exits, leaving Oberon with Hays.)

OBERON: Do you have anything to say?

(Oberon makes a gesture and unfreezes him.)

HAYS: *(Belligerently.)* I don't know how you did that, it's probably a gas or something, but I could *sue you* for *assault and battery!* And don't you think I wouldn't —

(Wham!! Oberon has done it again. Hays is frozen.)

OBERON: Don't you mortals ever learn? You keep making the same mistake, over and over. You don't *believe!*

REINHARDT: *(Off.)* Quickly now! No time to lose! Come quickly!

OBERON: . . . Heh, heh. I have an idea. Come.

(Oberon hurries off, forgetting that Hays can't move.)

Oh, right.

(He snaps his fingers, unfreezing Hays's legs — and Hays backs off after Oberon like a broken robot. As Oberon and Hays leave, the cast of the movie enters, all in costume, led by Reinhardt. They include Olivia as Hermia, Lydia as Helena, Powell as Lysander, Cagney as Pyramus, and Brown as Thisbe. Warner and Daryl enter with them.)

DARYL: Hurry up! Make it quick! No time to lose! Everyone on the set please. We're at the palace. On set quickly, please.

REINHARDT: *(Urgently arranging the actors.)* Ve only have fifteen minutes, I vant to get this in one take, so act very happy or I vill kill you.

LYDIA: Sorry. But why is Helena happy again?

REINHARDT: *(Impatiently.)* Because she has just married the man she loves.

LYDIA: Is this her first marriage or her second or third?

REINHARDT: Her first!

LYDIA: Did she have a prenuptial agreement?

REINHARDT: *I DON'T KNOW VHAT SHE HAD, NOW SIT DOWN, VE ARE LOSING TIME!* Good. Ladies and gentlemen. You are at the Palace in Athens watching a play entitled "Pyramus and Thisbe." Love has triumphed and all is well.

(Suddenly, there is thunder and lightning — and Will Hays comes stampeding in wearing an ass head. It grows out of his shoulders and is part of his body. He runs wildly around the stage, trying desperately to get the head off.)

OLIVIA/LYDIA: *AHHHHHHHHHHHHHHHHH!*

HAYS: *HEE HAW HEE HAW HEE HAW HEE HAW!!*

POWELL: *Who's that?!*

CAGNEY: *What is it?!*

DARYL: *What do you want?*

HAYS: *I annnnnnt taaaaawk! I annnnnnnt taaaaaawk!*

> *(Hays bolts, and Daryl, Cagney, Powell, and Brown chase the creature around the stage. When they catch him, they try to pull his head off.)*

BROWN: *Maybe he's from wardrobe!*

HAYS: *I'm noooooot! I'm noooooot!*

WARNER: *Well he better stop it. That's an expensive costume!*

CAGNEY: *And it's mine! Now take it off!*

HAYS: *I caaaaaan't! I caaaaaaan't!*

WARNER: *Boys, take it off him!*

CAGNEY: *All right, fuzz face, don't move!*

DARYL: *Stay where you are!*

CAGNEY: *Powell, grab him!*

POWELL: *Hey, come back here!*

BROWN: *Get him!*

HAYS: *HEE HAW HEE HAW HEE HAW HEE HAW!!!*

DARYL: *I got him!*

CAGNEY: *Now pull his head off!*

HAYS: *Pleeeeeeese stop! Pleeeeeeese stop!*

WARNER: Who *are* you?!

HAYS: Wiiiiiiiiill Hays! Wiiiiiiiiill Hays!

EVERYONE: Will Hays?/That's Will Hays? [Etc.]

REINHARDT: Will Hays??? . . . That's good.

> *(Hays grabs a pad and pencil from the director's desk.)*

WARNER: Wait. He's writing something down. *(He snatches the paper and reads.)* "If you will remove this ass head, I will withdraw my objections to the movie."

> *(Everyone cheers.)*

BROWN: But it's stuck like glue!

> *(Hays grabs the pad back and scribbles some more.)*

WARNER: Wait. He says: *(Reading.)* "I think the actor who plays Oberon can do it."

> *(Hays snatches back the pad and scribbles some more. Warner reads.)* ". . . The son of a bitch."

REINHARDT: But where *is* Oberon?

(Oberon and Puck have silently entered by this time.)

OBERON: I'm right here.

WARNER: Can you do it?

OBERON: Of course I can. It's just a costume.

(To Hays.) Do you want me to take it off?

HAYS: Yes pleeeeeese! Yes pleeeeeese!

OBERON: And are you begging me, like Niobe, all tears?

(Hays goes down on his knees and clasps his hands together. To Puck:)

Do you think we should?

PUCK: Oh, why not.

(Oberon removes the head. Hays staggers backward. The cast react: "It is him!" "Will Hays!")

WARNER: *(Angry.)* Hays?! What the hell are you doing?!

HAYS: *(Purple with rage.)* . . . How dare you . . . *How dare all of you!!! I could sue every single one of you for this! And I could stop this foolish movie!*

REINHARDT: *(Taking the note from Warner and holding it up.)* Except that you made a contract.

(Silence.)

HAYS: . . . All right, *fine*! Make your stupid movie. I'll be revenged on the whole pack of you!

(He stomps out, and the cast of the movie express relief.)

REINHARDT: Go. Everyone. Take a break. Fifteen minutes. And when you get back, go to Sound Stage Three and ve vill *continue* making movie.

(A cheer from the actors. They and Reinhardt wander off happily, chatting among themselves. As they go, Lydia and Warner find themselves face to face.)

WARNER: Lydia.

LYDIA: Jack.

(Then they both speak at the same time.)

BOTH: I know you'll never forgive me, but —

(They stop, surprised.)

BOTH: What did you say?

WARNER: You go first.

LYDIA: No, please, be my guest.

WARNER: . . . I was saying that I'm sure you'll never forgive me for hitting you like that.

LYDIA: And *I* thought you'd still be mad at me for making such a fuss over Daryl. Jack, I-I-I don't know what happened! It was like a brain seizure or somethin'.

WARNER: It made me so jealous.

LYDIA: You were magnificent.

WARNER: I was?

LYDIA: Like Othello when he thought that Desdemonia was unfaithful.

("Desdemonia" is her mispronunciation.)

WARNER: *(Astonished.)* Lydia . . . ?

LYDIA: This Shakespeare stuff really gets to you.

WARNER: Let me ask you a question: will you marry me?

LYDIA: Let me ask *you* a question. Do you still have that three-carat ring?

WARNER: Lydia!

LYDIA: I'm kidding, I'm kidding. Of course I want to marry you. Then I can *really* boss you around.

(They kiss.)

Now where's my ring?

WARNER: Right here.

LYDIA: Ooh! Ahh! Ooh! I love it! Look at this! *(She puts it on and they stroll off together.)* Listen, I got a great idea for our next movie. Another Shakespeare. "War and Peace!"

(And they're gone. Puck hurries up to Oberon.)

PUCK: Master, we must go. It's any moment now.

OBERON: Anon, good Robin.

PUCK: Lord, what fools these mortals be. And yet, there is some . . . greatness about them. I'll be waiting for you in the parking lot.

(As Puck exits, Olivia reenters.)

OLIVIA: There you are.

OBERON: Olivia —

OLIVIA: Lunch?

OBERON: I can't have lunch.

OLIVIA: We'll have dinner then.

OBERON: I can't have dinner with you.

OLIVIA: Why not?

OBERON: Because I have to go away.

OLIVIA: What do you mean?

OBERON: I'm leaving here in a few minutes.

OLIVIA: But when do you get back?

OBERON: I'm not coming back. I can't. I'm sorry.

(Shocked silence. Olivia is stunned.)

OLIVIA: *(With rising panic.)* But why? Why are you leaving? Did I do something wrong?

OBERON: Never.

OLIVIA: But you can't just walk away! There must be some reason!

OBERON: You have to trust me. It can't be stopped.

OLIVIA: No! I don't want you to go!

OBERON: Trust me.

OLIVIA: *But I love you! (She holds him and weeps.)* Please. Don't go. Don't you know how I feel? *(She weeps in his arms.)*

OBERON: Shhhh. It will be all right.

> *(Lulling her to sleep; carrying her to some pillows on the floor.)*
> I know a bank where the wild thyme blows,
> Where oxslips and the nodding violet grows,
> Quite over-canopied with luscious woodbine,
> With sweet musk-roses and with eglantine.
> There the snake throws her enameled skin
> Weed-wide enough to wrap a fairy in.
> *(She sleeps. He has a petal of the Western flower in his hand.)*
> And with the juice of this I streak your eye
> So that the next thing now that you espy
> Shall be the only love that you recall.
> And you shall never dwell on me at all
> Or feel the ache of grief, the tear of pain,
> And only in your inmost dreams will I remain.
> *(He lays her down on the ground. He kisses her. At this moment, Powell enters.)*

POWELL: Hi. Sorry. Your friend said you wanted to see me?

OBERON: Yes. I have to go now.

POWELL: Olivia . . . ? Is she asleep?

OBERON: She's waiting for you to wake her up.

POWELL: For *me*? You don't mean you've talked to her?!

> *(Oberon nods.)*
> Really?

OBERON: Wake her and see.

> *(Powell kneels at Olivia's side. As he does, Oberon gestures and makes himself invisible. Zzzzing! As Powell gently shakes Olivia's shoulder, then speaks to her, Oberon stays and watches over the resolution that he's wrought, like a benevolent spirit in a Giotto fresco.)*

POWELL: Hello?

(Olivia opens her eyes and smiles. Then looks confused.)

OLIVIA: . . . What happened? Was I asleep? . . . Dick? Oh, Dick, it's so good to see you!

POWELL: I'm only here because of . . . Where did he go . . . ?

OLIVIA: Oh, I had the strangest dream. I thought I was in love with . . . a spirit of some sort. From another world.

POWELL: Sounds like a pretty nice dream.

OLIVIA: It was.

POWELL: Would you like to get some lunch with me at the commissary?

OLIVIA: I'd love to.

(They embrace. Then they head off together.)

POWELL: Then maybe after dinner we can go dancing, would you like that? I've got to warn you, though, I'm a really good dancer . . .

OLIVIA: I'll be right there.

(He exits; and she lingers for a moment. She looks around. Something very strange and very wonderful has happened to her, and she doesn't quite know what it is.)

(Reinhardt strolls on and speaks in the half-light.)

REINHARDT: The next morning, as if by some miracle, the actor Victor Jory changed his mind and asked to come back and play Oberon. And by the end of the month, Mickey Rooney's leg was healed and he returned to play the role of Puck. Two months later, the shooting was finished; six months later, the movie was released. Alas, I directed no more movies in Hollywood. But I tell you this. I never forgot what I learned in that year of shadows.

(He exits.)

(Olivia takes one last look at where Oberon must be:)

OLIVIA: Good-bye.

(She runs off. Oberon watches her go as the lights fade.)

OBERON: Good-bye.

(The lights fade slowly on Oberon, standing alone.)

END OF PLAY

AFTERWORD
On Comedy

When I was in my twenties I fell in love with a form of comic drama that I call the Great Tradition. It is a specific form of drama, as defined and ritualized in its way as the Noh drama of Japan or the masked drama of Greek tragedy. It is not social comedy or the comedy of manners. It is not satire and is not mere farce. It begins with Shakespeare's greatest comedies, *A Midsummer Night's Dream, Twelfth Night, Much Ado About Nothing,* and *As You Like It,* and continues to the present day. It does not include some of the best comedies ever written such as *The Alchemist* in the seventeenth century and *Private Lives* in the twentieth. The comedies in the Great Tradition are simply different in kind and represent a specific way of looking at the world and expressing it on the stage.

Following Shakespeare, the Great Tradition shows up intermittently, sometimes with many decades between sightings. The names of the plays themselves may not mean much, but let me name them first and then describe what binds them together, thus allowing them to be called a tradition of comedy.

The first time we spot the Great Tradition after Shakespeare is at the end of the Restoration period in the works of John Vanbrugh, particularly in his plays *The Relapse* and *The Provoked Wife.* These are followed closely, in the early 1700s, by two comedies by George Farquhar, *The Recruiting Officer* and *The Beaux' Stratagem.* What we see in all these plays is the loosening up of the strict conventions of the earlier Restoration comedies, those "aren't-we-terribly-witty-as-we-talk-of-nothing-but-mistresses-and-cuckolding" sort of plays by Etherege and Congreve (brittle and brilliant though they certainly are). In Vanbrugh, good nature begins to return to the theater. There are still fops, but they begin to laugh at themselves and so bring light into the room. And in Farquhar, where the plays are set in the country instead of the town, there is a whole new world of characters to enjoy, from highwaymen to rowdy innkeepers.*

The next notable instances of this comic tradition appear clustered in the last third of the eighteenth century. They begin with Garrick and Colman's buoyant *The Clandestine Marriage* (which was made into a commercial movie in 2001) and Garrick's own *The Lying Valet*, which has gone largely unappreciated for the past two hundred years. It is worth remembering that Garrick was as great a comedian as he was a tragedian and that one of his most famous roles was that of Sir John Brute, the man who puts on a dress in Vanbrugh's *The Provoked Wife*.

Next, in 1773, comes Oliver Goldsmith's triumphant masterpiece *She Stoops to Conquer*, followed closely by Richard Brinsley Sheridan's *The Rivals* (1775) and *The School for Scandal* (1777), then John O'Keeffe's *Wild Oats* in 1791. I am not certain if it has ever been appreciated as such, but the thirty-year period from the mid-1760s to the mid-1790s is second only to Shakespeare's heyday as the high point of dramatic comedy in the English language. (Notice that I did not say "by English authors" since most of these playwrights were Irish.)

This period is followed by a long hiatus until Dion Boucicault wrote the youthful, zesty *London Assurance* in the early 1840s. His leading character, Sir Harcourt Courtly, is obviously a direct descendant of Vanbrugh's Lord Foppington and, if anything, even more hilarious. Then, at the end of the century come George Bernard Shaw (who loved to mock the Great Tradition and call it hooey while at the same time paying homage to it), and then Wilde's *The Importance of Being Earnest*, which came, saw, and conquered the Great Tradition and set it on its head. Among the best plays of the twentieth century in this tradition are J. B. Priestley's *When We Are Married*, Thornton Wilder's *The Matchmaker*, Kaufman and Hart's *The Man Who Came to Dinner*, and Tom Stoppard's *On the Razzle*.

*I had the good fortune to "coauthor" an adaptation of Farquhar's *The Beaux' Stratagem* with Thornton Wilder. He began the adaptation in 1939 but gave it up in 1940 about halfway through due to other commitments. Some sixty-five years later, well after Wilder's death, the Wilder Estate asked me to complete it. The world premiere was presented by the Shakespeare Theatre Company in Washington, D.C., directed brilliantly by Michael Kahn, and it is now frequently performed around the country. (It is published by Samuel French.) How interesting that of all the dozens of classics Wilder could have chosen to adapt for the modern stage, he chose *The Beaux' Stratagem*. This is yet another example of Wilder's brilliance.

During the long spell in the nineteenth century when good comic plays were in scarce supply, the spirit of high comedy bounded irrepressibly into view in the glorious comic operas in the *buffa* tradition. (It is no coincidence that the original title of *Lend Me A Tenor* was *Opera Buffa.*) These include the operas of Rossini, like *The Barber of Seville* and *La Cenerentola*, and their great successors by Donizetti, *La Fille du Regiment, L'Elisir d'Amore,* and *Don Pasquale.*

In the twentieth century, the tradition takes two more unexpected turns, showing up in the screwball film comedies of the 1930s and 40s (such as *Bringing Up Baby, Hail the Conquering Hero,* and about twenty others) and in the comic strain of the American musical (such as *Guys and Dolls, The Music Man,* and *Kiss Me Kate*).

For anyone who believes that any of the plays mentioned above are old-fashioned and rusty, the fact of the matter is that they have all been entertaining audiences for centuries. Audiences do not go to these plays because they are antiques. They are not. They are funny and often moving comedies that fill their audiences with a sense of joy and fulfillment: joy because the plays make us laugh, fulfillment because they are beautifully plotted, beautifully written, and beautifully balanced. They are works of art. One might call them great comic romps disguised as good literature.

All the plays in this tradition have a specific set of characteristics in common, and by identifying these characteristics we begin to get a feel for the genre.

First, all these plays are innately romantic. They are love stories and they are not cynical. Take the noisy, touching story of Sir Peter and Lady Teazle in Sheridan's *The School for Scandal.* It could have been another cynical tale of a young wife being unfaithful to an older husband; but Sheridan gives Lady Teazle a soul and a conscience and, more to the point, gives Sir Peter Teazle a sense of humor about himself. Sir Peter's first speech in the play is as follows: "When an old bachelor takes a young wife, what is he to expect! Tis now six months since Lady Teazle made me the happiest of men, and I have been the miserablest dog ever since . . ." Thus, from the first, we are rooting for the Teazles' marriage. Indeed, all the plays in the Great Tradition are marriage comedies, ending in single marriages, multiple marriages, or remarriages. (Interestingly, the first comedy in history to get to marriage via divorce is *The Beaux' Stratagem.*)

Second, the plays in this tradition often transport their characters outside the "real world" to worlds that can be turned upside down, like the forest of Arden in *As You Like It*, or the remote country inn of *She Stoops to Conquer.* The town of Bath functions this way in Sheridan's *The Rivals* (as it does in Jane Austen's *Northanger Abbey*); so do the country estates in Wilde's *The Importance of Being Earnest* and Boucicault's *London Assurance;* and so does Hollywood in Kaufman and Hart's *Once in a Lifetime.* The moral seems to be "Leave home and find a little freedom." Usually this is found by going from the city to the countryside, but sometimes it is the other way around.

Third, one of the main building blocks of comedy in the Western tradition is the effort of parents to thwart the sexual urges of their children. It is no coincidence that the main plot of *A Midsummer Night's Dream* opens with a father angrily declaring

> *Full of vexation come I, with complaint*
> *Against my child, my daughter Hermia.*

Or that the opening line of *The Matchmaker* is "I tell you for the hundredth time you will never marry my niece." Indeed, we sometimes see father and son competing for the same girl.

Other characteristics of this genre of comedy include a ticking clock in the form of a time crunch that makes the action feel speeded up; strong comic premises, such as disguising a girl as a boy or having a character mistake a house for an inn; multiple plots; and the physical robustness of farce and slapstick. Another critical hallmark of this form of comedy is confusion and mistaken identity, often involving disguise and sometimes cross-dressing. Indeed, it is rare to find a comedy in the Great Tradition that does not contain some form of mistaken identity.

A subtle but important characteristic of these comedies is that they are always written — to take a metaphor from music — in sonata form. They are all in three parts, or movements, progressing from the statement to the development to the recapitulation. (This is regardless of how many acts or intermissions they may have.) In *Anatomy of Criticism,* Northrop Frye famously describes the cyclical nature of drama, using the seasons as a metaphor, and he refers to this kind of comedy as part of the mythos of spring, where "there is usually a movement from one kind of society to another . . . At the end of the play, the device in the plot that brings the hero and heroine together causes a new society to crystallize around the hero."

Finally, in the end, I believe that what binds these plays together is a deep-rooted sense of optimism. It has taken me a long time to understand this, and it is not a trivial observation. As the writer Louis Kronenberger says, "Comedy is not just a happy as opposed to an unhappy ending, but a way of surveying life so that happy endings must prevail." At the moment, of course, it is not fashionable to admire works of art of this kind. Yet all the works of art that I have just described contain not only a sense of humanity but, ultimately, a sense of hope for the possibility of joy.

Think of Marlow, Kate, and Tony Lumpkin as they battle their way through the matrimonial stakes in *She Stoops to Conquer*. Think of the fop of all fops Sir Harcourt Courtly as he makes his final amends in *London Assurance*. Think of Earnest in *Earnest* and the extravagant play-quoting Rover finding his one true love in the Quaker Lady Amaranth in *Wild Oats*. Think above all of Beatrice and Benedick at the end of the wedding scene in *Much Ado About Nothing* and the embattled heroines Viola in *Twelfth Night* and Rosalind in *As You Like It*. Graver interpretations of these plays proliferate at the moment, as they should: plays are mirrors of the age. But at bottom (and Bottom would agree), these plays, no matter how you slice them, leave us with a strong sense that with resolution, courage, and the right attitude to the wide world, we can survive anything that life throws at us. This notion is exhilarating, and the tradition behind it is continually inspiring.

A WORD ON PRODUCTION

Writing plays and producing plays are two different things, of course, and once the writing stage has passed, I think it is useful to bear in mind how, as a practical matter, stage comedy should be played.

The first rule of playing comedy is never try to be funny. I cannot emphasize this enough. Whenever an actor tries to be funny, it is not successful. Whenever a director adds comic "business" for its own sake, the "business" feels forced, no one looks good, and the enterprise fails.

The second rule, a corollary of the first, is that the actors must always talk to each other, and they must do it from a place of honesty. That is the key word: honesty. If the actors tell the story honestly, not stopping along the way for extraneous "business," the laughs will take care of themselves. This does not mean that comedies of the kind I write should not to be played with high style. They must be. But the comedy must grow out of the situation and must never be forced.

Another important rule of stage comedy is that the stakes must always feel immensely high. What is happening onstage must be nothing less than life and death for the characters involved. In *Lend Me A Tenor*, if Tito does not show up, the entire opening night festivities will fail and Saunders will be out of a job. At the same time, if Max does not succeed in singing the role of *Otello*, he will never get to show Maggie what he is worth, and he will lose her. Similarly, in *Leading Ladies,* if Leo and Jack do not convince Florence's household of their new identities, they will lose two million dollars. Then the stakes change and become even higher: If Leo does not pull off his deception, he will lose Meg forever. All these circumstances are of life-and-death importance to the characters in the play, and they must be played that way.

Finally, stage comedies must be played with energy. The cardinal rule is to *always* pick up your cues unless there is a specific reason for a pause. There is a tendency today, no doubt because of the prevalence of movie acting, to leave a little pocket of air before saying a line. This is a mistake. Again, if a pause is called for, then by all means take it. But if no pause is indicated, then jump on your cue and take out the air cushion. A good high comedy should feel like a ping-pong game where the ball never hits the ground.

I recently saw a college production of *Leading Ladies* in North Carolina where the director and actors simply did everything right: the director made certain that the actors talked to each other, and no one tried to be funny in ways that the story and the dialogue did not suggest. They did not add comic "business," and most importantly, they told the story with an eye on the long arc of the piece as well as the arc of each individual scene. The result was exhilarating, and this production will remain one of my fondest memories.

• • •

Two days after sending these introductory materials to the publisher, I was reading a pamphlet by George Bernard Shaw entitled *The Art of Rehearsal*. In it, Shaw offers advice to a boyhood friend on how to direct plays; and in the course of the advice, Shaw makes the following comments. The first is about the importance of honesty in performance:

> The beginning and end of the business from the author's point of view is the art of making the audience believe that real things are happening to real people.

The second comment is about pacing:

> *Never have a moment of silence on the stage except as an intentional stage effect.* [Italics by Shaw.] The play must not stop while an actor is sitting down or getting up or walking off the stage. The last word of an exit speech must get the actor off the stage. He must sit on a word and rise on a word; if he has to make a movement, he must move as he speaks and not before or after; and the cues must be picked up as smartly as a ball is fielded in cricket. This is the secret of pace, and of holding an audience. It is a rule which you may set aside again and again to make a special effect; for a technical rule may always be broken on purpose. But as a rule of thumb it is invaluable. I once saw a fine play of Masefield's prolonged by half an hour and almost ruined because the actors made their movements in silence between the speeches.

Shaw knew his plays and he knew his staging; and I found this advice to be so remarkably similar to what I have written above that I thought it should be included here.

KEN LUDWIG is an internationally acclaimed playwright whose many hits on Broadway, in London's West End, and throughout the world have made his name synonymous with modern comedy. He has won the Laurence Olivier Award, London's highest theater honor, in addition to three Tony Award nominations and two Helen Hayes Awards. His work has been performed in over thirty countries in at least twenty languages. His musical *Crazy For You* ran for over four years on Broadway and London, and his Broadway play *Lend Me A Tenor* was called "one of the two great farces by a living writer" by *The New York Times.* He was commissioned by the Royal Shakespeare Company to write *Shakespeare in Hollywood,* and he cowrote an adaptation of *The Beaux' Stratagem* with Thornton Wilder at the request of the Wilder Estate. His play *Moon Over Buffalo* was produced on Broadway and at the Old Vic in London, and his adaptation of *Treasure Island* was produced at the Theatre Royal, Haymarket, in London, and won the 2009 AATE Distinguished Play Award for Best Adaptation. His adaptation of *The Three Musketeers* had its world premiere at the Bristol Old Vic, and he directed the world premiere of *Leading Ladies* for the Alley Theatre. Other Broadway plays and musicals include *Twentieth Century* and *The Adventures of Tom Sawyer.* Over the years, his shows have starred, among others, Carol Burnett, Lynn Redgrave, Alec Baldwin, Mickey Rooney, Anne Heche, Joan Collins, Robert Goulet, Frank Langella, Hal Holbrook, Dixie Carter, and Otto Schenck. He has received the Edwin Forrest Award for outstanding contributions to the American theater, and he received an honorary doctorate from York College. He studied music at Harvard with Leonard Bernstein and theater history at Cambridge University in England.